SEATTLE

ALLISON WILLIAMS

CONTENTS

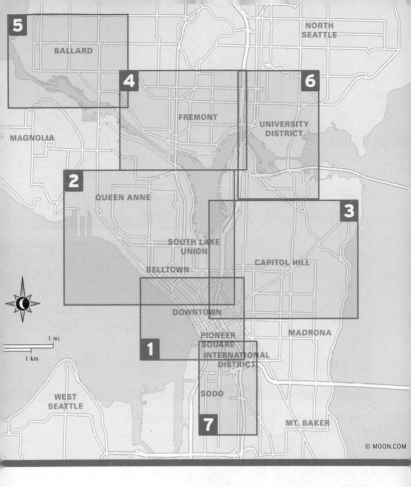

MAPS

1. Gas Works Park

2. Seattle Great Wheel

3. King Street Station

4. Pike Place Market

5. Seattle Central Library

6. Seattle Aquarium

DISCOVER
SEATTLE

More than 50 years have passed since a world's fair transformed this northwestern port into a global city—just look at the Space Needle for evidence of that era's endless optimism and vision. The city of Seattle, built on a series of hills between a lake and a bay, is today a mature metropolis.

The vibe is more about achievement than status; it's not cool to work so hard that you can't kayak a little before dinner or jam with your folk-rock quartet on the weekend. The healthy arts and music scene has grown beyond '90s grunge. But never fear—the city hasn't completely outgrown its youthful exuberance. It's still the home of the bustling coffee shop and the ambitious start-up. Creative energy explodes from tech minds, performers, and chefs who, like the Space Needle, reach for the stars.

6

Evidence of past success is around every corner in Seattle. Starbucks, once a tiny coffee shop near Pike Place Market, occupies downtown with the same ubiquity it's achieved around the world. Amazon, the online bookstore turned tech monolith, has colonized the South Lake Union neighborhood and helped turn its forgotten blocks into a bustling cultural center. Microsoft, which began here and is headquartered just outside of town, has left its mark—not just of its business, but also of the entities it helped build, like the campus of the philanthropic Bill & Melinda Gates Foundation and Paul Allen's football stadium and music museum.

Seattle is a place of experiments, of legalizing marijuana and raising the minimum wage by leaps and bounds. The city is growing so fast it sometimes feels like a living being, one figuring out this brave new world at the same time it's creating it. With just enough history to build considerable civic pride, Seattle encourages looking to the horizon—or perhaps just to the sunsets that illuminate the Olympic Mountains on clear nights. Sure, it rains sometimes, but that makes the beautiful days all the sweeter.

10 TOP
EXPERIENCES

1 **Watch Fish Fly at Pike Place Market:** The seafood counter may be the most famous part of this downtown landmark, but there's enough produce, spices, crafts, buskers, and fresh-made doughnuts to fill an entire day (page 60).

2 **View Masterpieces at the Seattle Art Museum:** Discover a peerless collection of Pacific Northwest art (page 62).

3 **Explore Seattle Center:** This collection of museums, sights, green spaces, and fountains entices visitors to spend as much time as possible here (page 68).

4 **Take in the Views from the Space Needle:** The city's symbol offers sky high views from its observation deck (page 69).

5 Get Out on the Water: Take advantage of Seattle's waterfront bounty by boat, kayak, or stand-up paddleboard (page 166).

>>>

6 Go Back in Time at the Museum of History and Industry: Interactive exhibits, artifacts, and curiosities offer insight into the city's past, as well as some glimpses into its future (page 73).

>>>

7 **Observe the Hiram M. Chittenden Locks:** Boats big and small gain passage to the Ship Canal through these locks, next to a special thoroughfare made just for salmon (page 78).

>>>

8 **Embrace Coffee Culture:** The craze for caffeine was born here, and the city's blocks are full of corporate coffee chains and indie outposts alike (page 93).

<<<

9 **Experience the Seattle Sound— Live:** This is the city that Jimi Hendrix called home and where Kurt Cobain found fame before his tragic end (page 129).

>>>

10 **Drink Craft Beer:** An abundance of local, artisanal breweries place the city at the forefront of this hoppy trend (page 143).

EXPLORE
SEATTLE

THE BEST OF SEATTLE

Seattle is an international city with arts, food, science, and the outdoors to explore. To make the most of a short trip, focus first on the city's core, and then venture out onto the water or to one of the city's parks. Stay in a hotel in the downtown core, like Hotel Max, for the easiest travel around the city.

This itinerary assumes you won't need a car for the first three days and includes information on using public transportation to get around.

> ### DAY 1:
DOWNTOWN AND
QUEEN ANNE

Start the day like any other day—at **Starbucks.** The location in Pike Place Market isn't quite as "original" as the T-shirts and mugs would have you believe, but it's an interesting reminder that the chain used to be just another local coffee stand. Java in hand, explore **Pike Place Market** and its long rows of craft and food stands. Watch fish fly at **Pike Place Fish Market,** and venture past the **Gum Wall.**

the view from the Smith Tower observatory

BEST VIEWS

COLUMBIA CENTER SKY VIEW OBSERVATORY
The second-highest public viewpoint west of the Mississippi is near the top of Seattle's biggest skyscraper (page 63).

SMITH TOWER
An observation deck at what used to be the tallest building in the West offers a 360-degree view of the city, waterfront, and distant mountains (page 66).

SPACE NEEDLE
Besides the 360-degree panorama from the observation deck of Seattle's famous landmark, you can, as of 2018, gaze straight down through a rotating glass floor (page 69).

LAKE VIEW CEMETERY
The gentle hills of tombstones look out on Lake Washington, and, on clear days, the snow-topped Cascade Mountains to the east (page 75).

GAS WORKS PARK
From its spot on the north end of Lake Union, this funky park has a clear view of the Seattle skyline, including the Space Needle (page 76).

WEST SEATTLE WATER TAXI
The passenger-only water taxi from downtown to the West Seattle neighborhood across Elliott Bay offers sensational skyline views from its deck and, on sunny days, the whole city seems to spread out before you from the West Seattle ferry dock (page 84).

THE NEST
Located atop the Thompson Hotel, this rooftop bar boasts indoor space and an outdoor patio with sensational views of Elliott Bay and Pike Place Market (page 130).

KERRY PARK
For the classic shot of downtown Seattle—with Mount Rainier in the background, when it's clear—head to this Queen Anne pocket park (page 167).

the Seattle Center Monorail

Walk south along 1st Avenue to the *Hammering Man* at the **Seattle Art Museum,** and venture inside to view one of the West Coast's best art collections. From there it's only a few blocks down University Street to the waterfront—just aim for the **Seattle Great Wheel.** Take a boat ride on **Argosy Cruises**—it would be a shame to leave Seattle without getting on the water at least once.

Once you're back on dry land, walk to Westlake Center. From here take the **Seattle Center Monorail** to **Seattle Center.** You're probably starving, so make a stop just west of the monorail terminal at the Seattle Center Armory, which hosts small outlets of some of the city's best cheap eateries. Seattle Center alone contains enough entertainment for a week, so pick your poison: science at the **Pacific Science Center** or rock and roll and pop culture at the **Museum of Pop Culture.** Topping either one will take something big—like, say, the **Space Needle.** Travel to the top to the observation deck and leave time to take in the full 360-degree view. The heights-averse will enjoy the on-the-ground delights of the **Chihuly Garden and Glass.**

For dinner, head to Belltown. Hit up one of the city's memorable restaurants: **El Gaucho** is known for steak, while **Six Seven** earns acclaim for both seafood and its waterfront location.

>> **PUBLIC TRANSIT:** To get to Belltown from Seattle Center, take the Route 4 bus from 5th Ave. N and Broad St. to 3rd Ave. and Vine St.

Return downtown to see the **Seattle Symphony** at Benaroya Hall or a rock band at the **Showbox.**

>> **PUBLIC TRANSIT:** To get downtown from Belltown, hop on a southbound Route 1, 2, 3, or 4 bus from the intersection of 3rd Ave. and Vine St. Exit at 3rd Ave. and Union St.

> **DAY 2:**
SOUTH LAKE UNION AND BALLARD

Start the day with *tres leches* French toast at **Cactus** in South Lake Union. Walk to Yale Avenue for some quick shopping at **REI** or follow Terry Avenue north to **Lake Union Park** and the **Museum of History and Industry** to learn the story of Seattle and its high-flying, computer-inventing ways. Look for the seaplanes taking off and landing on Lake Union just outside.

It's time to head north into Ballard to try some of the neighborhood's best cuisine. Have lunch at **La Carta de Oaxaca** or go for the pizza at **Stoneburner.**

>> **PUBLIC TRANSIT:** To get to Ballard from Lake Union Park, pick up a northbound Route 40 bus from Westlake Ave. N and Mercer

ACTIVE IN SEATTLE

BIKE SHARES
JUMP and LimeBike makes it easy to grab a bicycle for a quick ride (page 170).

BURKE-GILMAN TRAIL
This bike trail goes from Ballard to Woodinville, passing through the University of Washington and some of the city's quiet residential neighborhoods (page 170).

AGUA VERDE PADDLE CLUB
Rent a kayak or stand-up paddleboard for a quick paddle on Lake Union, then head upstairs for Mexican food and margaritas (page 171).

DISCOVERY PARK
Trails meander through the park's meadows and forests, while the expansive beach leads to an old lighthouse (page 172).

GREEN LAKE PARK
The city's runners love the three-mile trail that circles this park's urban lake (page 172).

St. Disembark at NW Leary Way and 15th Ave. NW.

Next, walk west on Northwest Market Street to reach the **Hiram M. Chittenden Locks.** It's fun to watch the gates open and the locks fill as boats move in and out, and there's also a fish ladder with underground viewing windows. When you're ready for dinner, retrace your steps to Ballard Avenue and wait in line for the city's best oyster bar at **The Walrus and the Carpenter.**

Bars in Ballard are among the city's best, so take a tipple at **Noble Fir** or **King's Hardware,** and drink as the anglers once did on these very streets.

Head back downtown to finish

the brick water tower at Volunteer Park

the night with music at **Dimitriou's Jazz Alley.**

>> **PUBLIC TRANSIT:** To return downtown from Ballard, take a southbound D Line bus from 15th Ave. NW and NW Leary Way to 3rd Ave. and Virginia St.

>DAY 3:
CAPITOL HILL AND WEST SEATTLE

If something exciting is happening in Seattle, it'll either start or end in Capitol Hill. Begin the day at one of the neighborhood's many indulgent breakfast spots, like **The Wandering Goose,** where the biscuits are so good they've inspired a children's storybook.

Then it's time to visit **Volunteer Park,** one of the city's prettiest green spaces. Climb to the top of the brick water tower for a workout with a view, or gaze at the Space Needle through the middle of the circular *Black Sun* sculpture. If it's open (it's undergoing renovations in 2019), venture inside the **Seattle Asian Art Museum,** guarded by twin camel statues, or

enter an urban botanical jungle inside the glassy walls of the conservatory. Kids will be drawn to the playground, but **Lake View Cemetery** next door attracts fans of the late Bruce Lee, buried here.

>> **PUBLIC TRANSIT:** To get to Volunteer Park, take the Route 10 bus from the intersection of 15th Ave. E and E Harrison St. Exit at 15th Ave. E and E Prospect St.

With More Time

DAY 4

UNIVERSITY DISTRICT
When the cherry trees are in bloom, the campus of the University of Washington becomes a grove of brilliant blossoms bursting in pink and white. The rest of the time there are plenty of classic quads, plus repositories for the best in science and culture: the Burke Museum of Natural History and Culture and the Henry Art Gallery. Shop at one of the many bookstores near campus, like the comfy Third Place Books.

Save pennies by eating as the college students do, popping into a bustling lunch spot on the street known as simply "the Ave." Leftovers are practically a guarantee at Thai Tom, while Mexican Agua Verde Cafe is best enjoyed after renting kayaks from the paddle club next door. Pop into The Blue Moon Tavern to see where some of Seattle's literary rock stars once hung out.

INTERNATIONAL DISTRICT
Burn off all that food with several rounds at the Seattle Pinball Museum, where admission includes unlimited play. Sports fans should take a tour at CenturyLink Field or Safeco Field. Once you've worked up an appetite again, go for a casual meal at Canton Wonton House or take your time at Red Lantern.

After dinner, wander the aisles at Asian market Uwajimaya, a kind of international crossroads in the middle of Seattle.

Capitol Hill is bursting with restaurants, so the options for lunch are endless. Try the upgraded diner fare at **Skillet Diner,** or wander down the hill to the options at **Melrose Market,** a collection of eateries selling everything from oysters to burgers.

After all that culture and fine dining, it's time to hit the beach. Make your way to **West Seattle** via water taxi to the sands of Alki Beach, the spot where the city's founders first arrived. Today there's a miniature Statue of Liberty, volleyball courts, and a long stretch of waterfront for strolling. Before hopping the water taxi back to Seattle, grab a snack or a beer at **Marination Ma Kai.**

>> **PUBLIC TRANSIT:** To get to the water taxi pier, take a westbound Route 106 or 550 bus to Pioneer Square Station, then walk to the waterfront. Once in West Seattle, hop on a westbound Route 37 or 775 bus to Alki Ave. SW and 61st Ave. SW.

Finish the night back in Capitol Hill—dancing at **Q** and drinks at the bustling **Quinn's Pub** will have you up late.

>> **PUBLIC TRANSIT:** To return to Capitol Hill from the water taxi pier, take an eastbound Route 12 bus from the intersection of Marion St. and 1st Ave. Disembark at E Madison St. and Broadway.

BEST DRINKS

ROB ROY
Skilled bartenders carve a single large ice cube for every old-fashioned, helping the classic outshine the newer-fangled cocktail bars in town (page 132).

CHUCK'S HOP SHOP
This popular bottle shop has dozens of beer taps. Try local varieties and get an expert's opinion on hoppy IPAs, dark porters, or semisweet ciders (page 136).

CANON
Capitol Hill's best cocktail bar regularly appears on national best-of lists, and its whiskey library is basically the booze equivalent of the Library of Congress (page 136).

Fremont Brewing

FREMONT BREWING
This brewery's Interurban IPA, named for a long-gone Seattle railway line, is a classic version of the popular Pacific Northwest style of beer (paget 144).

WOODINVILLE
This destination just outside the city has big wineries with castle-sized tasting rooms along with intimate one-man winemaking operations, not to mention a brewery (page 217).

SEATTLE WITH KIDS

Though Seattle is best known for its very adult technology industry and cloudy weather, it's a perfect retreat for kids—as long as they like to explore, play, and get dirty.

Stay at the **Hotel Monaco** or **Hotel Ballard,** which have adult style but less bustle, or the **Fairmont Olympic Hotel,** which has a glassed in swimming pool that kids will love.

>DAY 1

The entire **Seattle Center** complex is perfect for children, starting with—of course—the **Seattle Children's Museum.** The other attractions are ideal for kids, like the IMAX theater and hands-on exhibits at **Pacific Science Center,** which teach everything from global climate to parts of the human body.

Be sure to toss a coin into the pools that sit between the buildings—it's good luck. The **Space Needle** will thrill all the way from the elevator ride to the 360-degree revolving glass floor on top, and even **Chihuly Garden and Glass,** where the outdoor glass

mural by Paul Horiuchi in the Seattle Center

sea anemone and clownfish at the Seattle Aquarium

Seattle Great Wheel

sculptures look like a scene from *Alice in Wonderland*, is surprisingly family friendly. Every kind of dining preference can be catered to at the Armory, with its food court of local favorites, and the International Fountain outside was made to be played in.

Down on the waterfront, the **Seattle Aquarium** has giant tanks of fish, a wily octopus, and feeding shows with harbor seals. Check up front for details on the day's events. Next door, the **Seattle Great Wheel** thrills the child in all of us, especially when it dips over the dark Elliott Bay water.

Most restaurants in Seattle are somewhat family friendly, save the most formal. Get the whole family to try oysters at **Elliott's Oyster House,** or rely on tried-and-true fried treats at **Ivar's Acres of Clams** on the waterfront.

>DAY 2

As stuffy as the name sounds, the **Museum of History and Industry** was made for young explorers. Just venture upstairs to the working periscope, or try the interactive history exhibits that explain how nature, calamity, and ingenuity built the city. Plus, the **Center for Wooden Boats** next door rents toy sailboats for use on the pond next

Museum of History and Industry

BEST PEOPLE-WATCHING

PIKE PLACE MARKET
People gather around to watch fish-mongers toss halibut to each other, but observing the looks of delight and surprise from the crowd is almost as fun. Bonus: Buskers play and sing throughout the market (page 60).

PIONEER SQUARE
During the first Thursday of every month, the neighborhood's art galleries stay open late and fill with art appreciators (page 65).

INTERNATIONAL FOUNTAIN
The Seattle Center fountain is the kind that kids can run through on a hot day, so it's the ideal spot to laze on the grass and people-watch (page 68).

OLYMPIC SCULPTURE PARK
The zigzag walkways of this outdoor sculpture park welcome art lovers and visitors, plus pedestrian commuters and cyclists who pass through the park's striking modern art on their way into and out of downtown (page 72).

VOLUNTEER PARK
Capitol Hill is home to one of the city's biggest artistic communities, and Volunteer Park often welcomes the neighborhood's eccentrics; don't be surprised to see acrobats or sword fighters on sunny days (page 169).

to the museum, and the grass outside is perfect for watching seaplanes take off from Lake Union.

Over in Ballard, the **Hiram M. Chittenden Locks** combines a botanical garden with a working nautical operation. It's easy to spend an entire afternoon watching the engineering feat that moves boats up and down, passing them into the Ship Canal that links the city's lakes to Puget Sound. Across the locks, an underground fish ladder allows

salmon to make their annual move to fresh water.

For dinner, make your way toward Fremont, to the **Frelard Pizza Company.** Located on the border of Ballard and Fremont, this thin-crust pizza joint has a play area for kids.

Hiram M. Chittenden Locks

>DAY 3
Get breakfast at **Macrina Bakery** in SoDo. A block south, the **Living Computers: Museum + Labs** has working computers on display, some hundreds of times bigger than the cell phones kids are familiar with. Ask about which ones have working computer games from the past. Meanwhile, the **Seattle Pinball Museum** is much more low-tech. The playable machines, which are included in the cost of admission, range from decades old to brand new, but the goal is the same—keep hitting buttons and prevent the little ball from disappearing.

End your day with dinner in the International District. **Shanghai Garden** is a good choice for families.

A RAINY DAY IN SEATTLE

The great thing about Seattle rain is that it's rarely a torrential downpour, but rather a gentle sprinkle that barely fazes the locals.

>MORNING

Start a rainy day in **Pike Place Market,** almost completely covered and home to the cozy **Crumpet Shop.** Even the flying fish and the flower stalls are under cover, and local travel book shop **Metsker Maps** is the best place to daydream about your next trip. Skip the Gum Wall outside and head to the shelter of the oldest **Starbucks.** If the crowds are too much, try the French charm of **Le Pichet** for lunch; the bistro stays warm the old-fashioned way, with wine and good service.

Pike Place Market

>AFTERNOON

Lose yourself in some of the West Coast's best museums, including the spacious **Seattle Art Museum** downtown. Galleries collect Native American art and works from around the Pacific Rim. To get a taste of the city's lush and green surroundings without getting

Seattle Art Museum, featuring the *Middle Fork* sculpture by artist John Grade

BEST FOR ROMANCE

SEATTLE GREAT WHEEL
During slow periods, you can score a private ride in a gondola as it rotates over Elliott Bay. The VIP ride costs more but comes with comfier seats and a champagne toast (page 64).

WASHINGTON PARK ARBORETUM
From roses to rhododendrons, there are thousands of beautiful flowers to serve as the backdrop to a romantic stroll (page 81).

MATT'S IN THE MARKET
Though everything around it is busy and bustling, this small restaurant manages to be intimate and comfortable. Plus it's close to the flower stalls in Pike Place Market (page 89).

CANLIS
The city's famous fine-dining destination is removed from the fray, offering views of Lake Union and exceptional service (page 99).

FRAN'S CHOCOLATES
Rumor is President Obama purchased some chocolates from here. The delicate sea-salt-topped caramels are a love affair all their own (page 181).

soaked, head to the glassed-in conservatory at **Volunteer Park,** which is like a tropical mini-vacation on a dreary Northwest day. The cozy **Wandering Goose** isn't far, where hot biscuits are constantly coming out of the oven, and the neighborhood's two bookstores are perfect for rainy days. **Ada's Technical Books and Café** is for quirky sci-fi and non-fiction biographies of science greats, while **The Elliott Bay Book Company** is for everything else. Check for readings happening in the downstairs events room, or find a seat in the café in back.

>EVENING
Do what the locals do on a rainy night: Warm up with company and local beer. Though it sounds depressing, the former mortuary space at **Pine Box** is actually quite welcoming and often bustling, even on weeknights. Serious beer nerds can easily spend an entire evening at **Chuck's Hop Shop** and barely make a dent in the bottle and draft offerings, while wine fans can get their fill at chic French bistro **Café Presse.**

the Volunteer Park conservatory

THE BEST OF TECH

Museum of Pop Culture

>MORNING

Start the day with the most charming transportation in the city: the **Monorail.** It creaks and shudders its way through downtown Seattle, an aging but still beloved sight. At the Seattle Center Monorail tsserminus, the **Museum of Pop Culture** offers a peek into the science that has yet to (and may never) arrive. Bring an open imagination to the science-fiction galleries, home to artifacts that painted the best science pop culture could dream up.

Across the street, the **Bill & Melinda Gates Foundation Visitor Center** shows how one of the biggest technology companies in the world, Microsoft, built a fortune that's now used to improve lives around the world, often using innovative yet simple technologies. One of the Gates's pet projects is building a better toilet; see how they've revolutionized the costs, environmental impact, and sanitation of one of life's necessities.

>AFTERNOON

Tucked away in an industrial neighborhood south of downtown, the **Living Computers: Museum + Labs** recalls an era where a computer took up an entire room. Many of the exhibits are turned on and available for experimentation.

Living Computers: Museum + Labs

>EVENING

End the day with the classic space age monument of Seattle, the **Space Needle.** Though built more than half a century ago, the Space Needle is remarkably earthquake-stable and still looks as spiffy as it did when it became the centerpiece of the world's fair.

PLANNING YOUR TRIP

WHEN TO GO

Summer in Seattle is a magical time. Not only does the region more or less shed its rainy reputation (though a gloomy or hazy day is always possible), the city is abuzz with outdoor festivals and events. **Labor Day weekend,** home to gaming convention PAX and music festival Bumbershoot, is one of the busiest times of the year. However, hotel prices reflect it; it's **cheaper** to visit during **fall or winter,** when the city's arts organizations are especially active. The weather in **spring** can be hit or miss, but it does mean **lower prices** and some beautiful days. Regardless of what's falling from the sky, the blooms around the city in March and April reflect the lush, green Northwest.

ENTRY REQUIREMENTS

When visiting the United States from another country, a **valid passport** is required. Depending upon your country of origin, a **visa** may also be required when visiting the United States. For a complete list of countries whose citizens are exempt from needing a visa, visit the State Department's website (http://travel.state.gov).

Canadian citizens can visit the United States without a visa, but must show a passport or enhanced driver's license at the border. All car, train, and bus crossings may entail questioning from border control agents about the purpose of the visit, destination (including hotel address), and purchases made while in the country. To protect the agricultural industries of each country from the spread of pests and disease, the transportation of fresh fruit and plants may be prohibited. There is a limit on the amount of alcohol and tobacco visitors can bring into the country. More information on crossing into the United States can be found at the Customs and Border Protection website (www.cbp.gov).

TRANSPORTATION

Visitors from far-flung locations often arrive via **Sea-Tac International Airport,** located south of the city. Those driving in likely arrive via the interstate, either I-5 from the north and south or I-90 from the east. Trains arrive at **King Street Station** from the north, south, and east.

Within Seattle, public transit consists of King County Metro's bus system, the Link Light Rail train, two Seattle streetcar lines, a water taxi, and the Washington State Ferry system. All but the ferries accept the **ORCA card,** a reloadable card that can be purchased at any Link Light Rail station, including the one at Sea-Tac Airport. The bus system is far-reaching and cheap, but can be hard for visitors to decipher. The Link Light Rail is the **most useful** to visitors; it travels from the airport and stops in Pioneer Square, downtown, and Capitol Hill. Cabs, as well as ride-sharing services like Uber and Lyft, operate throughout the city.

Driving in Seattle can be complicated, thanks to **thick traffic,** steep hills, and confusing one-way streets. Within the downtown core, it's best to walk or take a cab. However, to reach attractions farther afield, a car may come in handy. Car rental is available at the airport and in a few locations around the city.

RESERVATIONS

Reservations are encouraged for the **Space Needle** and **Underground Tour,** as well as rides on the **Seattle Great Wheel,** though they're available day-of on all but the busiest summer weekend days. Tours like Ride the Ducks often have **walk-up availability.** Hotel rooms can be hard to come by during big festivals like Bumbershoot, as well as during popular conventions. Musicals and music performances at big theaters like the Paramount, the Showbox, the Moore, and others often sell out in advance, so plan to buy tickets at least a month before (even earlier for big-name acts).

Fine-dining restaurants like **Canlis** and **El Gaucho** require advance reservations, and it can be hard to score a seat at cocktail bar **Canon** without one. Book a spot at Canlis about 2-3 weeks out; Canon reservations should be made at least a week ahead of time.

PASSES AND DISCOUNTS

The **Seattle CityPass** (www.citypass.com/seattle, $74 adults, $54 children 4-12) includes

DAILY REMINDERS

• **Monday:** Many museums are closed, including the Seattle Art Museum (seasonally) and Henry Art Gallery.

• **Tuesday:** The Seattle Art Museum, Seattle Asian Art Museum, and the Henry Art Gallery are closed.

• **Wednesday:** The Seattle Mariners play select daytime baseball games during the summer.

• **Thursday:** Many of the city's museums are open late, including the Seattle Art Museum and the Museum of History and Industry, and many are free. On the first Thursday of the month in Pioneer Square and the second Thursday of the month in Capitol Hill, art galleries stay open late and often kick off new shows.

• **Saturday:** The University District Farmers Market is held.

• **Sunday:** The Ballard Farmers Market is held. During the fall many restaurants offer Seahawks-specific menus and specials tailored to football games. The area around CenturyLink Field gets busy and rowdy on home-game Sundays. Street parking is free downtown. Admission is free at the Henry Art Gallery.

admission to five city attractions for one ticket price. It works for the Space Needle, Seattle Aquarium, Argosy Cruises Harbor Tour, either the Museum of Pop Culture or the Woodland Park Zoo, and either Chihuly Garden and Glass or the Pacific Science Center. It saves up to 45 percent on admission fees if you visit all the attractions and must be used within nine days. The pass is ideal for visitors hoping to hit a lot of big sights in a single trip, with enough time to take a little break in between each one.

Many museums are **free** on the

first **Thursday** of the month, including the Seattle Art Museum, Burke Museum of Natural History and Culture, Henry Art Gallery, Living Computer Museum, Museum of History and Industry, Wing Luke Museum, and the Seattle Asian Art Museum.

The Olympic Sculpture Park, Klondike Gold Rush National Historical Park, and the Center for Wooden Boats are always free.

Seattle Free Walking Tours offers, yes, **free walking tours** of Pike Place Market and downtown, and sustains itself through tips and donations.

on the Underground Tour

GUIDED TOURS

The **Underground Tour** is one of the city's most famous attractions. It ventures down to the buried storefronts and streets that disappeared during construction that reshaped the city. **Savor Seattle Food Tours** (206/209-5485, www.savorseattletours.com, $44-74) offers walking tours of Pike Place Market and downtown areas, as well as farther-flung neighborhoods with active culinary scenes.

Other popular tours include the **Ride the Ducks,** a tour via amphibious vehicle that rolls through downtown and then motors through Lake Union. **Show Me Seattle** (206/633-2489, http://showmeseattle.com, $44-99) does tours via minibus.

CALENDAR OF EVENTS

MARCH

Seattle is known as a nerd town, so it's no wonder that the **Emerald City Comicon** (www.emeraldcitycomicon.com) has grown to be a giant festival of comic books, superheroes, and fantasy. Actor appearances, book signings, and film screenings draw attendees, many of whom don costumes.

The **Moisture Festival** (www.moisturefestival.com) claims to be the world's largest comedy/variety festival, running four weeks. It includes acts like jugglers, comedians, and aerialists, as well as burlesque.

APRIL

At **Taste Washington** (http://tastewashington.org), hundreds of wineries from across the state and dozens of local restaurants come together to show off Northwest flavors.

MAY

The decades-old **Northwest Folklife Festival** (www.nwfolklife.org) fills Seattle Center with musicians, dancers, crafters, and fans of Pacific Northwest traditions. There are thousands of performers on multiple stages, pulling from dozens of world-wide traditions to represent the mix of heritages within the city.

The **Seattle International Film Festival** (www.siff.net) runs for a month in late spring. It claims to be the largest and most-attended film festival in the country, and tickets to screenings are available to the public.

hydroplane race at Seafair

JUNE

Things go fast at **Seafair** (www.seafair.com), the city's annual summer festival that stretches June-August. Hydroplanes race around Lake Washington at more than 150 miles per hour, and fighter jets turn loops above a boat flotilla on the lake.

On the last Sunday in June, Seattle's annual **Pride Parade** (www.seattlepride.org) runs downtown along 4th Avenue. Coinciding with the parade and billed as the largest free Pride festival in the country, **Seattle PrideFest** (www.seattlepridefest.org) fills Seattle Center with vendors and performers.

On the longest day of the year and the official start of summer

WHAT'S NEW?

- **Transit extensions:** The extension of the **Link Light Rail** is one of the most exciting transportation upgrades of the decade. It opened the University of Washington campus and the Capitol Hill neighborhood to transit riders. The opening of the **Seattle First Hill Streetcar line** from Capitol Hill to Pioneer Square in 2016 was almost as momentous.

- **More restaurants:** Recent years have seen a boom of restaurant openings in Fremont and Ballard, including new favorites like **Tarsan i Jane, Copine,** and **RockCreek Seafood & Spirits.**

- **Waterfront renovations:** A recent renovation of the **seawall** downtown, which keeps the land from tumbling into Elliott Bay, has meant a facelift for the waterfront. The **Seattle Aquarium,** the **Seattle Great Wheel,** and other downtown attractions had to endure construction and limited access, but many used the opportunity to spruce up their own spaces.

- **Seattle Asian Art Museum** is closed as it undergoes renovations. It's projected to reopen sometime in 2019.

is the **Fremont Solstice** (http://fremontsolstice.com), a celebration of all things free and expressive.

JULY

The **Seattle International Beerfest** (www.seattlebeerfest.com) is a celebration of one of the city's favorite products and pastimes, with more than 200 ales, lagers, ciders, and barley wines available for the tasting at Seattle Center.

AUGUST

Even before Washington legalized recreational marijuana use in 2012, **Hempfest** (www.hempfest.

Fremont Solstice paraphernalia

org) was the largest pot-themed gathering in the world, hosting music performances, selling marijuana-related merchandise, and celebrating cannabis culture.

SEPTEMBER

The city's biggest music festival, **Bumbershoot** (www.bumbershoot. org), is named for something locals are proud to do without: umbrellas (it's British slang). Every Labor Day weekend, the Seattle Center grounds fill with arts of every stripe, from headlining bands to art shows and poetry readings.

Once upon a time, **PAX** (http:// west.paxsite.com) was just the Penny Arcade Expo, a small gaming gathering for tabletop and video game enthusiasts. But it quickly grew into a giant gathering, and now the Seattle version is called PAX West. Tickets sell out very quickly.

The beer is flowing and the pretzels are salty at **Fremont Oktoberfest** (http:// fremontoktoberfest.com), held in Seattle's funky and freethinking Fremont neighborhood over a late September weekend. Hundreds of different beers from local breweries are served in the beer garden.

OCTOBER

Like a good jazz song, the **Earshot Jazz Festival** (www.earshot. org) can't be contained; it's made up of dozens of performances that take place in venues around the city, from giant Benaroya Hall to The Elliott Bay Book Company in Capitol Hill.

DECEMBER

Seattle Center's annual holiday celebration, **Winterfest** (www. seattlecenter.com/winterfest) is made up of lights, a winter train, a skating rink, and holiday performances throughout the public space. Events last through the entire month of December.

NEIGHBORHOODS

Downtown and Pioneer Square

Map 1

Downtown Seattle is the nexus for much of the city's **business and commerce,** and most of the city's hotels are here, as is Pike Place Market, home to Seattle's oldest Starbucks and some flying fish. The nearby **waterfront** includes some of the city's favorite destinations, like the Seattle Aquarium, the giant Seattle Great Wheel, and views

of the distant Olympic Mountains. Parking is difficult, so most people navigate the central core by foot.

Pioneer Square, accessible from most downtown hotels via a short walk, is **old Seattle,** its history evident in the **ornate architecture.** It's also home to a bevy of **art galleries.**

TOP SIGHTS

- Pike Place Market (page 60)
- Seattle Art Museum (page 62)
- Seattle Central Library (page 63)

TOP RESTAURANTS

- Matt's in the Market (page 89)
- Cherry Street Coffee (page 94)

TOP NIGHTLIFE

- The Triple Door (page 128)
- White Horse Trading Company (page 130)

TOP ARTS AND CULTURE

- Seattle Art Museum (SAM)
  Gallery (page 152)
- 5th Avenue Theatre (page 152)

TOP RECREATION

- Argosy Cruises (page 165)
- Underground Tour (page 165)

TOP SHOPS

- Metsker Maps (page 177)

TOP HOTELS

- Fairmont Olympic Hotel (page 200)
- Thompson Hotel (page 200)

GETTING THERE AND AROUND

- Link Light Rail stations: Pioneer Square,
  University Street, Westlake
- First Hill Streetcar: western terminus
  at South Jackson Street near
  Occidental Avenue South
- Major bus hubs: 3rd Avenue near Pike and
  Pine Streets; Convention Place Station
- Ferries: Seattle Ferry Terminal
- Water Taxi: Pier 50

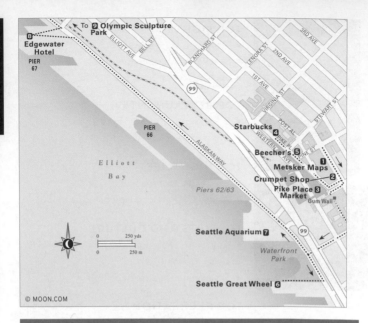

DOWNTOWN WALK

TOTAL DISTANCE: 1.25 miles
WALKING TIME: 1 hour

Any exploration of downtown should focus on Pike Place Market. There are as many opinions of the market as there are stalls in its covered main passage. Depending on who you ask, it's a delightful collection of local fare, a crowded tourist hub, the best place for fresh fish downtown, or basically a three-ring circus. But it's undeniably the heart of downtown Seattle. Oh, and call it "Pike Place Market" or simply "the market." Nothing identifies a newbie more than the incorrect "Pike's Market."

The market is open almost every day, closed only on Thanksgiving and Christmas. While some stands stay open until 6pm and nearby restaurants buzz with activity into the night, morning is the ideal time to visit (and to do this walk) in order to catch the farm stands and the tables of flowers and fruit bursting with inventory.

The indoor/outdoor complex is walkable from most downtown hotels. If you must drive, most of the parking garages nearby have day rates.

1 Start on 1st Avenue South, among the stores that make up the outer shell of the market. Some of the best for browsing are between Pike and Pine Streets, including **Metsker Maps,** which combines a killer travel

Pike Place Market

book section with beautiful maps and charts that are more art than navigation tools.

2 Carbo-load at the **Crumpet Shop,** on 1st Avenue just north of Pike Street (and three doors down from Metsker). It's a small café devoted to the British breakfast pastry that's like a softer version of an English muffin. It only makes sense to add a cup of tea.

3 Exit the café and take a right to reach the intersection with Pike Street after just a few steps. Turning right again, you'll enter **Pike Place Market.** Straight ahead, directly under the neon sign that reads "Public Market Center," is the famous Pike Place Fish Market where fishmongers toss halibut and salmon to each other, putting on a show for the crowds. Don't hesitate to take out the camera: The workers ham it up, maneuvering the fish around for cheek kisses or moving a flounder's mouth with a hidden string. If you'd rather not carry around a fillet of raw fish for the rest of the day, try an oyster shooter in a souvenir shot glass. From the hubbub around the fish stand, step back to take in the market, including the iconic red neon sign above and a pig statue below that actually serves as a piggy bank, collecting change for social service organizations. On Pike Place itself, pedestrians crowd the street (car traffic is allowed here, so be cautious). The eastern side of the thoroughfare has fruit stands and bakeries that open directly to the street, while the western side has entrances into the covered market with its smaller individual stalls.

4 As you inch north on Pike Place past Stewart Street, you'll see a crowd of people around a coffee shop you might have heard of. The so-called original **Starbucks** isn't exactly where the coffee giant began—that shop no longer exists—but this nearby location has the original risqué logo and plenty of coffee acolytes snapping photos.

5 Head south down Pike Place again, toward the fish counter and past the talented buskers stationed around the market. Along the way, stop in at **Beecher's** to peruse the staggering amounts of cheese. Continue south down Pike Place until you reach Pike Street, where you first entered the market. Beyond the pig statue at this intersection is a set of outdoor stairs that will lead you to the city's grossest attraction. Once at the bottom of the stairs, follow the cobbled Post Alley downhill about 30 feet to the Gum Wall. People stick gobs of multicolored gum to the brick building exteriors, some even spelling out messages.

6 The angled Post Alley continues down to Union Street. At Union, turn right and head west toward Elliott Bay. Cross Western Avenue after one block and walk down the stairs to reach the waterfront, walking under Seattle's aging Viaduct and crossing Alaskan Way to reach Waterfront Park. The park consists of bay-front docks with a statue of Christopher Columbus and benches. Take a left at Alaskan Way to reach Pier 57, packed with souvenir shops and the towering **Seattle Great Wheel.** Even on a cloudy day, it offers soaring looks at the cheerful white ferries that cross Puget Sound and the gigantic tankers that inch into Seattle's port.

7 Next, walk north along Alaskan Way to the other side of Waterfront Park, where the **Seattle Aquarium** sits on another pier jutting out into the bay. You could spend a whole day visiting the giant Pacific octopus, harbor seals, and coral reef fish inside.

Seattle Aquarium

8 Outside the museum, it's time to continue north along the waterfront, so turn left onto Alaskan Way. Just a few hundred yards farther is empty Pier 63, like a giant outdoor deck that extends into the water, perfect for taking pictures of the Olympic Mountains across Puget Sound. Keep going to pass a small marina and the city's cruise terminal. At this point, you'll be crossing into the waterfront portion of Belltown. (For more information

Olympic Sculpture Park

on Belltown, see page 36.) Continue walking to reach the **Edgewater Hotel,** where the Beatles famously stayed half a century ago—they stuck fishing poles out the window straight into Elliott Bay.

9 Just under a mile from the aquarium, Alaskan Way bends east and becomes Broad Street. Here, the **Olympic Sculpture Park** begins. Right next to the road's sharp turn, look for a giant pair of eyes, a sculpture by Louise Bourgeois. The park is dotted with dramatic sculptures from the likes of Alexander Calder (the giant red piece called *The Eagle*) and Richard Serra. Wander the zigzagging paths, making your way up toward Western Avenue (two blocks east of where you entered the park), and be sure to duck inside the vivarium that holds a nurse log growing new plants—a kind of biological sculpture. It's a short cab ride back to the center of downtown, or you can follow either Western Avenue or Elliott Avenue south to return to Pike Place Market, for just under a mile.

Queen Anne and Belltown Map 2

Though Queen Anne Hill is **residential,** at its base is Seattle Center, one of the city's signature attractions. The surrounding blocks have **shops, restaurants,** and **bars** that appeal to locals. Some of the city's best **elegant dining** is here, like How to Cook a Wolf, and Canlis. The hotels, while not fancy, are cheaper than in downtown.

Belltown was once downtown's scrappy sibling, growing quickly with tall condos and attracting loud nightlife. **Increased retail** and **new eateries** have changed its reputation. Belltown makes a good home base for more **adventurous** travelers who want to walk everywhere.

Recent years have seen **South Lake Union** become one of the city's most active **business neighborhoods,** home to the headquarters of Amazon, the Seattle headquarters of Facebook, and biotechnology research companies. Westlake Avenue is pedestrian-friendly, but parking can be difficult.

TOP SIGHTS
- Seattle Center (page 68)
- Space Needle (page 69)
- Olympic Sculpture Park (page 72)
- Museum of History and Industry (page 73)

TOP RESTAURANTS
- Canlis (page 99)

TOP NIGHTLIFE
- Bathtub Gin and Co. (page 132)
- Rob Roy (page 132)

TOP ARTS AND CULTURE
- Seattle Repertory Theatre (page 155)
- Pacific Northwest Ballet (page 155)
- Cinerama (page 155)

TOP SHOPS
- Endless Knot (page 183)
- Feathered Friends (page 184)

TOP HOTELS
- Edgewater Hotel (page 203)
- Ace Hotel (page 203)

GETTING THERE AND AROUND
- Monorail stops: Seattle Center, Westlake Center
- Major bus routes: 3rd Avenue; Denny Way (Route 8); Fairview Avenue North (Route 70)
- South Lake Union Streetcar: southern terminus at Westlake Center; northern terminus at Fairview Avenue North and Aloha Street

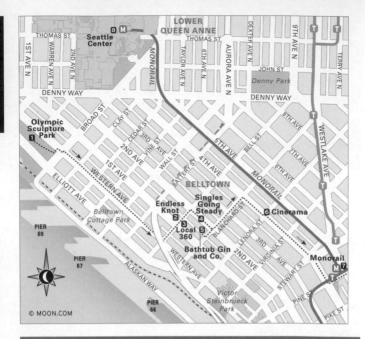

QUEEN ANNE AND BELLTOWN WALK

TOTAL DISTANCE: 1 mile (walking), 2 miles total
WALKING TIME: 30 minutes

Sandwiched between downtown and Queen Anne, Belltown is an active urban neighborhood, lined with shops, bars, and restaurants. A wander through the streets starting in the afternoon makes for a nice way to spend the day.

1 Start in the **Olympic Sculpture Park,** an outdoor, waterfront art park on acres that were once industrial lands. Now they're sculpted, multilevel lawns punctuated by the works of Alexander Calder and Jaume Plensa. Exit at the corner of Broad Street and Western Avenue, near the park's pavilion, and head southeast on Western Avenue toward downtown.

2 Once you've popped under the elevated Alaskan Way roadway, turn left on Bell Street and trudge up the hill (it's short!) to cross 1st Avenue. Women looking for effortless, fun Seattle fashion will want to pop into the boutique **Endless Knot** on the northern corner of the intersection.

3 Just across the street, you'll see **Local 360**—which tries to source its ingredients within a radius of 360 miles, serving up some delicious meals if you're ready for a sit-down bite, or you might just pause for a local beer.

4 Continue up Bell Street another block to 2nd Avenue and turn right, where you'll find the punk vinyl shop **Singles Going Steady,** fun for browsing.

5 Walk to the end of the block and turn right on Blanchard Street. Walk half a block south and turn right into the alleyway in between 1st and 2nd Avenues. Depending on your timing—it opens at 5pm daily— you can duck in for a tipple at the speakeasy **Bathtub Gin and Co.,** or note its location for later. Look for a door among the brick exteriors. Once you actually locate the bar, it's easy to find a cozy nook inside.

6 Back on Blanchard, head northeast the handful of blocks to 4th Avenue and turn right. After a block, the blue and red **Cinerama** marquee is impossible to miss, as is its stunning mural that wraps around two sides of the building. Inside is one of the last remaining movie screens of its kind, curved to show specialized three-strip films. Check to see if your timing is right to catch whatever's playing, or note showtimes for later.

7 Follow 4th Avenue a few more blocks east to reach Westlake Center. Pass through the plaza to enter the three-story shopping center, then head to the top floor to board the **Seattle Center Monorail.** At once rickety (yet safe) and space-age, it's a remnant from the mid-20th century, when Seattle represented the city of the future. Enjoy the brief ride—it takes about two minutes. There's only one stop on this elevated, mile-long route, and it's rare to have to wait more than 10 minutes to board.

Seattle Center's International Fountain

8 Step out of the Monorail into **Seattle Center,** a 74-acre complex full of museums and performance spaces. Back in 1962 this was the site of the world's fair. From here, the city is your oyster and you can choose your own adventure. The Seattle Center encompasses the Space Needle, Museum of Pop Culture, and Chihuly Garden and Glass, among other attractions. At its heart is the domed International Fountain. Since the world's fair, the area has been a gathering spot to lounge and unwind.

Capitol Hill

Map 3

If downtown is where Seattle works, Capitol Hill is where it plays. This bastion for LGBT culture has grown to become a **dining and nightlife mecca,** plus home to some of the best **small boutiques** in town. The twin thoroughfares of Pike and Pine Streets fill with pedestrians every evening, with crowds spilling out of bars and lining up at **outdoor food stands** late into the night.

Despite being crammed with **restaurants and shops,** there are few places to stay in Capitol Hill, though private rentals via AirBnB and similar companies help bring newcomers to its streets. Because the hill overlooks downtown, it's **easy to reach** for most city visitors—though it means a steep walk uphill. Parking is famously difficult on the Hill, so cabs are popular with the partying crowd.

TOP RESTAURANTS
- Skillet Diner (page 105)
- Stateside (page 108)

TOP NIGHTLIFE
- Chuck's Hop Shop (page 136)
- Canon (page 136)
- Unicorn (page 141)

TOP RECREATION
- Volunteer Park (page 169)
- I-5 Colonnade Park (page 169)

TOP SHOPS
- Ada's Technical Books and Café (page 185)
- The Elliott Bay Book Company (page 185)
- Melrose Market (page 187)

TOP HOTELS
- Hotel Sorrento (page 204)

GETTING THERE AND AROUND
- Link Light Rail station: Capitol Hill
- First Hill Streetcar: northern terminus at Broadway and Denny Street
- Major bus routes: Pike and Pine Streets

CAPITOL HILL WALK

TOTAL DISTANCE: 2.5 miles
WALKING TIME: 1 hour

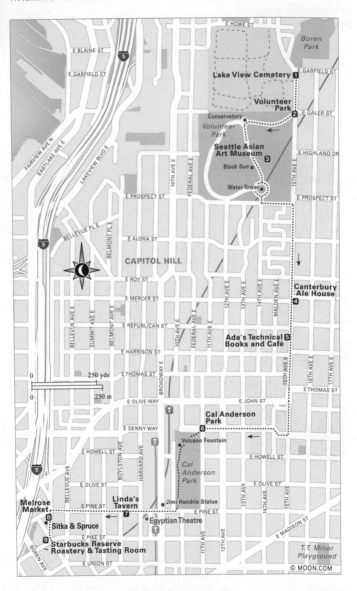

E HOWE ST

Boren Park

E BLAINE ST

E GARFIELD ST

Lake View Cemetery 1

Volunteer Park 2

E GARFIELD ST

E GALER ST

Conservatory

Volunteer Park

Seattle Asian Art Museum 3

E HIGHLAND DR

Black Sun

Water Tower

E PROSPECT ST

E PROSPECT ST

FAIRVIEW AVE N

EASTLAKE AVE E

LAKEVIEW BLVD E

10TH AVE E

FEDERAL AVE E

15TH AVE E

BELLEVUE PL E

BELMONT PL E

E ALOHA ST

CAPITOL HILL

E ROY ST

E MERCER ST

Canterbury Ale House 4

12TH AVE E

13TH AVE E

14TH AVE E

MALDEN AVE E

E REPUBLICAN ST

BELLEVUE AVE E

SUMMIT AVE E

BELMONT AVE E

10TH AVE E

FEDERAL AVE E

11TH AVE E

Ada's Technical Books and Café 5

15TH AVE E

16TH AVE E

17TH AVE E

E HARRISON ST

E THOMAS ST

E THOMAS ST

0   250 yds

0   250 m

E OLIVE WAY

E JOHN ST

Cal Anderson Park 6

BROADWAY E

E DENNY WAY

Volcano Fountain

E HOWELL ST

BOYLSTON AVE E

HARVARD AVE E

E HOWELL ST

Cal Anderson Park

E OLIVE ST

E OLIVE ST

13TH AVE E

14TH AVE E

15TH AVE E

Linda's Tavern 7

Jimi Hendrix Statue

E PINE ST

Melrose Market 8

E PINE ST

Sitka & Spruce

Egyptian Theatre

E MADISON ST

E PIKE ST

BOREN AVE

Starbucks Reserve Roastery & Tasting Room 9

11TH AVE E

12TH AVE E

14TH AVE E

E MADISON ST

T.T. Minor Playground

E UNION ST

© MOON.COM

The city's best nightlife is in Capitol Hill—this is where Seattle hangs out. Wander through two of the city's best parks in the evening, pay your respects at memorials to two famous Seattle residents who died too young, then be sure to stop for a drink at some of the 'hood's many, many watering holes.

VOLUNTEER PARK AND 15TH AVENUE EAST

1 Begin the walk on a somber—but not morbid—note at **Lake View Cemetery,** entering at 15th Avenue East near East Garfield Street. The beautiful old graveyard holds the tombs of some of the city's founders, plus the graves of two local martial artists who died tragically young: Bruce Lee and his son, Brandon. The gates close around dusk.

2 Exit the cemetery the same way you entered and take a right on 15th Avenue East, walking south just a few hundred feet to **Volunteer Park.** Enter the park where 15th Avenue intersects with East Highland Drive. As the sun dips toward the Olympic Mountains to the west, turn left (south) at the glassed-in conservatory (the botanical attraction closes at 4pm) and make your way to the center of the park. You can see the Space Needle through the *Black Sun* sculpture by Isamu Noguchi, which is said to have inspired the Soundgarden song "Black Hole Sun."

gravestones of Bruce and Brandon Lee in Lake View Cemetery

Seattle Asian Art Museum

3 The **Seattle Asian Art Museum** is undergoing renovations in 2019, but the art deco exterior, guarded by twin camel statues, is a perennial park highlight. Continue south out of Volunteer Park. Before exiting, you'll pass the 1906 brick water tower. Ascend 107 steps inside to reach an observation level with windows facing all directions. See the Olympic Mountains and the Space Needle from one side and Lake Washington from the other. As the sun dips and reflects east, the Cascade Mountains past Lake Washington may be painted in a purple evening alpenglow.

4 Exit the park by walking south from the water tower, putting you on East Prospect Street. Just one block up the hill takes you to 15th Avenue East, where you'll turn right and walk five blocks, or a third of a mile, to **Canterbury Ale House,** which has an impressive beer selection on tap. This is a locals' bar, packed to the gills during Seahawks football games.

5 With a belly full of beer, head another tenth of a mile (just over a block) south on 15th Avenue East to reach **Ada's Technical Books and Café,** located in a small house with a porch. This warm home to sci-fi, fantasy, and nonfiction tomes is open until 9pm, its café dishing out tea, coffee, and small bites. The store isn't large, but expect to spend a lot of time browsing.

6 Continue another third of a mile south on 15th Avenue East to Denny Way. You'll pass a hospital on your left and a Safeway on your right. At Denny, turn right (downhill), going four blocks to 11th Avenue East and the northeast corner of **Cal Anderson Park,** full of Capitol Hill's student and young artist population enjoying the evening. Take in the volcano-shaped fountain in the northwest corner, near the new light-rail station; it spills into a large reflecting pool. As you continue diagonally to the southwest corner, you'll end up near sports courts that mostly host games of bike polo. From here, the corner of East Pine Street and Nagle Place, walk one block west to Broadway. At Broadway, turn right and walk a few feet up the sidewalk to the statue of guitar god Jimi Hendrix, commissioned and owned by the proprietor of the art supply store just next to it. Hendrix was born in Seattle in 1942 and died of a drug over-dose at age 27.

7 Return to East Pine Street and turn right to continue west (down-hill) toward downtown. Both Pike and Pine Streets are famous for their barhopping crowds in the evenings, but this is a calmer stretch of the neighborhood's famous corridor. Pass the Egyptian Theatre, an old movie house saved by the massive Seattle International Film Festival, and popular longtime dive **Linda's Tavern.** On either side of the street, new glassy luxury apartment buildings rise above old Capitol Hill brick facades, with a few old shops and businesses hanging on in a neighbor-hood bursting at the seams.

8 Continue west on East Pine Street for a third of a mile (five blocks), then turn south (left) onto Melrose Avenue. **Melrose Market** is to your right, a refurbished brick building that now houses an oyster bar, several shops, a wine bar, and one of the city's best Northwest-focused restaurants, Sitka & Spruce. Pick from the myriad dining establish-ments and settle in for dinner.

Starbucks Reserve Roastery & Tasting Room

9 Follow Melrose Avenue south for a block to end . . . at a Starbucks? Yep. The **Starbucks Reserve Roastery & Tasting Room** is no mere java stand, but a sprawl-ing space with copper pipes and coffee galore—and it's open until 11pm. Try a late-night caffeine jolt or order from the cocktail menu If you're ready for a nightcap.

Fremont   Map 4

Its nickname is the **Center of the Universe,** but Fremont isn't really in the middle of anything. Located just a little closer to the center of town than Ballard, it's known for its off-kilter sense of style. Most of the bars and restaurants in the area embrace this **funky vibe.**

However, Fremont's unusual character hardly makes it a joke. Restaurants here are quiet homes to **fine cuisine.** Famed sandwich shop Paseo has devotees that line up out the door. With no hotels, Fremont is **welcoming to visitors** but not overrun with them, a free little enclave in the middle of a tech-heavy city.

TOP SIGHTS

- Gas Works Park (page 76)
- Fremont Troll (page 77)

TOP RESTAURANTS

- Manolin (page 114)
- Paseo (page 117)

TOP NIGHTLIFE

- Fremont Brewing (page 144)

TOP SHOPS

- Archie McPhee (page 188)

GETTING THERE AND AROUND

- Major bus routes: North 34th Street; North 36th Street; Leary Way
- Biking: Burke-Gilman Trail (trailhead at Northwest 45th Street and 11th Avenue Northwest; east to Gas Works Park)

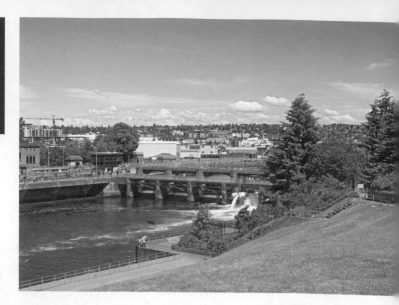

Ballard

Map 5

This northern Seattle neighborhood is like a second Capitol Hill, though a bit **calmer** and more **mature.** Ballard Avenue is home to one of the best stretches of **independent retail** in the city. The neighborhood's **dining scene** is no longer a secret thanks to restaurants like The Walrus and the Carpenter, which attracts hours-long lines. The weekly **Ballard Farmers Market** is the best in the city.

Though Ballard isn't close to much, it's home to one of the city's best non-downtown accommodations, the Hotel Ballard. Its sister property across the street, Ballard Inn, has smaller rooms but even more charm. The neighborhood is best enjoyed by foot. It's a home base for the visitor who wants a different Seattle experience but still expects a **wide range of options.**

TOP SIGHTS
- Hiram M. Chittenden Locks (page 78)

TOP RESTAURANTS
- The Walrus and the Carpenter (page 118)
- Stoneburner (page 121)

TOP NIGHTLIFE
- King's Hardware (page 147)
- Noble Fir (page 147)

TOP RECREATION
- Burke-Gilman Trail (page 170)

TOP SHOPS
- Ballard Farmers Market (page 190)
- Bop Street Records (page 191)

TOP HOTELS
- Hotel Ballard (page 205)

GETTING THERE AND AROUND
- Major bus routes: Northwest 45th Street and Northwest Market Street (Route 44); 15th Avenue Northwest (D Line)
- Biking: Burke-Gilman Trail (Golden Gardens Park south to intersection of Northwest 54th Street and 32nd Avenue Northwest)

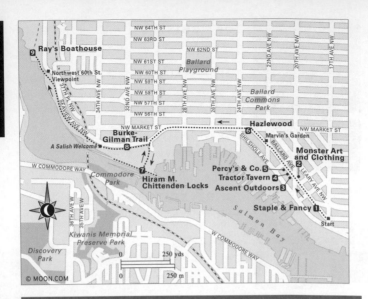

BALLARD WALK

TOTAL DISTANCE: 1.8 miles
WALKING TIME: 35-45 minutes

Though Ballard was originally settled by Scandinavian fishermen, its busiest blocks are not directly on the waterfront. Start this walk about two hours before sundown, so that by the time you reach Ray's Boathouse, you can soak in the sunset views as you eat dinner. Start your tour of the neighborhood where **Ballard Avenue meets 17th Avenue NW.** Finding parking is always a problem in Ballard, but this end of the neighborhood is a little quieter (more parking may be available on Shilshole Avenue, one block southwest of Ballard Avenue).

1 Head northwest on Ballard Avenue. In less than a block, you'll pass the restaurant **Staple & Fancy.** The "staple" portion of the menu has plenty of Italian bites that work as delicious fuel for an evening walk. Before you leave, peek through the interior windows to The Walrus and the Carpenter, a popular oyster bar whose wait times are legendary.

2 Ballard Avenue gets busier in a few blocks, with the artsy **Monster Art and Clothing** at the corner of 20th Avenue NW. If the evening air is getting chilly, purchase a pair of goofy printed socks from the wall of footwear. Wearing socks with sandals is a Seattle tradition.

3 Cross Ballard to reach **Ascent Outdoors,** an outdoor store known for its used clothing racks and gear-geek staff.

4 A few doors farther northwest on Ballard Avenue, peruse the music show flyers outside **Tractor Tavern.** Most nights there's a lively concert going on inside, so make a note of what shows are worth seeing later. On Sundays, this part of Ballard fills with booths selling produce and crafty goods during the Ballard Farmers Market, which spans NW Vernon Place to 22nd Avenue NW.

Monster Art and Clothing

5 Enter **Percy's & Co.,** just a few doors past Tractor Tavern, and head all the way through the apothecary-themed bar to the patio out back. This airy, west-facing space stays warm with the last of the day's sun. After enjoying a drink, continue one block northwest. Where Ballard Avenue meets 22nd Avenue NW, the intersection forms a small park called Marvin's Garden, which is anchored by a brick bell tower. The bell dates back to the turn of the 20th century, when Ballard was its own

the stage at Tractor Tavern

Percy's & Co.

city. The park is named for the onetime "honorary mayor" of the neighborhood, Marvin Sjoberg.

6 Take a left to go west when Ballard Avenue dead-ends into NW Market Street, popping into wee cocktail haven **Hazlewood** for a leisurely drink.

7 Continue west on NW Market Street for four blocks, then veer left on 54th Street, passing an outdoor rock climbing wall. It's just a block farther to the entrance of the **Hiram M. Chittenden Locks,** a combination of lush gardens, wildlife management tools, and fascinating industrial equipment at work.

8 Once you tear yourself away from watching the ships pass through, head back toward NW 54th Street to join the paved **Burke-Gilman Trail,** which runs parallel to NW 54th. Stay alert; the path is crowded with bikers nearly year-round. Just a few dozen feet west of the locks, along the trail, is a statue of a behatted tribal figure holding a blue and red circle, a work titled *A Salish Welcome.* The

Burke-Gilman Trail

Hiram M. Chittenden Locks

bronze, aluminum, and glass sculpture honors the life of the salmon—notice them carved into the disc lofted above the figure's head. The water just inside the locks, much of Ballard's working waterfront, is known as Salmon Bay.

9 Continue up the Burke-Gilman Trail, which runs next to train tracks and maintains Ballard's industrial feel. Pause when the trail passes Seaview Avenue. This small, open green spot, dotted with a few benches, offers views into Shilshole Bay and the shores of Magnolia just across the water. Look for a rainbow Seattle Parks sign labeling it "Northwest 60th Street Viewpoint." Walk north on Seaview Avenue, which runs parallel to the Burke-Gilman Trail here. You've arrived at waterfront **Ray's Boathouse,** where the more casual upper level has a deck boasting perfect sunset views of Puget Sound. Don't leave before scanning the waters of Puget Sound for wildlife; orcas have been known to play among the sailboats and skiffs here.

University District

Map 6

It's right there in the name: This neighborhood is all about the **University of Washington,** which has 44,000 students and dominates the landscape on the western edge of Lake Washington. Husky Stadium, named for the school's mascot, rises from one end of the campus, and a large section of the neighborhood is **pedestrian quads** and classroom buildings. **The Ave,** or University Way, is packed with **breakfast spots** and cheap **takeout joints,** perfect for student life. The nearby University Village shopping center is rather upscale, with lots of home design and clothing stores.

TOP RESTAURANTS

- Din Tai Fung (page 121)
- Portage Bay Cafe (page 122)

TOP NIGHTLIFE

- The Blue Moon Tavern (page 148)

TOP ARTS AND CULTURE

- Henry Art Gallery (page 158)

TOP SHOPS

- Glassybaby (page 193)
- University Village (page 194)

GETTING THERE AND AROUND

- Link Light Rail station: UW/Husky Stadium
- Major bus routes: Northeast Pacific Street and 15th Avenue Northeast (Route 43); Northeast 45th Street and 15th Avenue Northeast (Route 44)

International District and SoDo

Map 7

The International District was historically the center of Seattle's **immigrant culture,** especially Japanese and Chinese communities. Today it is home to a number of **Asian restaurants** and businesses. SoDo stands for either "south of downtown" or, as longtime locals insist, "south of the Dome," referencing the Kingdome stadium that was demolished in 2000. It's an **industrial area** adjacent to the Port of Seattle, but the old warehouses are increasingly home to **shops, live music, and restaurants.** It's not an easily walkable district, and

when there's a football, soccer, or baseball game, or a big concert, traffic snarls are common.

TOP RESTAURANTS
- Tamarind Tree (page 124)
- Fuji Bakery (page 125)

TOP RECREATION
- CenturyLink Field (page 173)

TOP SHOPS
- Uwajimaya (page 194)

GETTING THERE AND AROUND
- Link Light Rail stations: International District, Stadium, SoDo
- Major bus routes: 4th Avenue South (Routes 131, 132)

SIGHTS

Much of Seattle's sights revolve around the futuristic, innovative energy of the city, from the *Hammering Man* in front of the art museum to the Tomorrowland-

Hammering Man, designed by Jonathan Borofsky, stands in front of the Seattle Art Museum.

like Seattle Center. It doesn't matter what the weather is—Pike Place Market is open even in the rain, and the top of the Space Needle is a thrill even on a cloudy day. The Seattle Art Museum puts classic Old West photography next to modern installations and a large collection of Native American art, while the Museum of History and Industry takes a playful, often hands-on approach to the city's weird and tech-filled history.

The urban core of the city first grew up around Pioneer Square, just south of today's busiest and biggest buildings, where the white Smith Tower is just one architectural gem preserved from an earlier era. More recent buildings, like the skyscraping Columbia Tower, are reflective glass giants, while at their feet is a walkable city.

Higher up Capitol Hill, the city's nightlife and dining hub, sights like Lake View Cemetery are a calm balance to the bustle; visitors flock to the graves of Bruce Lee and his son. In Ballard, the sea-going roots of the city are remembered at the striking new Nordic Museum and are still alive at the working Hiram M. Chittenden Locks. And in the University District, the University of Washington is a sight unto itself, holding a world-class education facility and multiple museums. It's hard to see all of Seattle, because every corner is different and inviting.

HIGHLIGHTS

✪ **MOST POPULAR MARKET:** The seafood counter and its flying fish may be the most famous part of **Pike Place Market,** but there's enough produce, spices, crafts, buskers, and fresh-made doughnuts to fill an entire day in the downtown landmark (page 60).

✪ **BEST CULTURE:** Inside the **Seattle Art Museum** is a peerless collection of Pacific Northwest art (page 62).

✪ **BEST BOOK NOOK:** The glass **Seattle Central Library** looks like a greenhouse for books, and its seemingly infinite collection is free to wander (page 63).

✪ **BEST PLACE TO SPEND A WHOLE DAY:** The collection of museums, sights, green spaces, and fountains at **Seattle Center** entices visitors to spend as much time as possible here (page 68).

✪ **MOST ICONIC PERCH:** The **Space Needle** has been the city's symbol for decades, offering sky-high views from the observation deck with a glass floor (page 69).

✪ **BEST OUTDOOR ART:** Once a forgotten industrial site, the **Olympic Sculpture Park** has turned a few waterfront blocks into a cutting-edge art destination (page 72).

✪ **UNIQUE CITY VIEW:** Look for the periscope inside the **Museum of History and Industry** for a peek out at Lake Union (page 73).

✪ **BEST RUST:** The views of downtown from **Gas Works Park** are almost as spectacular as the industrial ruins that populate this former gasification plant (page 76).

✪ **BEST FAIRY TALE CHARACTER:** Peek under the Aurora Bridge to find a monster-sized statue called the **Fremont Troll,** poised to eat a car (page 77).

✪ **MOST IMPRESSIVE FEAT OF ENGINEERING:** Boats big and small gain passage through the Ship Canal at the **Hiram M. Chittenden Locks,** next to a special thoroughfare made just for salmon (page 78).

Olympic Sculpture Park

Downtown and Pioneer Square

Map 1

DOWNTOWN

✪ Pike Place Market

Around every corner of Pike Place Market, the city's most popular attraction, are stands selling fresh veggies, bright bouquets of flowers, local cheese, and handmade crafts, as well as performers busking for change. This nine-acre farmers market is one of the oldest continuously operated markets in the country. The market was born in 1907, when Seattle was evolving from a small port town into a bustling city of commerce. Local purveyors started pulling wagons full of produce to the spot; shortly after, the permanent arcade, comprising a long line of stalls, was built by a Klondike gold rusher.

The main arcade, on the west side of Pike Place, runs underneath the two famous red neon signs (one reads "Public Market Center," the other "Public Market") atop the market building at Pike and Pine Streets. It houses most of the traditional produce, flower, fish, and craft stalls. The buildings to the south and east mostly house small restaurants and food counters. More than 20 buildings make up the area known as "the market."

Pike Place, which runs right

flowers at Pike Place Market

through the market's densest area, is technically still a road, but the high numbers of pedestrians and lack of parking mean that it's unwise to drive through. The pedestrian-only Post Alley, home to several bars and gift shops, cuts through the buildings to the east, between Pike Place and 1st Avenue.

Pike Place Fish Market (86 Pike Pl., 206/682 7181, www.pikeplacefish.com; 6:30am-6pm Mon.-Sat., 7am-5pm Sun.) draws the biggest crowds in the complex. Here, halibut, salmon, and crabs are tossed through the air from one fishmonger to another, a practice that started early in the fish stand's market life to hurry purchases back behind the counter, where they were weighed and wrapped. The centrally located stand, topped with a "World Famous" sign, is 90 years old, recently sold to a group of its employees so its singular tradition can continue. The counter also sells oyster shooters in souvenir shot glasses ($3.50) as well as cookbooks.

On the eastern side of Pike Place and facing the main arcade is **Starbucks** (1912 Pike Pl., 206/448-8762, www.starbucks.com; 6:30am-9pm daily). The chain's first location was a few doors down, but this early outpost retains a few old-timey touches, like a logo whose mermaid mascot is more bare-breasted than the version that's been exported worldwide. Lines for a latte or vintage-style Starbucks swag often snake out the door. Here you can also purchase the Pike Place Special Reserve blend, only available at this "original" Starbucks.

Seattle's stickiest attraction is the **Gum Wall** (1428 Post Alley, enter at Pike St. and Pike Pl.), located down an alley near the entrance to the market. It started when patrons of a nearby

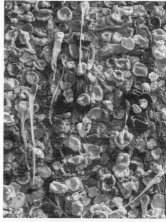
Gum Wall

improv theater began leaving their gum on the building's exterior.

Next to the north end of the market, **Victor Steinbrueck Park** (2001 Western Ave., 206/684-4075; 6am-10pm daily) offers waterfront views and two traditional cedar totem poles. It makes for a good photo op after a visit to the market.

MAP 1: Bordered by Western Ave., Virginia St., 1st Ave., and Pike St., 206/682-7453, www.pikeplacemarket.org; market 9am-6pm Mon.-Sat., 9am-5pm Sun., individual shop hours vary

NEARBY:

- Dine with a view at **Matt's in the Market** (page 89).

- Blend Japanese and Spanish cuisine at **Japonessa** (page 92).
- Tip back a local beer at **Pike Brewing Company** (page 128).
- Top off your outfit at **Goorin Brothers Hat Shop** (page 179).
- Hoard foodie gifts at **DeLaurenti** (page 181).
- Indulge your chocolate cravings at **Fran's Chocolates** (page 181).

TOP EXPERIENCE

✪ Seattle Art Museum

The art on display at the Seattle Art Museum ranges from the traditional to the cutting-edge, with artists like John Singer Sargent and Jackson Pollock represented. There are also galleries of Northwest art, including collections of Western paintings and native art. Outside, a line of video screens displays nature and city images, and occasionally even live shots from below the museum. In the middle of busy downtown, the museum has a tiled archway entrance at 1st Avenue and University Street; otherwise, the four-floor gallery space looks like the exterior of a modern office building. With the galleries stacked atop each other and connected by escalators, there isn't much breathing room here. It's easier to maneuver around the school groups by visiting on weekday mornings.

The museum offers three ways to take an audio-guided tour: via app (available on the museum's website), cell phone (206/866-3222), or handheld device (available at the front desk, free). Admission is free the first Thursday of the month (but the museum gets very crowded), and periodic SAM Remix events open the galleries extra-late on Friday nights and feature a raucous dance party. To find

Big Picture: Art After 1945 at the Seattle Art Museum

the museum, just look for Jonathan Borofsky's *Hammering Man*—the moving sculpture that stands guard in front of the museum (and takes a break only on Labor Day).

MAP 1: 1300 1st Ave., 206/654-3100, www. seattleartmuseum.org; 10am-5pm Wed. and Fri.-Sun., 10am-9pm Thurs.; $25 adults, $23 seniors, $15 students, children free

NEARBY:

- Get lost in the wine list at **Purple Café and Wine Bar** (page 88).
- Linger through the chef's tasting

menu at **Heartwood Provisions** (page 90).

- Find classic Seattle fusion cuisine at **Wild Ginger** (page 94).
- Have a literary tipple at **Bookstore Bar & Café** (page 130).
- Shop for future museum pieces at **Seattle Art Museum (SAM) Gallery** (page 152).
- Buy gifts that you'll want to keep for yourself at **Watson Kennedy Fine Home** (page 179).

Seattle Central Library

❂ Seattle Central Library

There are a million books inside the Seattle Central Library and nearly as many glass panels on its unusual exterior. Being inside is something like visiting a greenhouse, but one that grows books. The windowed building was designed by Dutch architect Rem Koolhaas and has enough glass to cover more than five football fields.

Groups of five or larger can book free tours of the space, but everyone can wander for free and access the cell phone tour (206/686-8564). Head to the 3rd floor for the largest public space and a café, and then venture to the floors known as the Books Spiral— four stories of stacks, connected by an incline ramp, that slowly spiral upward. Readings and events occur daily in the library's auditorium and other meeting spaces. For a quieter experience and views of the skyscrapers just outside, head to Level 10, the Betty Jane Narver Reading Room.

MAP 1: 1000 4th Ave., 206/386-4636, www.spl.org; 10am-8pm Mon.-Thurs., 10am-6pm Fri.-Sat., noon-6pm Sun.; free

Columbia Center Sky View Observatory

How high do you want to go? Visit Columbia Center Sky View Observatory for the absolute tallest observation point in the city (yes, taller than the Space Needle). From the carpeted lobby, you can see almost to Canada through the windows—just look for Mount Baker to the north, and know that everything past it is another country. The spot feels like a rather bland waiting room with a killer view, though there are a few informational displays to tell you what you're looking at and a café that serves coffee and local beer and wine. The Olympic Mountains to the west are one of the most prominent sights, and even on a cloudy day you'll likely see the busy port and Elliott Bay below. The view at 902 feet off the ground makes this the second-highest publicly accessible spot west of the Mississippi, and the waits are much shorter and the ticket prices much lower than at the Space Needle. On the way up to the 73rd floor, visit the 40th-floor Starbucks, the chain's highest outpost in the world.

MAP 1: 701 5th Ave., 206/386-5564, www.skyviewobservatory.com; 10am-8pm daily; $22 adults, $19 seniors, $16 children 5-13, children under 5 free

WATERFRONT

Seattle Aquarium

From its spot atop two piers, the Seattle Aquarium dangles over the waters it celebrates. In the lobby, the giant Window on Washington Waters tank is filled with local fish, and throughout the day divers pop inside to show off its inhabitants. Look for the mottled orange of the rockfish, which can live up to 100 years but develops eye problems in captivity. (The Seattle Aquarium's vet has extensive experience in eye surgery and even hopes to someday provide prosthetic eyes for the creatures.) The aquarium has touch tanks and bird exhibits, plus octopuses and hundreds of jellyfish. Larger habitats house sea and river otters, and a new amphitheater-style area holds three harbor seals.

Check at the front desk for the schedule of daily animal feedings. The giant Pacific octopus encounter is memorable for the animal's graceful movements, while the marine mammal introductions feature the cuddly otters and seals, with trainers showing off the animals' learned behaviors. More than 100 viewers can gather around the harbor seal exhibit. The café has pizzas, sandwiches, some seafood entrées (sustainable ones only, of course), and microbrews, and the outdoor balcony is open on days with decent weather.

MAP 1: 1483 Alaskan Way, 206/386-4300, www.seattleaquarium.org; 9:30am-5pm daily; $29.95 adults, $19.95 children 4-12, children under 4 free

Seattle Great Wheel

When the Seattle Great Wheel popped up on Seattle's waterfront in 2012, it took the city by surprise—and it carried a million riders in less than a year. The 175-foot Ferris wheel is the tallest of its kind on the West Coast, and the enclosed cars can hold eight people each. From inside each gondola, the views shift from downtown Seattle to Elliott Bay and the Olympic Mountains across Puget Sound, and the end-of-the-pier location means that you'll dangle over the dark-blue water. One of the cars is not like the others: The VIP gondola has leather seats and a glass floor, and a ride inside ($50) comes with a champagne toast, commemorative T-shirt, and the ability to skip the line.

MAP 1: 1301 Alaskan Way, 206/623-8600, www.seattlegreatwheel.com; 10am-11pm Sun.-Thurs., 10am-midnight Fri.-Sat. summer, 11am-10pm Mon.-Thurs., 11am-midnight Fri., 10am-midnight Sat., 10am-10pm Sun. fall-spring; $14 adults, $13 seniors, $9 children 3-11, children under 3 free

Ye Olde Curiosity Shop

Ye Olde Curiosity Shop is indeed a shop, but it's also a historic Seattle attraction. In 1899 it opened as the Free Museum and Curio, mainly showing off artifacts from Alaska that gold rushers had brought back. The preserved mummy named Sylvester is the shop's biggest attraction; the body was supposedly dug from the Arizona desert in 1895 and may have been mummified by natural dehydration, though a CT scan revealed the bullet that killed him. There's also a large collection of shrunken human heads, conjoined cow bodies, walrus tusks, and the Lord's Prayer engraved on a single grain of rice. The wares for sale are a little less exotic—souvenirs, porcelain collectibles, and saltwater taffy, plus Northwest Native American totem poles and masks. You can also buy a shrunken head replica made of goat hide.

totem pole in Pioneer Square

MAP 1: 1001 Alaskan Way, 206/682-5844,
www.yeoldecuriosityshop.com;
9am-9:30pm daily summer; 10am-6pm
Sun.-Thurs., 9am-9pm Fri.-Sat. winter

PIONEER SQUARE
Pioneer Square

Pioneer Square is a small public space located on the north end of the neighborhood of the same name. It sits at the corner of Yesler Way and 1st Avenue and comprises a city block of shrubs, trees, and an ornate iron pergola that dates to the 1909 Alaska-Yukon-Pacific Exposition. A giant totem pole in the middle of the square represents the fraught history of Seattle's relationship with indigenous tribes: The first one to stand here was stolen from Alaskan Tlingit Indians in the 19th century; after it was set afire in the 1930s, Tlingit carvers created a new one as a gift. Much of the architecture around the square is classic Victorian and Edwardian, the structures built on fill that buried the first iteration of the town after a fire ravaged the area.

During the Klondike gold rush, the neighborhood filled with saloons and outfitters where prospectors would prepare for the trip to Alaska. Since the 1960s, Pioneer Square's buildings have been preserved and protected; pay attention to moldings, ceilings, and arched entryways when exploring the shops around the square.

MAP 1: Yesler Way and 1st Ave., www.
pioneersquare.org

Klondike Gold Rush
National Historical Park

When you think "gold rush," you probably picture California or Alaska, not Seattle. But the Klondike Gold Rush National Historical Park, run by the National Park Service, is located in the middle of the Pioneer Square neighborhood. It's not actually a park, but rather a museum in the old stone Cadillac Hotel, where prospectors stayed in Seattle before heading north to the goldfields. The museum tells the story of how Seattle served as the gateway to the Klondike region.

One central display shows off newspaper articles detailing the great excitement that arose in 1897 when gold from the Klondike River in Alaska and Canada arrived via steamship at American ports. Prospectors came to Seattle to outfit themselves for the trip north, and even Seattle's own mayor quit to join the stampede. The Royal Canadian Mounted Police, worried that all those people were going to starve in the wilderness, began requiring that each person bring a year's worth of food. Fun hands-on exhibits and gold-panning demonstrations show how the Seattle economy grew from that gold rush—and how poorly most prospectors fared.

Smith Tower

MAP 1: 319 2nd Ave. S., 206/220-4240, www.nps.gov/klse; 9am-5pm daily summer, 10am-5pm daily winter; free

Smith Tower

The Space Needle is weirder looking and the Columbia Tower is taller, but the Smith Tower is a beautiful historic building that used to be the tallest in the West, at 484 feet. Built in 1914, the pointy white tower was long a symbol of the city. On the 35th floor—reached on an original Otis elevator—an observation deck offers a 360-degree view of the city, waterfront, and distant mountains. The room is decked out in Chinese wood furniture and porcelain and teak ceiling tiles. A corner of the observation floor is now a cocktail bar called Temperance, while a self-guided tour covers local bootlegging history via ornate exhibits on the ground floor. Don't miss the interactive screen that debunks the tower's best-known myths and legends.

MAP 1: 506 2nd Ave., 877/412-2776, www.smithtower.com; 10am-9pm daily; $19 adults, $15 seniors, $15 children 6-12, children under 6 free

Waterfall Garden Park

Tucked behind high walls on an unassuming corner of Pioneer Square is Seattle's own secret garden. It's easy to pass the iron gates that mark the park's entrance without noticing that there's a waterfall just inside this small courtyard. Water flows down a two-story rock wall next to small tables with chairs, making it a popular place for local workers to spend a relaxing lunch. Look for a plaque that recognizes 100 years of UPS; the company was started on this site.

MAP 1: 219 2nd Ave. S.; 8am-5:30pm daily summer, 8am-3:45pm daily winter; free

TO THE SKIES: THE MUSEUM OF FLIGHT

Museum of Flight

You might think you like airplanes, but until you've been to the **Museum of Flight** (9404 E. Marginal Way S, South Seattle, 206/764-5720, www.museumofflight.org; 10am-5pm daily; $24 adults, $20 seniors, $15 children 5-17, children under 5 free), you don't really understand what it means to be obsessed. Welcome to one of the biggest air and space museums in the country. It has 150 planes and flying machines, many hanging in a giant glass pavilion, including the Mach 3 Blackbird, the fastest plane ever built, along with early airmail biplanes, a sailplane, WWI fighters, and a Huey helicopter. A big red barn—the original Boeing airplane factory—traces the history of flight and the Boeing industry in Seattle. Outdoors you'll find a sort of parking lot for cool old airplanes, including a supersonic Concorde jet and the first jet to serve as Air Force One; walk through the 707 and see where President Kennedy sat on his flights. Also at the museum is a 3D theater and flight simulators.

One of the most exciting parts of the Museum of Flight is the space exhibits, including a full-size replica of an International Space Station lab and a Soyuz module used by Charles Simonyi, a billionaire who used his Microsoft money to visit space (and fund the gallery that houses many of the museum's space artifacts). In the center of the room is the giant Space Shuttle Trainer, a full-scale replica of the now retired spacecraft. It never went to space, but every shuttle astronaut trained on it. Tours ($20-25, reservations recommended) are available for a peek inside the crew compartment, though any museum visitor can peer inside the cargo bay—Queen Elizabeth once dined inside it when she visited NASA in Houston, Texas.

The museum building is located next to Boeing Field/King County International Airport's airstrip, used by Boeing, private aircraft, and a handful of commercial flights—which means that there are a few airplane parking spaces for visitors who fly in. For everyone else, the museum is reachable by car or mass transit. It sits south of downtown and takes about 20 minutes—though the route is prone to traffic—by car. Take I-5 south from the city to exit 158, then turn right on East Marginal Way. The museum is a half mile later, and parking is free. Metro Bus 124 connects the museum to downtown Seattle for an approximately 25-minute ride. Visit on the first Thursday night of the month for free admission 5pm-9pm.

Queen Anne and Belltown

Map 2

QUEEN ANNE

✪ Seattle Center

Born as the fairgrounds of the 1962 World's Fair, Seattle Center is a giant play space, workshop, stage, and meeting spot. Beyond its signature tall white arches—part of the Pacific Science Center, designed by the same architect who designed New York City's World Trade Center—is the domed International Fountain and 74 acres of performance spaces, museums, parks, and art installations like the 150-foot-long Grass Blades. Seattle Center serves as the city's collective backyard, or perhaps its welcoming parlor—a number of festivals take place on the grounds celebrating music, art, and culture. One lawn has a giant, multicolored outdoor glass mosaic by Paul Horiuchi, and a pagoda made of Japanese cypress houses a bell that was given to Seattle by its sister city, Kobe, Japan.

Seattle Center comprises many of the city's big-name attractions, such as the Space Needle, the Museum of Pop Culture, the Chihuly Garden and Glass, and the Bill & Melinda Gates Foundation.

Although the building has had many uses both during and after the world's fair, today the Armory, one of Seattle Center's buildings, serves as a pavilion boasting a truly gourmet food court. Some of Seattle's most popular restaurants have outposts here, including Skillet Street Food, Mod Pizza, Bigfood BBQ, and Eltana Wood-Fired Bagels. Order from the counter and then head outside if the weather's good; public bathrooms are also available in the building.

MAP 2: 305 Harrison St., 206/684-7200, www.seattlecenter.com

NEARBY:

- Learn something new about the world at Pacific Science Center (page 69).
- Feel like Alice in Wonderland at Chihuly Garden and Glass (page 71).
- Enjoy everything from brunch to late-night happy hour at Toulouse Petit (page 100).

- Toss back a throwback cocktail at **Tin Lizzie Lounge** (page 133).
- Snack like a king at **Triumph Bar** (page 134).
- Make a quiet escape to **Mercer Street Books** (page 183).

TOP EXPERIENCE

✪ Space Needle

The city's retro icon was born as a sketch on a cocktail napkin by one of the 1962 World's Fair planners, and the 605-foot Space Needle was built in less than a year. Today, elevator operators give a short history of the tower during the trip to the top. At 520 feet, the **Observation Deck** (8am-midnight daily; $32.50-37.50 adults, $27.50-32.50 seniors, $24.50-28.50 children 4-12, children under 4 free) features indoor and outdoor binoculars and information on what you can see (or what you'd see if the clouds would clear); a snack bar, wine bar, and gift shop are located inside. An extensive renovation in 2018 added a new feature, a revolving glass floor with views straight down. Timed tickets can be purchased in advance; lines often wrap the Space Needle's base, so plan ahead. The needle's revolving restaurant is in the process of being reconceived.

MAP 2: 400 Broad St., 206/905-2100, www.spaceneedle.com

Seattle's most recognizable icon

NEARBY:

- Get psychedelic at the **Museum of Pop Culture** (page 71).
- Find out how the world's biggest fortune is being spent at the **Bill & Melinda Gates Foundation Visitor Center** (page 72).
- Dine on creative Thai at **Pung Kang Noodle Place** (page 102).
- Plunge into divey **Mecca Café and Bar** (page 134).
- See a hit play at **Seattle Repertory Theatre** (page 155).
- Tour the city by land and sea with **Ride the Ducks** (page 167).

Pacific Science Center

Life-size dinosaurs and bigger-than-life IMAX films live at the kid-friendly

SEATTLE'S WORLD'S FAIR

Even Elvis discovered Seattle in 1962 when the Century 21 Exposition put the city on the map. The world's fair was meant to show off Washington State as the center of jet-age progress, proving it was more than an out-of-the-way region often confused with Washington, D.C.

With the country in the middle of the space race against the Soviet Union, expo organizers believed the home of Boeing had to show off its science and technology above all. Over breakfast meetings in the city's finest hotel, the Olympic, a group of businessmen dreamed up the infrastructure that would become Seattle's icons—Seattle Center, the Monorail, the Space Needle. A giant replica of a dam had water falling down six spillways, and a glass elevator called the Bubbleator took riders through a World of Tomorrow exhibit. There was even a visit from a famous cosmonaut, Gherman Titov, who achieved some notoriety at his world's fair press conference when he proclaimed, "I don't believe in God. I believe in man." Four days later, U.S. astronaut John Glenn agreed that he didn't see God in space, but only because God was too big for such an appearance.

For all the showing off, the fair was mostly about fun. The country tasted its first Belgian waffles at a popular stand in the outdoor area called the Gayway. Rides and games for the kiddies were out front, but an observant visitor could find Show Street, where the bawdy Gracie Hanson hosted a topless girlie show.

The Shah of Iran, a British prince, Bob Hope, and Lassie all popped by the six-month fair, but of the almost 10 million visitors, none was more adored than Elvis Presley. He shot the film *It Happened at the World's Fair* and, in his off hours, avoided the fair crowds by going on double dates around town with a production assistant—one was even to see an Elvis movie.

When the Century 21 Exposition finally closed in October 1962, its most anticipated guest, President John F. Kennedy, bowed out, claiming a cold. The festivities went on without him, and a few days later it was revealed that the Cuban Missile Crisis, not congestion, had kept JFK away.

Pacific Science Center. During the 1962 World's Fair, this was the U.S. Science Pavilion, and there's a retro midcentury feel to the outdoor pools and boxy buildings. The exhibits inside are much more up-to-date, and include a weather globe and interactive health displays. Warm and humid, the Tropical Butterfly House is filled with 500 tropical butterflies every week; animal exhibits, such as the one that houses the East African naked mole rat, include residents known to be a little less glamorous. Outside, the *Sonic Bloom*'s sculptured flowers show off the power of the sun's radiation by glowing with solar energy. Laser shows take place regularly, arranged to pop or psychedelic tunes, and visiting history and art exhibitions come to the newly renovated gallery space. Two IMAX theaters show nature films and popular cinema, and a planetarium has free shows.

MAP 2: 200 2nd Ave. N, 206/443-2001, www.pacificsciencecenter.org; 10am-6pm daily summer, 10am-5pm Mon. and Wed.-Fri., 10am-6pm Sat.-Sun. winter; $23.95 adults, $21.95 seniors, $17.95 children 6-15, $13.95 children 3-5, children under 3 free; IMAX and special exhibits extra

Seattle Children's Museum

Located downstairs in the Seattle Center Armory building, the Seattle Children's Museum appeals to tots 10 and younger—in fact, you'll need to have a kid of that age to enter. The building holds small but brightly colored hallways and exhibit rooms. Exhibits are hands-on and image based, like the Global Village where the dresser drawers and table are filled with clothing and food from around the world. There is

Seattle Children's Museum

MAP 2: 305 Harrison St., 206/753-4940, www.chihulygardenandglass.com; hours vary by season, open daily; $29 adults, $24 seniors, $18 children 4-12, children under 4 free

Museum of Pop Culture

What would you do with a billion dollars? Microsoft cofounder Paul Allen started, among other things, the Experience Music Project in honor of Jimi Hendrix and his hometown's musical heritage. The Frank Gehry-designed building has since morphed into the Museum of Pop Culture. Outside the museum's guitar tower are interactive booths for trying out keyboards and turntables. Downstairs, an animatronic dragon overlooks a fantasy exhibit (pull his tail—he'll move), which also has a giant magical tree and interactive exhibits about fantasy archetypes. Also downstairs, the *Infinite Worlds of Science Fiction* exhibit includes a *Star Trek* captain's chair and *Doctor Who* props.

MAP 2: 325 5th Ave. N, 206/770-2700, www. mopop.org; 10am-7pm daily summer, 10am-5pm daily winter; $28 adults, $25 seniors and students, $19 children 5-17, children under 5 free

Seattle Center Monorail

The lumbering old metal Monorail skates down a mile-long track to the center of downtown, a reminder of the city's once extensive plans for public transportation. The trip from Seattle Center to Westlake Center is great fun for transportation junkies or tourists looking to see the city from a few stories up, but it's not much of a time-saver for commuters. Still, the train rumbling above 5th Avenue or through the Museum of Pop Culture, which was built around it, remains one of the enduring sights of Seattle.

a construction zone, play bus, and a big art studio. There is both interior and exterior access to the museum—enter from the outside or from within the Armory.

MAP 2: 305 Harrison St., 206/441-1768, www.thechildrensmuseum.org; 10am-5pm Tues.-Sun.; $11.50 adults and children, $10.50 seniors, children under 1 free

Chihuly Garden and Glass

You can't go far in the Pacific Northwest without seeing some spectacular glass art. Chihuly Garden and Glass celebrates the country's most famous glassblower, Dale Chihuly, with a gallery of his works and a fanciful garden of glass sculptures. Prepare to feel like Alice wandering around Wonderland as you walk through spaces consisting of, for instance, a glass ceiling overflowing with anemone-like works. The attached Collections Café reflects Chihuly's penchant for collections—each table center has handfuls of his fish decoys, shaving brushes, 1950's cameras, inkwells, or other items housed under glass. And the gift shop includes not just patterned T-shirts and postcards but Studio Edition Glass Artwork and Fine Art Prints from Chihuly Studio.

Museum of Pop Culture

MAP 2: Thomas and Broad Sts.,
206/905-2600, www.seattlemonorail.com;
7:30am-11pm Mon.-Fri., 8:30am-11pm
Sat.-Sun. summer, 7:30am-9pm
Mon.-Thurs., 7:30am-11pm Fri.,
8:30am-11pm Sat., 8:30am-9pm Sun. winter;
$2.50 adults, $1.25 seniors and children
5-12, children under 5 free

Bill & Melinda Gates Foundation Visitor Center

Although Bill Gates first made his mark as the founder of Microsoft, he's now trying to solve the world's biggest problems of health and extreme poverty through his foundation. The Bill & Melinda Gates Foundation Visitor Center is a chance to highlight what the foundation does. The ash- and apple-wood displays explain how the Gates's money helps smaller organizations deliver health care and crop assistance. A giant interactive wall offers a timeline of the Gates family and the group itself. But perhaps the biggest emphasis is on toilets: In an effort to bring sustainable sanitation to people living in unhygienic conditions, the foundation's Reinvent the Toilet Challenge produced a waterless solar-powered toilet prototype that now stands in the lobby.

MAP 2: 440 5th Ave. N, 206/709-3100,
http://discovergates.org; 10am-6pm
Tues.-Sat. summer, 10am-5pm Tues.-Sat.
fall-spring; free

BELLTOWN
✪ Olympic Sculpture Park

What was once an oil company's waterfront land has been reborn as Olympic Sculpture Park, a series of zigzagging green spaces that hold massive works of art. The centerpiece is Alexander Calder's *The Eagle*, a twisted figure of red metal that is visible from the ferries that cross Elliott Bay. A glass bridge is decorated with images of the skyline, and the piece *Love & Loss* includes a prominent ampersand atop a tall spike. A Z-shaped path crosses the green space as it leads down to the water. In the vivarium, a 60-foot nurse log represents the intersection of art and nature, showing how a dying tree serves as an incubator for new plants. Outside, the sculpture park includes ginkgo and dawn redwood trees, plus meadow grasses and a shoreline often visited by seals. A pavilion holds restrooms and offices, plus a large space for events.

MAP 2: 2901 Western Ave., 206/654-3100, www.seattleartmuseum.org; sunrise-sunset daily, pavilion 10am-5pm Wed.-Sun. summer, 10am-4pm Wed.-Mon. winter; free

South Lake Union   Map 2

TOP EXPERIENCE

✪ Museum of History and Industry

When the Museum of History and Industry (MOHAI) moved to this former armory building in 2012, it spurred a renewed interest in the facility's mix of artifacts, hands-on exhibits, and curiosities—finally, the city's best museum about itself wasn't on the periphery, but close to downtown, in a striking four-story waterfront home.

Start your visit in the large atrium. The neon signs that take up one wall have interactive elements, and the opposite end of the airy main gallery has a tall sculpture made from pieces of a 19th-century schooner (walk inside it to view an underground portion). The center of the museum, an open cavern that reaches up to the ceiling, is filled with notable and nostalgic emblems of the city, like Boeing's first airplane and the city's most recognizable beer sign, a giant neon "R" that used to glow from atop the old Rainier brewery in south Seattle.

Hit the permanent True Northwest room upstairs, which tells the history of Seattle, or venture into the Bezos Center for Innovation. The latter, funded by Amazon founder Jeff Bezos, features interactive displays that salute the power of invention and experimentation. Head to the top floor to see a maritime exhibit and a working World War II-era periscope that offers a chance to peek out onto Lake Union. The middle floors have displays that explain the impact of events like the Great Seattle Fire of 1889 and the 1962 World's Fair. An old notepad bears the scribbling of a young Bill Gates.

The museum hosts regular programs for kids and adults, including history talks, extended hours on the first Thursday of the month, and occasional Maker Days with included crafts. There are free audio tours available at the front desk. Outside the museum, floating in Lake Union, are several historical ships and tugboats (some give tours) and a small pond. Toy sailboats can be rented from the Center for Wooden Boats next door.

MAP 2: 860 Terry Ave. N, 206/324-1126, www.mohai.org; 10am-5pm Fri.-Wed., 10am-8pm Thurs.; $19.95 adults, $16.95 seniors, $15.95 students, children free

NEARBY:
- Stroll the docks at the **Center for Wooden Boats** (page 74).
- Eat a delicious brunch or hit happy hour at **Cactus** (page 104).
- Play mad scientist with your burger at **Lunchbox Laboratory** (page 104).

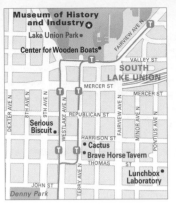

- The food is no laughing matter at **Serious Biscuit** (page 105).
- Cozy up with the happy hour crowd at **Brave Horse Tavern** (page 135).
- Sail model boats on a tiny pond at **Lake Union Park** (page 168).

South Lake Union Streetcar

The city of Seattle has almost as many forms of transportation as it has hills. The South Lake Union Streetcar, opened in 2007, is one of the more limited ways to get around. Its route begins at Stewart Street and 5th Avenue and travels through the South Lake Union neighborhood and up the east side of Lake Union. From the outside, the streetcar doesn't look very different from the city's light-rail, but it runs alongside automobiles on the street, not on a segregated track. The streetcar runs from downtown toward the Eastlake neighborhood, and is mostly useful to commuters going between the two. Still, it's a convenient tool for anyone hopping from MOHAI to downtown, since there's a stop right outside the museum. Both streetcars—there's a line that runs from Pioneer Square to Capitol Hill—are generally more subdued than the city's sometimes crowded and loud buses.

MAP 2: Stewart St. and 5th Ave.; 6am-9pm Mon.-Thurs., 6am-11pm Fri.-Sat., 10am-7pm Sun.; $2.25 adults, $1 seniors, $1.50 children 6-18, children under 6 free

Center for Wooden Boats

The Center for Wooden Boats, located right next to MOHAI, promotes ship-building and sailing. On a clear day, the organization does so by renting rowboats, pedal boats, and sailboats. The center is largely water-bound, comprising a collection of docks and tied-up boats of every size, and you can wander through to peek at the vessels and the people who maintain them. Even if you're not hanging around for a boat rental ($25-50 per hour), the short maze of floating docks makes a nice ramble before or after a MOHAI trip, and members love to show off their craft.

The center, which maintains a collection of historical wooden boats, always has some craft on display and holds regular lectures and story times for kids. On the first Thursday afternoon of the month there's usually a toy boat-building event for children ($3 suggested donation). For anyone nervous about their seafaring skills, there's no shame in renting a model

Center for Wooden Boats

boat (Sat.-Sun. May-Oct., $5 suggested donation) for use on a nearby pond. The 39-inch models resemble the sailboat *Pirate* on display at the center.

Every Sunday, rain or shine, the center offers free public boat rides on its fleet of historical schooners, steamboats, and yachts; sign-ups begin at 10am. Because the boats change from week to week, the number of openings varies. Rides around Lake Union are usually less than an hour and take place midday, shortly after sign-ups begin. No advance reservations are available unless you're a member of the center.

MAP 2: 1010 Valley St., 206/382-2628, www.cwb.org; 12:30pm-8pm Mon. and Wed.-Fri., 10am-8pm Sat.-Sun. summer, 10am-5pm or dusk Tues.-Sun. winter; free

Capitol Hill   Map 3

Seattle Asian Art Museum
Operated by the Seattle Art Museum, the Seattle Asian Art Museum is located in the middle of Volunteer Park in a beautiful 1933 building, adorned with giant art deco glass doors. It once housed the entire SAM collection. Though Seattle's Pacific Rim location is an easy explanation for why the collection started with a focus on Chinese and Japanese art, today the collection includes works of Indian, Korean, and even Himalayan origin, and traveling exhibitions visit as well. Replicas of Ming dynasty camel statues sit outside, flanking the entrance, making perfect props for a photo. The museum closed in 2017 for renovations to expand the space and is projected to reopen in 2019.

Volunteer Park is a 15-minute walk from the Capitol Hill light-rail station, and is on the 10 and 49 Metro Bus lines from downtown.

MAP 3: 1400 E. Prospect St., 206/654-3100, www.seattleartmuseum.org

Seattle Asian Art Museum

Lake View Cemetery
Capitol Hill's cemetery lives up to its name, with a vista down to Lake Washington and the Cascades beyond. The cemetery feels like an extension of adjacent Volunteer Park; its flowering trees and green lawns are an excellent place for a respectful stroll. Many of Seattle's founders and notable names are buried here, including the leader of the Denny party and the founder of Nordstrom. But the most famous graves are of father and son: Bruce Lee and Brandon Lee, who both died tragically young after making their marks in martial arts entertainment.

The cemetery is located right next to Volunteer Park, also close to the 10 and 49 bus lines and a 20-minute walk from the Capitol Hill light-rail station. MAP 3: 1554 15th Ave. E, 206/322-1582, http://lakeviewcemeteryassociation.com; 9am-dusk daily

Seattle University

Though the University of Washington is the city's biggest educational campus, Jesuit-founded Seattle University has a lovely 50-acre plot on Capitol Hill, its fountains and small quads tucked just between the city's hospital district and the crowded blocks of bars on Pike and Pine. The central Chapel of St. Ignatius (7am-10pm Mon.-Thurs., 7am-7pm Fri., 8am-5pm Sat., 8am-10pm Sun.), designed by architect Steven Holl, is a modern building whose design plays with color, lenses, and light. At different times of the day, sunlight—when it's able to gleam through Seattle's clouds—hits strategically placed glass lenses and bounces off surfaces painted a specific color, causing the nave, choir, and other corners of the chapel to glow in different shades. A large reflecting pool next to a stark modern bell tower shimmers in the sun.

Seattle University is a 10-minute walk from the Capitol Hill light-rail station along Broadway, or a five-minute ride on the First Hill Streetcar. It's also on the Metro Bus 12 line from downtown.
MAP 3: 901 12th Ave., 206/296-6000, http://seattleu.edu

Fremont

Map 4

✪ Gas Works Park

There's something beautiful about the industrial ruins in Gas Works Park, even if state ecologists are still testing the former metal refineries and their tanks for pollution. The gasification plant, built on the north end of Lake Union on what was then known as Brown's Point, closed in 1956 after half a century of operation. It took decades to be reborn as a park, the project spearheaded by University of Washington's Richard Haag. The landscape architect liked the ghostly industrial towers, deciding to preserve them as part of the park. The boiler house became a picnic shelter, and another building became a children's play area. The big metal ruins are fenced off from the public, and there's no lake access or swimming allowed in this

Gas Works Park

waterfront park because of contaminants. However, the city views—and the kite-flying—are perfect from atop the park's biggest hill, which is topped with a sundial.

You can reach Gas Works on the 31 or 32 Metro bus from near the Space Needle or from the University District, then a five-minute walk south.

The Fremont Troll crushes a car under the Aurora Bridge.

MAP 4: 2101 N. Northlake Way,
206/684-4075, www.seattle.gov/parks;
6am-10pm daily

Lenin Statue

The Fremont neighborhood is famously liberal and independent, calling itself the Center of the Universe (a county council-approved moniker since 1994) and bragging about the number of bicycle commuters that pass its bridge every day using a digital counter on the bike path. But the larger-than-life statue of Russian communist Vladimir Lenin on one Fremont corner is perhaps its most idiosyncratic statement. The seven-ton bronze was originally erected in Slovakia, then taken down in 1989 and brought to Seattle a few years later by a local who found it in a scrap heap. The 16-foot-tall Lenin appears mid-stride with fire and guns around him, in an otherwise unremarkable square. The statue (technically for sale by the family of the original importer) is controversial among residents, but it's often dressed up to reflect the holiday—with a tutu for Gay Pride or topped with a star for Christmas. Other nearby sculptures, of a children's entertainer and of commuters waiting for a train, are also decorated regularly.

The 40 Metro bus from downtown stops about a block away from the statue.

MAP 4: Fremont Pl. N and N. 36th St.,
http://fremont.com/about/lenin

✪ Fremont Troll

Built by a group of artists in 1989, the Troll statue under the Aurora Bridge has grown so famous that the short road it sits on has been renamed Troll Avenue. The Troll was fashioned to look like it's pulling itself out of the ground under the bridge, with just its head and torso showing. The statue, some 18 feet high, is built out of concrete and rebar. In one hand the Troll grasps a real Volkswagen Beetle, buried nose-first because the car had been totaled in a crash before it was incorporated into the art piece. (At one point the car held a time capsule with a bust of Elvis Presley, but it was quickly stolen—and graffiti remains a problem at the site.) Occasional plays and "Trollaween" parties are held at the Troll, but it's mostly just a spot for excellent vacation photos. Because it's located on a busy street, prepare to park several blocks away and walk.

To party with the troll via public transportation, take Metro bus 31 and 32 from Seattle Center or bus 62 from downtown; stop at Troll Avenue.

MAP 4: 3405 Troll Ave. N, http://fremont. com/about/fremonttroll-html

Woodland Park Zoo

The 92-acre Woodland Park Zoo holds more than 1,000 animals of more than 300 species, many of which are endangered. Nearly a million people visit the zoo every year, making it one of the city's busiest attractions. An African Savanna area has giraffes, hippos, gazelles, and zebras, and the Tropical Asia exhibit has elephants and orangutans. Keepers give demonstrations with different raptor species, and grizzly bears are fed salmon every day (even though their exhibit has a stream stocked with fish). Head to the elephant barn first thing in the

Woodland Park Zoo

morning to see the animals bathed, and ask about when the gorillas get their afternoon snack packs filled with food and toys. The zoo gives discounts for taking public transportation and on some rainy days; check the website before going.

From downtown Seattle, Metro bus 5 goes to the zoo's west entrance at North 55th Street and Phinney Avenue. Bus riders get $2 off admission with proof of ridership.

MAP 4: 5500 Phinney Ave. N, Green Lake, 206/548-2500, www.zoo.org; 9:30am-6pm daily spring-summer, 9:30am-4pm daily fall-winter; spring-summer $18.75 adults, $1.75 seniors, $11.75 children 3-12, children under 3 free; fall-winter $12.75 adults, $12.75 seniors, $8.75 children 3-12, children under 3 free

Ballard   Map 5

✪ Hiram M. Chittenden Locks

For the mechanically minded, there's nothing like an afternoon watching the locks, operated by the U.S. Army Corps of Engineers and opened in 1917. The locks are both a working waterway, acting as a gateway between

Puget Sound and Lake Union, and a lovely park. The sound, with its changing tides, is rarely level with the Ship Canal that leads to Lake Union, so vessels enter a small tank-like enclosure where the water level rises and falls, much like the famous setup on the Panama Canal. During busy summer weekends, there's a line of sailboats, pleasure yachts, commercial fishing craft, and sightseeing boats waiting for their turn to either explore Puget Sound or return to a protected marina on the lake.

In summer and early fall, salmon hurl themselves up a series of tanks to travel upstream to spawn. Visitors can travel across the canal between lock openings (which rarely take more than a few minutes) to visit an underground passage with windows into the fish ladder. During the migration there are often naturalists on hand to explain the process.

Even when the fish aren't present, there's plenty to see at the locks, including a visitors center and the Army Corps of Engineers' only botanic garden. One of the groundskeepers started the garden in the early 20th century, asking boat captains that came through the locks to bring him seeds from around the world; the

Carl S. English Jr. Botanical Garden is named for him. Now there are more than 500 species of plants, including the dawn redwood, which English helped revive when it was thought extinct. Free tours are held in the summer.

Reach the locks via Metro buses 17 or 29 from downtown, or the 44 from the University District light-rail station.

MAP 5: 3015 54th St. NW, 206/783-7059, www.nws.usace.army.mil; grounds 7am-9pm daily, fish ladder 7am-8:45pm daily, visitors center 10am-6pm daily May-Sept., 10am-4pm Thurs.-Mon. Oct.-Apr.; free

NEARBY:

- Enjoy a breakfast pizza at **Stoneburner** (page 121).
- Pair a game of Skee-Ball with your beer at **King's Hardware** (page 147).

Hiram M. Chittenden Locks

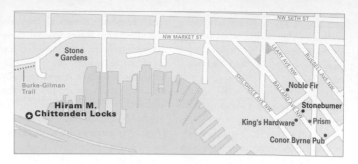

- Sip craft beer at **Noble Fir** (page 147).
- See who's playing at **Conor Byrne Pub** (page 148).
- Scale the climbing walls of **Stone Gardens** (page 170).
- Browse earthy clothing designs at **Prism** (page 190).

Nordic Museum

Although much of the Northwest can trace some roots to Scandinavia, Ballard in particular was founded by people of northern Europe—Norway, Denmark, Finland, Sweden, and Iceland. So it's no wonder that a Nordic Museum was born in the neighborhood. It was located in a 1907 school building 1980-2018 before opening a new version on the waterfront, much closer to the heart of Ballard. The ultra-modern structure has a boxy shape and a glassy entrance, with tall ceilings and white interior walls. The two-floor Fjord Hall welcomes visitors, and interior bridges link exhibit rooms that tell the story of Nordic immigration to the United States in the 19th century, especially the immigrants' work in the fishing and lumber industries. Other rooms highlight contemporary life and art. Regular storytelling and lecture events celebrate the oral history of the region, and folk school classes teach wood carving, painting, and more (fees required).

Reach the building, located near the Ballard Locks, via Metro buses 17 or 29 from downtown, or the 44 from the University District light-rail station.

MAP 5: 2655 NW Market St., 206/789-5707, www.nordicmuseum.org; 10am-5pm Tues.-Wed. and Fri.-Sun., 10am-8pm Thurs.; $15 adults, $12 seniors, $10 students and children 5-18, children under 5 free

University District — Map 6

University of Washington

Locals say "UW" or the shorter "U-Dub" when they're talking about the sprawling University of Washington, which serves almost 50,000 students. This current campus was first a fairground, host to the 1909 Alaska-Yukon-Pacific Exposition, though the university itself dates back to 1861. Students crowd the central Red Square, an expansive redbrick space bordered by examples of the university's gothic and modern architecture, between classes or relax on grassy

cherry blossoms at the University of Washington

quads. The busiest gathering space on football game days is the rebuilt Husky Stadium on Lake Washington.

The campus is a beautiful place to wander any time of year, but during cherry blossom season, usually in February or March, the college's trees erupt into a beautiful display of white, pink, and purple blooms. These trees are most evident in the quads around Red Square. There are also several large sculptures like Barnett Newman's *Broken Obelisk* and a Robert Irwin installation behind the Henry Art Gallery. Free tours of the university are meant for prospective students and their families, last 75 minutes, and are led by current students. Advance registration is required through the office of admissions.

The Link Light Rail has one terminus at the University of Washington, located next to the football stadium and just east of the main campus. Several bus lines also serve the university from downtown, including Metro buses 43 and 70.

MAP 6: 1401 NE Campus Pkwy., 206/543-9686, www.washington.edu

Burke Museum of Natural History and Culture

What's cooler than dinosaur skeletons? How about the bones of a giant sloth?

The remains of the latter were found at Seattle-Tacoma International Airport and delivered to the Burke Museum of Natural History and Culture at the University of Washington, where they are now on display. The fossils of a mastodon and stegosaurus are even more massive, mounted in the museum's midcentury building fronted with Northwest Native American carvings over the door.

This is the state's oldest public museum, even older than Washington's statehood, and it's now devoted to the cultural heritage and biodiversity of the Pacific Northwest. Inside, the bones of that sloth and the other extinct animals are displayed in front of painted backdrops, almost dwarfing the small exhibit rooms. There also are treasures that didn't come out of the dirt, like a wall mural tracing the course of evolution and a collection of Pacific cultural art. Outside, an ethnobotanical garden has dozens of local plants that were used in various aspects of Native American life. Thanks to the museum's out-of-the-way location, it rarely gets crowded, though construction of a new building across the parking lot and the big move to a new space in fall 2019 may lead to some exhibit closures.

The museum is a 10-minute walk from the University of Washington light-rail station, through campus, or on the Metro bus 70 from downtown. **MAP 6:** 17th Ave. NE and NE 45th St., 206/543-5590, www.burkemuseum.org; 10am-5pm daily; $10 adults, $8 seniors, $7.50 students and children 5 and older, children under 4 free

Washington Park Arboretum

Washington Park Arboretum, part of the University of Washington, is more than a simple garden: It's a natural sanctuary that holds more than 20,000 trees on more than 230 acres, including well-regarded collections of maple, pine, oak, and mountain ash. Trails circle the park, and yes, there are plenty of flowers, too. Rhododendrons, the state flower, are bushy plants with large, soccer-ball-sized bunches of blooms, and are best seen in spring (Mar.-May). Wetlands on Lake Washington are populated with waterfowl. The Graham Visitor Center has maps and a small gift shop, but most infrastructure here is devoted to the many weddings and events held on the grounds. The maps show the tangle of trails that criss-cross the park space, but none are long enough to be a real hike, so it's best just to wander on any footpath that looks appealing, especially down toward Duck Bay for water views. Because it's in a residential area away from the rest of the university, a trip to the arboretum is a time investment. Plan to enjoy the gardens for a few hours to make it worthwhile.

Reach the gardens by Metro bus 43 from downtown or the University District (followed by a 10-minute walk), or via a 20-minute walk from the University District light-rail station, along busy Montlake Boulevard.

MAP 6: 2300 Arboretum Dr. E, Madison Park, 206/543-8800, http://depts. washington.edu/wpa; visitors center 9am-5pm daily; free

Japanese Garden

Japanese Garden

Though the Japanese Garden shares land with the arboretum, like a little island within the larger park, it's operated by the city, not the university, so there's a fee to enter. The walled garden is especially popular when the cherry trees bloom in early spring, but the manicured lawns and koi ponds are beautiful year-round. Tea ceremonies ($10 adults, $7 children) are held on occasional weekend days (see website for specific dates), and a community center inside the formal garden has periodic art displays. Access the garden through a gatehouse on the southern end of the arboretum.

MAP 6: 1075 Lake Washington Blvd. E, 206/684-4725, http:// seattlejapanesegarden.org; 10am-5pm Tues.-Sun. Mar. and Oct., 10am-7pm daily Apr.-Sept., 10am-4pm Tues.-Sun. Nov.; $8 adults, $4 seniors, students, and children 6-17, children under 6 free

International District and SoDo

Map 7

SIGHTS

INTERNATIONAL DISTRICT

Seattle Pinball Museum

Go ahead, touch the exhibits at this museum; it's practically required. All of the vintage games at the Pinball Museum are playable, from the 1969 King Tut game—some machines are even older—to the nearly new America's Most Haunted. The small space gets crowded easily and feels more like a tightly packed two-story arcade than a museum, though it's heaven for pinball enthusiasts. There isn't much (beyond informational placards mounted above each machine) for anyone not willing to play. The staff is friendly, and a concession stand sells vintage-style sodas and local beer. Admission includes unlimited play. Children must be seven years or older to play. Look for a neon sign on the ground floor of a brick office building to find the small space.

The museum is easily accessible from the International District/Chinatown light-rail stop, the First Hill Streetcar stop at 7th Avenue and Jackson, and the 41 Metro bus stop from downtown.

MAP 7: 508 Maynard Ave. S, 206/623-0759, www.seattlepinballmuseum.com; noon-6pm Sun., Mon., and Thurs., noon-8pm Fri.-Sat.; $15 adults, $12 children

Wing Luke Museum of the Asian Pacific American Experience

At the Wing Luke Museum, the focus is on Asian American history, from immigrant stories and community portrait galleries to special films and exhibits on Bruce Lee, perhaps the city's most famous Asian American figure. Visiting the museum entails touring the four-story space, a restored hotel and shop in the town's historic International District, and includes a look at the pressed-tin ceilings of the family association room, once the meeting room for one of the social clubs that were the center of Chinese American culture in Seattle. Tour guides explain how immigrants once lived, ate, and played mah-jongg together in the clubs. But the museum goes beyond the Chinese experience to explore many facets of Asian life in the Pacific Northwest, from contemporary art to the story of how Filipinos worked in Northwest canneries or the South Asian diaspora that shaped Washington, with the historic building providing a transporting experience. Admission is good for the whole day, so you can pop out for food after the 45-minute tour and then return later to wander the exhibits. There are also additional extended tours of Chinatown, its local dumpling,

Seattle Pinball Museum

FOLLOW THAT WATER TAXI!

A water taxi makes the trip between West Seattle and downtown.

Located on the tip of a peninsula that juts into Puget Sound, **West Seattle** is a chilled-out respite from the bustle of downtown. This is Seattle's own little beach town. Spend a day out here and see for yourself.

Make your way to West Seattle via **water taxi.** The dock is at Pier 50, to the south of the Seattle Great Wheel, and you'll buy your ticket here before boarding (one-way $5.75, $2.50 seniors, children under 6 free); there's a discount for using an ORCA fare card. After enjoying the 10-minute dash across the water, you'll arrive at Seacrest Park in West Seattle.

Follow the coast north then west to reach **Alki Beach** (1702 Alki Ave. SW, 206/684-4075, www.seattle.gov/parks; 4am-11:30pm daily), where the city's white founders first came ashore. There are 2.5 miles of waterfront for walking, sunbathing, and volleyball, plus fire pits and picnic spots. Notable stops along the shore include a replica Statue of Liberty, a 1911 bathhouse, and a memorial to a shipwreck that occurred in the usually calm waters of Elliott Bay.

After spending some time at the beach, you may not be quite ready to leave. Check out these other West Seattle spots, if that's the case; all but Marination will require a cab or bus ride from the water taxi dock:

Eat at Marination Ma Kai (1660 Harbor Ave. SW, 206/328-8226, http://marinationmobile.com): What began as a food truck is now a mini-empire across Seattle, and this waterfront outpost is the most charming location. The counter serves Hawaiian-Korean fusion dishes like kalua pork sliders topped with slaw, a kimchi quesadilla, and a pork katsu sandwich. Snag a table outside while you're waiting for your food and enjoy one of Seattle's least commercialized, least crowded waterfronts.

Drink at Shadowland (4458 California Ave. SW, 206/420-3817, http://shadowlandwest.com): This bar is full of warm light from slender hanging lamps reflecting off shiny leather chairs. Though it's a bar first and performance space second, the bill can include DJs, singer-songwriter nights, and on Wednesdays, a circus performance.

Browse at Easy Street Records (4559 California Ave. SW, 206/938-3279, http://easystreetonline.com): One of the biggest names in Seattle vinyl, Easy Street buys used records and has an impressive selection. Merchandise includes work by local artists and in-the-know staff picks. An attached café names dishes after music figures—the Salad of John and Yoko has veggie bacon and avocado.

Sleep at Grove West Seattle Inn (3512 SW Alaska St., 206/937-9920, www.grovewestseattle.com): If the neighborhood really wins you over, you can stay a little longer by checking into this hotel that first opened in 1962, the year of Seattle's transformative world's fair. There's still plenty of retro charm to go around. Rooms have sleek, modern decor, and the free breakfast, parking, and Wi-Fi are unusual perks for the area.

barbecue, and specialty restaurants, and Bruce Lee hangouts ($20-43 including museum admission).

A walk to Wing Luke from downtown takes about 15 minutes, and it's about four blocks from the International District/Chinatown light-rail station.

MAP 7: 719 S. King St., 206/623-5124, www.wingluke.org; 10am-5pm Tues.-Sun.; $17 adults, $15 seniors, $12.50 students 13-18, $10 children 5-12, children under 5 free

SODO

Living Computers: Museum + Labs

It's almost hard to believe that it took so long for computers to get their own museum in tech-happy Seattle. This computer-first museum only opened in 2012. This modest space, home to about 60 microcomputers, macrocomputers, and mainframes, sits in the out-of-the-way industrial neighborhood of SoDo ("south of downtown") in a converted warehouse. Started by Microsoft cofounder Paul Allen, the museum collects vintage computers that date back to when a simple machine took up half a room. Best of all, the computers are turned on and ready to use; you can write code or play old games like Pac-Man and Oregon Trail. Some artifacts and photographs from computing history are behind glass, but most of the museum's collection consists of the ready-to-use computers; ask the friendly staff for help if a throwback Apple II doesn't seem intuitive. A free tour is included with admission, as is a virtual reality demo for visitors over 13 between noon and 4pm every day the museum's open. Though not on the usual tourist path, it's a must-visit for true computer nerds and stays refreshingly uncrowded on rainy days.

Reach the museum on the 21 Metro bus from downtown, or a 10-minute walk from the Sodo light-rail station.

MAP 7: 2245 1st Ave. S, 206/342-2020, www.livingcomputermuseum.org; 10am-5pm Wed.-Sun.; $16 adults, $14 seniors, students, and children 6-17, children under 6 free

Living Computers: Museum + Labs

RESTAURANTS

Of course there's seafood here. We can practically fish mussels and salmon right from the downtown piers. But the city is also becoming world renowned—think

Skillet Diner

James Beard Award-winning chefs—for its local sourcing and inventive methodology. Steak houses are experimenting with whole-animal butchery, while new restaurants are fusing cuisines like Spanish tapas and sushi.

The city's best-known chefs, names like Tom Douglas, Ethan Stowell, and Renee Erickson, gained fame for focusing on seasonal ingredients. Starbucks, once a funky little neighborhood coffee shop, has become a worldwide obsession, but you can still find independent roasters throughout the city.

Once upon a time, you couldn't pick up a menu in Seattle without seeing grilled salmon. The flaky fish is still a local favorite, but now you're as apt to find buttery halibut or the strange geoduck clam. Don't leave town without trying some oysters or mussels, most pulled from the briny waters of Puget Sound.

And then there's the Asian influence in the thriving International District, where the likes of ramen and dim sum are served up in unassuming nooks and fancy dining rooms alike.

Even as things change, there's still a place for classics like the Canlis salad, a high-end dish that hasn't changed in 50 years. It's made, tableside, at a fine-dining restaurant with a soaring view of the city, proof that some things never go out of style.

HIGHLIGHTS

✪ **BEST MEAL WITH A VIEW:** The round windows of **Matt's in the Market** look down on Pike Place Market and the shoppers below, but even the view can't compete with the high-end cuisine (page 89).

✪ **BEST COFFEE SHOP: Cherry Street Coffee** is a small local chain with friendly staff and plenty of hangout space (page 94).

✪ **FANCIEST MEAL:** A visit to the beloved Seattle institution **Canlis** means impeccable service and beautiful views (page 99).

✪ **BEST BACON:** The bacon jam at **Skillet Diner** comes spread on a meaty burger or by the jar so you can eat it with a spoon (page 105).

✪ **BEST CULTURAL FUSION:** By pulling from both French and Chinese influences, stylish **Stateside** has earned a reputation for spectacular flavors (page 108).

✪ **BEST FRESH FISH:** Fremont's **Manolin** is known for its ceviche's delicate flavors and delectable seafood entrées (page 114).

✪ **BEST PLACE TO JOIN A FOOD CULT:** Foodies love to line up for the Caribbean roast at **Paseo** (page 117).

✪ **BEST OYSTERS:** As magical as its Alice in Wonderland namesake, **The Walrus and the Carpenter** draws crowds for its baskets of mollusks (page 118).

✪ **BEST BREAKFAST PIZZA:** A slice is a legitimate morning meal at **Stoneburner** (page 121).

✪ **BEST BUDGET EATS:** Join University of Washington students at **Din Tai Fung** with world-famous (and affordable) dumplings (page 121).

✪ **BEST PANCAKE STACK:** The breakfast bar at **Portage Bay Cafe** is the fruit, nut, and whipped cream heaven dreams are made of (page 122).

✪ **BEST PLACE TO TRY PHO:** There are dozens of varieties of soup at **Tamarind Tree,** but the classic pho is the best (page 124).

✪ **MOST INTERNATIONAL BAKERY:** At **Fuji Bakery,** the Japanese pastries are crafted from local and foreign-sourced ingredients (page 125).

PRICE KEY

$	Entrées less than $15
$ $	Entrées $15-25
$ $ $	Entrees more than $25

Downtown and Pioneer Square

Map 1

PACIFIC NORTHWEST

Purple Café and Wine Bar $$$

You almost have to lean back to see the top of the wine tower in the two-story Purple Café and Wine Bar. This cavernous space fills with patrons during happy hour and on weeknights, feeding as many business diners as theatergoers. The menu is filled with the kind of rich bites that pair well with wines—wild boar rillettes and cheese flights, plus a killer braised bacon poutine. It's almost overkill, what with the sandwiches, pizzas, pastas, and other entrées fighting for attention, but the wine list has international scope and wit—the madeira varietal, for example, is described as "the Chuck Norris of wine."

MAP 1: 1225 4th Ave., 206/829-2280, www.thepurplecafe.com; 11am-11pm Mon.-Thurs., 11am-midnight Fri., noon-midnight Sat., noon-11pm Sun.

SEAFOOD

Elliott's Oyster House $$$

Though salmon may be the Pacific Northwest's signature seafood, oysters aren't far behind. The bays of Puget Sound, especially along Hood Canal, grow some of the best oysters in the world. The waterfront Elliott's is on a pier close to the aquarium and the Seattle Great Wheel, with sizable outdoor dining areas perfect for when the sun peeks through the clouds. The oyster list changes with the season, with most grown locally. During happy hour (3pm-5pm Mon.-Fri.) the price per shucked oyster changes on the hour, starting at $1.50 apiece. The dinner menu goes far beyond oysters, however, with crab cakes, prawn risotto, and, of course, salmon, here baked on alderwood planks.

MAP 1: 1201 Alaskan Way, 206/623-4340, www.elliottsoysterhouse.com; 11am-10pm Sun.-Thurs., 11am-11pm Fri.-Sat.

Etta's $$$

Preeminent restaurateur Tom Douglas has flashier offerings than Etta's, but the small waterfront joint is one of his most hip, with multicolored, functional decor and a view toward Pike Place Market and the waterfront. The square booths resemble futuristic cubicles, but this is hardly a place for work. The emphasis is on seafood, with a menu that includes oysters and a seafood stew. The salmon is prepared with Douglas's own "rub with love," a zesty meat rub that's also for sale, but the most decadent treat is a steamed Dungeness crab, served with butter.

Purple Café and Wine Bar

Fish-and-chips are made with cod, shrimp, or even fried oysters.

MAP 1: 2020 Western Ave., 206/443-6000, http://tomdouglas.com/restaurants/ettas; 11am-9pm Mon.-Thurs., 11am-10pm Fri., 9am-3pm and 4pm-10pm Sat., 9am-3pm and 4pm-9pm Sun.

Elliott's Oyster House

Steelhead Diner $$$

Despite its name, Steelhead is no coffee-and-toast place, but rather a well-appointed restaurant with views of Pike Place Market and an outdoor patio in one of the city's busiest areas. The bright-colored walls inside reflect the restaurant's modern take on Northwest food, where the burger comes with sautéed button mushrooms and the rib eye steak has a coffee crust. A special early-bird dish is served only until 6pm, but there's plenty to choose from after that, including an impressive list of vegetable dishes and salads. Nearly every meat is named for its origin, from the stream-raised rainbow trout to the black cod, confirmation that everything on offer originates in the Northwest.

MAP 1: 95 Pine St., 206/625-0129, www.steelheaddiner.com; 11am-10pm daily

Ivar's Acres of Clams $$

This iconic spot is Seattle's signature fast food. Locations are scattered throughout the region, but the downtown waterfront spot is the most popular. Ivar Haglund, a colorful Seattle character, opened the chowder and fish-and-chips spot in 1938, bringing crowds not only for the food but also the octopus wrestling and eating contests. The Pier 54 spot has a dining room and dockside fast food. It offers both white and red clam chowder, so chowder purists can argue over which is best. Fish-and-chips are made with Alaskan cod and Ivar's tartar sauce. Ivar's personal motto was "keep clam," and a statue commemorating him stands near the restaurant.

MAP 1: 1001 Alaskan Way, 206/624-6852, www.ivars.com; 11am-10pm Sun.-Thurs., 11am-11pm Fri.-Sat.

Seatown Seabar and Rotisserie $$

The Seatown Seabar and Rotisserie, located right next to Pike Place Market, is restaurateur Tom Douglas's most uncomplicated take on seafood. Oysters are popular with the after-work crowd, who quickly fill the long, bright-red bar on weekday evenings. There are also several kinds of Alaskan crab on the menu, plus rotisserie chicken. The all-day breakfast doesn't quite fulfill its promise, ending at 3pm—but it means that the chicken and biscuits or rich egg sandwiches can be lunch. The Rub with Love Shack counter next door sells the spices and rubs used at this and other Tom Douglas restaurants in town.

MAP 1: 2010 Western Ave., 206/436-0390, www.tomdouglas.com; 8am-10pm Mon.-Sat., 8am-9pm Sun.

NEW AMERICAN
✪ Matt's in the Market $$$

The beloved Matt's in the Market started in the mid-1990s as a tiny 23-seat eatery, and it's not much bigger today. As its name suggests, it's in Pike Place Market, on the 2nd floor of one of the buildings opposite the busy fish market stall. The upper-story location keeps it feeling like something of a secret, even though the staircase that leads to the restaurant is well marked. Inside the intimate eatery, tables sit atop gleaming black-and-white tile floors, and big curved windows look directly at the iconic market sign. The restaurant's chefs shop the market daily to create the menus, usually a short list of seafood or other meat dishes and simple, fresh salads.

MAP 1: 94 Pike St., No. 32, 206/467-7909, www.mattsinthemarket.com; 11:30am-2:30pm and 5:30pm-10pm Mon.-Sat.

Heartwood Provisions $$$
Finding a good compromise between downtown bustle and the quiet of a rural farmhouse, Heartwood Provisions is a stately destination on a busy avenue. The dining room is simple, with straight lines and warm, sleek wood surfaces. The menu is where the restaurant gets daring, combining Pacific Northwest meats and seafood with global flavors. Octopus is paired with ink sofrito, and chicken with quinoa tabbouleh. Delectable french fries come with a pimento-flavored ketchup, and the foie gras has a gingerbread crumb. The bar makes classic cocktails, and the service is friendly and relaxed, which balances the fine food. A reasonably priced chef's tasting menu ($75) makes for an event-ready meal.

MAP 1: 1103 1st Ave., 206/582-3505, http://heartwoodsea.com; 3pm-10pm Mon.-Thurs., 3pm-midnight Fri., 9:30am-2pm and 3pm-midnight Sat., 9:30am-2pm and 3pm-11pm Sun.

Matt's in the Market

Miller's Guild $$$
The grill is the thing at this meat-centric spot attached to the Hotel Max, one of downtown's more artsy places to stay. The restaurant's wood-fired grill cooks beef that's been dry-aged for 75 days, plus a daily selection that can include Wagyu rib eye and a lamb chop; look to the handwritten "From the Inferno" menu. Nose-to-tail butchery is taken seriously here, and Sunday's butcher-block special combines tastes from the whole menu in a single prix fixe meal. The morning breakfast is hearty, drawing on foraged mushrooms for the frittata. The exposed concrete and sleek chairs make for a modern interior, and keep it from feeling like an old-fashioned steak house. Sitting at the bar is the best way to get a look at the monster grill.

MAP 1: 612 Stewart St., 206/443-3663, http://millersguild.com; 7am-11pm Mon.-Fri., 8am-11pm Sat.-Sun.

RN74 $$$
Though it's located on a busy commercial block of downtown Seattle, Michael Mina's RN74 blocks out the bustle with dark shutters. Inside is an eatery with the feel of a modern Parisian bistro, featuring dark round booths topped with striking bottle-like light fixtures. The wine selections

are listed on a wall-mounted flipboard that resembles the schedule board of a train station, the letters clacking away every time it's updated. The excellent happy hour includes duck fat french fries and bacon-flavored hush puppies, a mix of snacky and elegant. The dinner menu is lengthy, with local fish, beef bourguignon, and steak frites made with Wagyu New York strip.

MAP 1: 1433 4th Ave., 206/456-7474, www. michaelmina.net; 4pm-9:30pm Mon.-Thurs., 4pm-10pm Fri.-Sat.

The London Plane

Damn the Weather $$

The name may be a common refrain during Seattle's rainy periods, but this Pioneer Square restaurant is delicate and hip, and there's often a wait on weekend nights. A bar takes up nearly half the small space and the bartenders specialize in creative cocktails, but the food is the real draw. Most offerings are small, meant to be combined into a larger meal. Fried cauliflower is topped with tahini, and seared squid has white beans and squid ink. Chicken-fat fries are a perennial favorite, and there's a changing menu of oysters and cheeses. The lunch menu is similar, with a few more salads and a sandwich option.

MAP 1: 116 1st Ave. S, 206/946-1283, http://damntheweather.com; 11am-11pm Sun.-Wed., 11am-midnight Thurs.-Sat.

The London Plane $$

The Pioneer Square neighborhood has blossomed in recent years, with bright new restaurants opening in quick succession and bringing the artsy blocks to life. This cheerful, two-floor eatery is part of a small complex that also holds a wine store and a flower shop. It draws crowds during weeknights and the First Thursday Art Walk, bringing groups to share a bottle of wine and small plates of locally sourced vegetables and meats. The 2nd-floor seats have a great view of the shelves packed with bottles and glassware, the bar lined with wooden stools, and the open kitchen. The menu offers a variety of meats, cheeses, and spreads like squash hummus, with a few more substantial plates of brisket or chicken.

MAP 1: 300 Occidental Ave. S, 206/624-1374, www.thelondonplaneseattle. com; 8am-5pm Mon., 8am-9pm Tues.-Fri., 9am-9pm Sat., 9am-3pm Sun.

Quality Athletics $$

Located just steps from CenturyLink Field where the Seahawks play, Quality Athletics is no sports bar. Instead of sticky floors and pitchers under charmless TVs, the restaurant adopts an old-fashioned sports theme with vintage trophies and a wall of lockers, more like the inside of an old-fashioned gentleman's club/locker room. The interior is otherwise bright, with tile decor and modern furniture (and yes, some TVs). The nachos are made with 12-hour smoked pork, and the burger has pickled onions. There's a rotating Seattle Freeze house-made frozen cocktail, named for the city's famously chilly attitude. For all the fancy touches, the place still gets rather rowdy during big Seahawks games, but it's much more sedate than the wild sports bars that surround the area.

MAP 1: 121 S. King St., 206/420-3015, http://qualityathletics.com; 11am-9pm daily

Radiator Whiskey $$

Radiator Whiskey is a hangout joint, one where the kitchen is open and so are the shelves stacked with dishes and napkins. The menu is scrawled across a blackboard, while barrels behind the bar echo the curved windows of the restaurant's 2nd-story Pike Place Market location. The barrels hold special whiskeys and barrel-aged cocktails, none of which come cheap; the lengthy whiskey menu is also easy to get lost in. Despite being in the middle of a tourist favorite, the bar draws locals and restaurant industry folks with its happy hour menu of "tot-chos"—nachos made with tater tots—and a "dirty" sandwich that comes with a Rainier tallboy and a shot of whiskey. Dinner still feels like a happy hour thanks to the crowds and buzz of the joint, though meat dishes like a lamb neck sloppy joe and beef brisket are certainly hearty. A smoked half pig's head will feed the whole table but must be ordered at least a day or two in advance (and farther ahead to guarantee availability).

MAP 1: 94 Pike St., No. 30, 206/467-4268, www.radiatorwhiskey.com; 4pm-midnight Mon.-Sat.

13 Coins $

In a town of rapid culinary innovation, 13 Coins used to be a staple that never changes—and never closes. Until 2018, that is, when it moved across town. Formerly in South Lake Union, the new Pioneer Square location of the 24-hour restaurant retains some of its signature design: high-backed leather counter seats as big as the armchairs in a suburban TV room, and lights that are low and moody. It has high-backed stools and booths so private you could comfortably plan a covert crime over the plate-sized Cobb salads or veal piccata. Though the name comes from Peruvian folklore, the menu is straight from the 1960s, when the restaurant opened; it features classic meat dishes, some with Italian influence but all ideal for big appetites. It's a spot for business lunches midday, and the late-night crowd isn't usually rambunctious.

MAP 1: 255 S. King St., 206/682-2513, http://13coins.com; 24 hours daily

JAPANESE FUSION
Japonessa $$

Latin food and sushi? It's an unexpected pairing, but this fusion restaurant near Pike Place Market has been wildly successful, holding down a busy corner of downtown for years. It fills quickly during happy hour with diners eager for sushi topped with jalapeño or cilantro. The drinks menu is equally experimental, with a chai old-fashioned and a Manhattan made with Japanese whiskey and sake. The sushi-averse will find a few selections on the menu, but the extensive list of traditional and creative rolls is the whole reason for scoring a table in this large, rather dim eatery.

MAP 1: 1400 1st Ave., 206/971-7979, www.japonessa.com; 11:30am-11pm Mon.-Thurs., 11:30am-1am Fri., noon-1am Sat., noon-11pm Sun.

KOREAN
Girin $$$

Though located close to the stadiums, where sports bars and hot dog stands are thick on the ground, this Korean

COFFEE CULTURE

Coffee is one of Seattle's signature offerings, next to beer, flannel shirts, and grunge music. The world's biggest coffee conglomerate, Starbucks, was born here, and the city's blocks are full of corporate coffee chains and indie outposts alike.

Though coffee has long been a restorative drink for Americans, back in the 1960s it wasn't associated with lifestyle. In the late part of that decade, small coffeehouses began to spring up around Seattle, more notable for their culture than their brew. In 1971, two coffee shops opened downtown—one of which was named Starbucks, after a character in *Moby-Dick*. At first, they got their beans from Peet's Coffee and Tea in California. In fact, they only sold beans— it took a few years before they brewed and sold individual drinks.

A few decades later, the new coffee culture really took root. It was the 1990s, a time of cultural explosion in Seattle. Salon-style coffee shops popped up on almost every block in the city, becoming places where counterculture, music, poetry, and activism could thrive.

Cherry Street Coffee

It wasn't just the culture of the coffee shop that changed. Simple drip coffee was no longer enough, and Starbucks helped popularize the cappuccino, the latte, and other espresso drinks. By the mid-1990s Starbucks had acquired the rights to the name Frappuccino, a frozen version of the drinks that were becoming a daily necessity to Americans.

Around the city, coffee shops began to stock soy milk, nonfat milk, and almond milk, plus sugars in artificial and imported varieties. People started bringing laptops in with them, and the Wi-Fi password became as closely coveted as a window seat with an electrical outlet.

Today, Starbucks is still dominant, with 104 stores and its global headquarters within the city of Seattle. But there are also local mini-chains like Cherry Street Coffee and one-off favorites like Monorail Espresso. Seattle's coffee culture has become America's coffee culture.

- **Cherry Street Coffee:** With outposts scattered around downtown, this small local chain offers good coffee and the comfort of a café (page 94).

- **Caffè Umbria:** European roots tie the Emerald City's craze to centuries of tradition (page 94).

- **Monorail Espresso:** Streetside and with an attitude, this is one of the city's purest expressions of coffee, with smooth espressos and well-blended lattes (page 95).

- **Starbucks Reserve Roastery & Tasting Room:** The best-known coffee shop in the world slows down to show off its java cred. (page 109).

- **Victrola:** This neighborhoody spot welcome locals and visitors alike (page 109).

spot is all style and elegance, with a wood-heavy theme that extends from the somber exterior to the beautiful interior that's broken up by an Asian-inspired log house that separates the large dining room. The Korean steak house menu includes oysters and set dinners that feature pairings of meats with kimchi and other sides. The *ssam* menu puts some of the same meats and vegetables next to leafy greens that can be used to make handheld mini-burritos. Other small plates are best shared between diners and paired with sake. Open for dinner only on weekends, there's a chef's tasting menu option for $45 or $65. Lunch is much more affordable, with a *ssam* lunch set around $15. Korean fried chicken is available on Mondays until the kitchen runs out of it.

MAP 1: 501 Stadium Pl. S, 206/257-4259, www.girinseattle.com; 11:30am-3pm Wed.-Fri., 4pm-11pm Sat.-Sun.

ASIAN
Wild Ginger $$

Considering Seattle's spot on the Pacific Rim, it's no surprise that a pan-Asian restaurant like Wild Ginger would do so well for so long. Inspirations come from throughout Asia, particularly Malaysia, Indonesia,

Wild Ginger

China, and Vietnam. Pad Thai shares the menu with satay and grilled boar. There's a special vegan menu and a live tank supplying clams and mussels. The restaurant's signature dish is the fragrant duck, served with puffy white steamed buns and plum sauce. The quarter-duck probably isn't big enough for your table, unless you're dining alone—it's that good. The large restaurant is across from Benaroya Hall, so the staff is adept at getting diners out in time for shows and concerts.

MAP 1: 1401 3rd Ave., 206/623-4450, www.wildginger.net; 11:30am-11pm Mon.-Sat., 4pm-9pm Sun.

COFFEE
✪ Cherry Street Coffee $

In a town that seems to have a Starbucks on every corner, Cherry Street Coffee is a nice combination of independent coffee spot and consistent chain, with eight locations downtown. Each shop features work from local artists and friendly baristas. Besides a wide array of coffee drinks made with Cherry Street's own bean blends, the café serves sandwiches, salads, and quiches. There's usually open seating, making this shop a good place to sit a spell, peer at the posters for local plays and art shows, and soak in the coffee culture of Seattle.

MAP 1: 700 1st Ave., 206/621-9372, www.cherrystreetcoffee.com; 6:30am-7pm Mon.-Fri., 8am-5pm Sat.-Sun.

Caffé Umbria $

The European roots of this Pioneer Square café go back to the 1940s, when founder Ornello Bizzarri opened a roastery in Perugia, Italy. His grandson opened his own coffee spot here in 1986, and the company now operates cafés in Portland and Chicago as well. (Plus there's another location in Ballard.) It's definitely an Italian spin on the coffee shop experience, with small metal tables for lingering espresso drinkers to savor the blended Arabica coffees. Umbria's roasters can roast 9,000 pounds of coffee per day. With large windows that open to the tree-lined brick street and panini and gelato on the menu, it's easy to mistake this block of old Seattle for the Old World.

MAP 1: 320 Occidental Ave. S, 206/624-5847, http://caffeumbria.com; 6am-7pm Mon.-Fri., 7am-7pm Sat., 8am-5pm Sun.

Monorail Espresso $

The downtown walk-up window hasn't been around as long as the monorail it's named after, but it sometimes feels like it. The few tables on the sidewalk mean that some customers lounge around, but most folks are on the go. The menu features the Frango Mint Mocha, named for a candy once sold by Seattle's defunct Frederick & Nelson department store, but is otherwise pretty simple. Then there's the other, more famous menu—one that lists prices for directions. (The central location means that the baristas get plenty of questions from lost tourists.) It's mostly a joke—they won't really charge $2 to point the direction to the Gum Wall—but it's still not in good form to ask for the way to the nearest Starbucks. The stand is cash only.

MAP 1: 520 Pike St., 206/422-0736; 6am-6pm Mon.-Fri., 8am-6pm Sat., 9am-5pm Sun.; cash only

Zeitgeist Coffee $

Pioneer Square's artsiest coffee stop dates back to the 1990s, when coffee culture became a defining characteristic of the city. The decor, however, feels very of the moment, as the name implies: There's exposed brick, exposed ducts hanging from tall ceilings, and warm blond wood panels on the wall. Art is the shop's secondary calling, with original pieces on the wall and large gatherings on First Thursday Art Walk nights. The written word gets its share of the space, with newspaper racks and a dictionary on display. There's breathing room and a number of tables to enjoy the lattes topped with delicate foam art, plus a sandwich if you want to linger over the dictionary.

MAP 1: 171 S. Jackson St., 206/583-0497, http://zeitgeistcoffee.com; 6am-7pm Mon.-Fri., 7am-7pm Sat., 8am-6pm Sun.

FRENCH

Loulay Kitchen and Bar $$$

Loulay owner and chef Thierry Rautureau calls himself The Chef in the Hat (and the eponymous hat also appears on the sign), but it's the only gimmick at this downtown restaurant. Located near the convention center, it's easily the best dining in the area. The two-story space feels at once both lofty and bustling, and the best tables overlook the action from the 2nd floor. Solo diners will appreciate the special table for one that makes the most of a small space while also being the best

Loulay Kitchen and Bar

seat in the house. The French menu includes classics like roasted chicken and braised short ribs, delivering delicate flavors and pitch-perfect preparations. Dinner's must-have dish (despite typically being a breakfast food) is the organic scrambled egg, which comes with white sturgeon caviar.

MAP 1: 600 Union St., 206/402-4588, www.thechefinthehat.com; 11am-2pm and 5pm-10pm Mon.-Fri., 8am-2pm and 5pm-10pm Sat., 8am-2pm and 4:30pm-9pm Sun.

Café Campagne $$

For a city halfway around the world from Paris, Seattle boasts a surprising amount of French cuisine. Pike Place Market's tucked-away Café Campagne recalls a French bistro, with its red doors and requisite mirrors. It has served popular brunches and meals for tired market-goers since the mid-1990s. The menu features black olive pasta, steak frites, and duck confit, all prepared in traditional style. Even the weekday breakfast is decadent, especially the brioche French toast made with bourbon egg batter. Happy hour offers carafes of wine and an impressive array of small bites.

MAP 1: 1600 Post Alley, 206/728-2233, http://cafecampagne.com; 8am-10pm daily

Le Pichet $$

The small Le Pichet is a taste of France in the middle of downtown Seattle, complete with sidewalk café, mirrors on the walls, and white tile floors. The menu is so French it's actually written in the language (with translations), but the most important thing to know is that the roasted whole chicken for two people takes an hour to cook. Good thing there are plenty of drinks and charcuterie selections to keep you occupied—it's worth the wait. For all the

French quality, there's nothing fussy about the restaurant. In fact, it's been voted both "Best Hangover Meal" and "Best Ambience" in the city.

MAP 1: 1933 1st Ave., 206/256-1499, www.lepichetseattle.com; 8am-midnight daily

MEDITERRANEAN
Lola $$

Tom Douglas's enduring Lola is a standby for downtown residents and workers, especially come weekend brunch. The bar area isn't huge but fills quickly on weekdays for a happy hour of kebabs and cocktails like the "Greece Lightning," made with ouzo. The Greek menu offers tagines, notably a seafood mix, and lamb a variety of ways, including in a burger. It doesn't quite feel like the Aegean seaside inside this space, with exposed pipework above and a mix of warm, earthy colors below. A long list of spreads made with fig, cauliflower, yogurt, and red pepper is served with pita fresh off the griddle; the sampler of all the spreads makes a good appetizer for the table. Brunch features a spicy Bloody Mary, more kebabs, and a special breakfast combo that includes octopus, yogurt, bacon, and eggs.

MAP 1: 2000 4th Ave., 206/441-1430, http://tomdouglas.com; 6am-11pm Mon.-Thurs., 6am-2am Fri., 7am-3pm and 4pm-midnight Sat., 7am-3pm and 4pm-11pm Sun.

ITALIAN
Il Terrazzo Carmine $$$

Though Pioneer Square generally attracts restaurants with a casual vibe, appealing to the young and buzzy crowds that have returned to the neighborhood, this longtime Italian eatery has remained consistently elegant and decidedly grown-up. Here, the tablecloths are white

THE FOOD TRUCK MOVEMENT

It wasn't long ago that food trucks didn't get much respect in the culinary world—they served cheap, fast food, making for a lunchtime staple. But as experimental restaurateurs looked for inexpensive ways to try out their concepts, small pods of food trucks became regular sights in American cities.

Many of Seattle's most popular food trucks eventually grow into brick-and-mortar restaurants. Skillet Street Food was a favorite long before it started building diners around the city to serve fried chicken and burgers with bacon jam. Marination Mobile perfected its Pacific Rim cuisine before settling down in bigger locations like Marination Ma Kai. Others have stayed mobile but are well known around town: Off the Rez serves Indian fry bread tacos, and Jemil's Big Easy serves Cajun-inspired gumbo and jambalaya. Both Seattle Chicken Over Rice and Now Make Me a Sandwich make, well, exactly what you'd expect.

Today, the best place to find food trucks is in **Westlake Park** (4th Ave. and Pike St.) downtown. Most trucks note their location on their own websites, but **SeattleFood-Truck.com** gathers all the info and publishes food truck locations by specific location and by neighborhood. Many trucks only set up shop during lunch hours, while others can be found parked outside happy hour joints in the early evening.

(albeit surrounded by farmhouse-style chairs) and the service patient, offering a dinner experience that starts with antipasti before moving to pastas and substantial entrées like osso buco or sweetbreads. Up front, the related bar Intermezzo Carmine has a bistro feel and luxe white leather bar chairs, ideal for having a glass of wine before dinner. Reservations are recommended.

MAP 1: 411 1st Ave. S, 206/467-7797, www.ilterrazzocarmine.com; 11:30am-4pm and 5pm-10pm Mon.-Fri., 5pm-10pm Sat.

The Pink Door $$

The Pink Door is a curious combination of restaurants. The outdoor patio, overlooking the waterfront and Pike Place Market, is that of a casual dining spot, but inside is a candlelit dining room where the reliable Italian menu is served under hoops and swings used by occasional cabaret and trapeze performers. The shows (with cover) can include burlesque performers and a balloon artist. The restaurant is indeed behind a pink door located on Post Alley, but it's much less hidden than it sounds. Look for a pointed finger sign directing the way.

MAP 1: 1919 Post Alley, 206/443-3241, www.thepinkdoor.net; 11:30am-10pm Mon.-Thurs., 11:30am-11pm Fri.-Sat., 4pm-10pm Sun.

CAFÉS AND BISTROS
Crumpet Shop $

A crumpet is a quintessentially British baked good, like an English muffin but spongier. This Pike Place Market-adjacent café specializes in crumpets topped with savory salmon, pesto, or sweet lemon curd. Morning specialties turn the crumpet into a breakfast sandwich base for egg and peppers or cream cheese. Commit to the British theme with orange marmalade or Stilton blue cheese and a cup of whole-leaf tea. The café can be bustling during morning hours and it can be hard to score space to eat your crumpet concoction, but few of the selections are well-suited to being eaten on the go, so plan on waiting for a table to open up.

MAP 1: 1503 1st Ave., 206/682-1598, www.thecrumpetshop.com; 7am-3pm Mon. and Wed.-Thurs., 7am-4pm Fri.-Sun.

Delicatus $

The city delicatessen gets an upgrade in Pioneer Square, where tour groups stream past and local office workers pop in for substantial sandwiches in a beautiful two-level space. The menu is broken into traditional sandwiches—a Reuben, a club—and what's called "progressives," including a prosciutto and mozzarella combination named for Seattle burlesque legend Gypsy Rose Lee, and the Duwamish—"filthy, just not toxic"—with shaved ham and pulled pork, named for the local polluted waterway. The eatery is open on weekends only when the nearby stadiums are open for home games.

MAP 1: 103 1st Ave. S, 206/623-3780, www.delicatusseattle.com; 11am-6pm Mon.-Fri.

DELIS
Salumi $

To find Salumi, just look for the line. The meat sandwiches at this Pioneer Square deli are incredibly popular. The long wait to reach the small counter is worth it, though, especially for a hot lamb, meatball, or the signature porchetta sandwich, big enough to leave you with leftovers. A private lunch table is available for up to eight people by reservation. Opened by the father of the now-infamous Mario Batali but sold in 2018 and reopened in a new space, there's now slightly more elbow room than before.

MAP 1: 404 Occidental Ave. S, 206/621-8772, www.salumicuredmeats.com; 11am-3pm Mon.-Sat.

BAKERIES
Le Panier $

In the midst of dozens of lunch spots in Pike Place Market, this French bakery draws crowds on most weekdays for its fresh pastries and the intoxicating smell of bread that wafts throughout the warmly lit space. Whenever the weather is halfway decent, the windows that open to the market's busiest thoroughfare are open. From the baskets of baguettes in the window to the macarons on display in the pastry case, it's a traditional French experience. Some of the ham-and-cheese croissants or filled puff pastries could practically serve as meals, but more substantial offerings include roast beef, BLT, and tuna sandwiches on fresh baguettes.

MAP 1: 1902 Pike Pl., 206/441-3669, www.lepanier.com; 7am-6pm Mon.-Sat., 7am-5pm Sun.

Queen Anne and Belltown

Map 2

PACIFIC NORTHWEST
✪ Canlis $$$

To be precise, Canlis isn't exactly a restaurant—it's more of an experience, a destination, and a landmark. Peter Canlis opened it in 1950, and it's run today by his grandsons in a beautiful midcentury building with a stone fireplace and angled windows overlooking Lake Union. Its signature service is all about personal touches, like the valet who doesn't take a name or offer a ticket, but simply remembers each driver's face and delivers the car as if by magic (the coat check works the same way). Meals come in a variety of tasting menus, but the Canlis salad is a must-try: greens and a dressing made of lemon, olive oil, and coddled egg prepared tableside. Main dishes are simple, well-prepared classics: grilled sea bass, slow-roasted chicken that takes an hour to prepare, and Muscovy duck breast for two. Dining at Canlis is an all-evening affair, and men are required to wear a suit or sport coat.

MAP 2: 2576 Aurora Ave. N, 206/283-3313, www.canlis.com; 5:30pm-10pm Mon. Thurs., 5pm-11:30pm Fri.-Sat.

AQUA by El Gaucho

SEAFOOD
AQUA by El Gaucho $$$

The original El Gaucho, located just a few blocks away, is a steak house; the AQUA location is the seafood version of that. The space, located at the end of a pier, is large enough to have the feel of a corporate restaurant, with a long wavy bar that fills with well-clad workers at happy hour. The lobster is from Maine, the halibut is from Alaska, and the steak is a New York strip. AQUA offers all the conventions of a high-end seafood restaurant, with spectacular water views and occasional outdoor seating.

MAP 2: 2801 Alaskan Way, 206/956-9171, http://elgaucho.com; 4pm-9pm daily

Six Seven $$$

There's more than seafood on the menu at the Edgewater Hotel's in-house restaurant, but with such sweeping views of Elliott Bay and the hotel's perch on a pier it seems a shame to order anything else. Arrive as close to sunset as possible, since these are among the few patio tables in the city that actually hover over the water. Selections include Alaskan crab legs and one of the city's old standbys, cedar-plank salmon (it's a classic for a reason). Sautéed diver scallops are served with little more than chimichurri and roasted tomatoes, though there is an array of side options that include lobster mac and cheese.

TOM DOUGLAS

There's no question who the most famous chef in Seattle is. Tom Douglas has started almost two dozen restaurants around town since his first in 1989, and he won his first James Beard Award back in the 1990s. Douglas runs a farm on the east side of the state and frequently appears on cooking shows like *Top Chef*. His style is centered on Pacific Northwest cuisine, especially seafood, but his restaurants range from Italian- and Greek-themed to biscuit and pizza spots and include **Seatown Seabar and Rotisserie, Etta's, Lola, Serious Biscuit,** and **Serious Pie,** a well as **Brave Horse Tavern,** serving local beers and pub fare.

ETHAN STOWELL

While Douglas has the biggest empire, he is by no means the only famous chef in town. Ethan Stowell oversees 13 restaurants, including the Italian **Rione XIII** and **Staple & Fancy** and small but beloved **How to Cook a Wolf.** Stowell is German-born but is also devoted to local Pacific Northwest ingredients, working a farm-to-table theme into almost every one of his eateries.

RENEE ERICKSON

Though Douglas and Stowell are the biggest names, Renee Erickson is quickly becoming the face of Seattle cuisine. Her restaurants are almost all seafood-focused, and they usually have whimsical names like **The Whale Wins** and **The Walrus and the Carpenter.** She focuses on shellfish and unusual seafood dishes. The dining spaces have the casual chic and buzzy young clientele that has come to define the Seattle dining scene.

EDOUARDO JORDAN

In 2017, a new star entered the scene. Edouardo Jordan's Salare had long been a neighborhood favorite, but his nearby **JuneBaby,** a Southern restaurant, quickly earned plaudits from national press, and the chef scored a James Beard Award in 2018.

MAP 2: 2411 Alaskan Way, 206/269-4575, www.edgewaterhotel.com; 6:30am-2:30pm and 5:30pm-9pm Sun.-Thurs., 6:30am-2:30pm and 5:30pm-9:30pm Fri.-Sat.

NEW AMERICAN

Toulouse Petit $$$

Very little is small about the New Orleans-themed Toulouse Petit. Located a 10-minute walk from Belltown and Seattle Center, the restaurant is crowded on weekend nights with flirty young professionals enjoying the late-night happy hour and tossing back sweet cocktails. Ornate fixtures, as might befit New Orleans' French Quarter, hang over booths and tables. The endless menu has appetizers, entrées, salads, seafood, charcuterie, "curiosities," oysters, pastas, steaks, and a prix fixe option—if you can't find something to eat at Toulouse Petit, you must really not like food. Some dishes have a Louisiana twist, and there is plenty of shrimp and spicy sausage. At brunch the party continues, this time with mimosas flowing freely and house-made fried beignets served with a chicory crème anglaise. The generous breakfast hash will sop up any mistakes you made the night before.

MAP 2: 601 Queen Anne Ave. N, 206/432-9069, www.toulousepetit.com; 9am-2:30pm and 4pm-2am Mon.-Fri., 8am-2am Sat.-Sun.

Black Bottle $$

The later it is, the busier it gets at this corner bistro located near the bottom of the hill that slopes toward the waterfront. Though the menu lists a variety of small, shared meat and seafood plates and veggie sides, it's known for flatbreads topped with in-season greenery and light meats. Look for the Seattle Nightcap made from chocolate liqueur and house-made espresso syrup. The space is often dim, with the exposed brick wall and dark tables sucking up the light, but it's loud enough to make up for it.

MAP 2: 2600 1st Ave., 206/441-1500, http://blackbottleseattle.com; 4pm-midnight Sun.-Thurs., 4pm-2am Fri.-Sat.

The 5 Spot $$

What kind of restaurant is The 5 Spot? It's a diner, plus a Florida seafood joint. Or a New Mexico cantina. Or a Texas barbecue restaurant. The menu has a permanent half and a rotating half, and the goofy decor changes with the theme. (The artwork is often connected to the door; look to see what changes when the front door swings.) Not every American cuisine style tackled here is perfectly realized, but no one can say the cooks are unadventurous. The comfy diner has a signpost noting all the places the menu has been, plus a cheap late-night menu and a hearty breakfast. It's where to go when you're fine with ending up just about anywhere.

MAP 2: 1502 Queen Anne Ave. N, 206/285-7768, www.chowfoods.com; 8am-11pm Mon.-Fri., 8am-3pm and 5pm-midnight Sat.-Sun.

How to Cook a Wolf $$

Sorry, but there's no wolf on the menu at Ethan Stowell's How to Cook a Wolf; the name comes from a book by midcentury food writer M. F. K. Fisher. The eatery does have endless fresh and finely crafted dishes, so it's just as well. Set in a local's neighborhood at the top of Queen Anne, it's more regularly visited by discerning Seattle diners, not tourists. Dishes are simple and rustic, drawing from Italian cuisine. The short menu usually has a handful of pastas and several small, sharable appetizers like chicken liver mousse or black bass. Order several of each to fill up, but expect a few extra tastes here and there from the kitchen.

MAP 2: 2208 Queen Anne Ave. N, 206/838-8090, www.ethanstowellrestaurants.com; 5pm-11pm daily

Local 360

Local 360 $$

Imagine Seattle in the middle of a circle with a radius of 360 miles. At Local 360, almost every ingredient comes from within that circle, including the lengthy spirits list. The restaurant goes for a funky feel, what with the rough-hewn wood walls, candlesticks, and peanut-butter-and-jelly bonbons on the menu (they come with a shot of milk, naturally). The young crowd comes here for snacks to go with cocktails, or perhaps even a whole meal of fried chicken or a pork shank. A slight touch of a Southern influence is evident from the grits, the collard greens, and the tasting flight of locally brewed moonshines.

MAP 2: 2234 1st Ave., 206/441-9360, www.local360.org; 11am-10pm Mon.-Thurs., 11am-11pm Fri., 9am-11pm Sat., 9am-10pm Sun.

THAI
Pung Kang Noodle Place $

Taking over the restaurant space of another Thai restaurant, Pung Kang offers a bright, colorful atmosphere full of beautiful meals loaded with vegetables. Sit at the counter for an even quicker meal, or move toward the back for larger tables. Though classic Thai noodle dishes are at the forefront, from pad Thai to noodle soups, the menu is also crammed with stir-fry dishes and curries made with braised beef or crispy pork belly. With its convenient location and speedy service, it's the perfect place to chow down on fried rice before hitting up nearby shows, movies, and overcrowded bars.
MAP 2: 517 Queen Anne Ave. N, 206/284-3700; 11:30am-9:30pm Mon.-Thurs., 11:30am-10pm Fri., noon-10pm Sat., 12:30pm-9:30pm Sun.

COFFEE
Caffe Vita $

Seattle is known for its coffee, and Seattle residents are known for being discerning about their coffee shop of choice. Most locals claim allegiance to one of the city's small chains, like Caffe Vita, which dates back to the 1990s. (Even restaurants brag about serving Caffe Vita's coffee.) The exposed brick and original paintings here give the shop all the indie bona fides it needs, but it's also known for its well-pulled espresso. The company occasionally offers a free public brewing class to demonstrate various styles; check the website for times.
MAP 2: 813 5th Ave. N, 206/285-9662, www.caffevita.com; 6am-7pm daily

Uptown Espresso $

Part of a local chain, this coffee shop earns character points with its collection of dining-room tables and walls laden with a hodgepodge of mirrors, framed oil paintings, and historical photographs. It's a quiet respite on a busy block of Queen Anne, where students hunker down with laptops or chat in small groups. The house coffee is known as Velvet Foam, a roast almost as creamy as the hot chocolate topped with whipped cream.
MAP 2: 525 Queen Anne Ave. N, 206/285-3757, www.velvetfoam.com; 5am-10pm Mon.-Thurs., 5am-11pm Fri., 6am-11pm Sat., 6am-10pm Sun.

STEAK HOUSES
El Gaucho $$$

A gaucho is a South American cowboy, but there's nothing rough-and-tumble about El Gaucho, a steak house with locations in Seattle, Portland, and Tacoma and across the lake in Bellevue. If you close your eyes, you can almost imagine you're back in the swinging '50s—and indeed, the restaurant was inspired by a supper club

El Gaucho

of that era. It's almost dinner theater, as an open charcoal grill isn't far from patrons dressed to the nines and a bananas Foster is set aflame as it's served at a leather banquette. Lobster tail and diver sea scallops are on the menu, but it's a shame to order anything but a dry-aged steak or perhaps the chateaubriand tenderloin, carved tableside.

MAP 2: 2505 1st Ave., 206/728-1337, www.elgaucho.com; 4pm-10pm Sun.-Thurs., 4pm-midnight Fri.-Sat.

PIZZA
Serious Pie $$

True to its word, this popular restaurant from Tom Douglas is dead serious about pizza. There are several outposts of this particular joint, serving pizzas fired to a smoky black around the edges in an apple-wood-fired oven. Toppings range from lamb sausage to Penn Cove clams, and the taps flow with locally made root beer and a daily house-made shrub. Beer comes in pitchers, but the wood floors and sophisticated communal table signify that this is no place to be frivolous about pizza.

MAP 2: 316 Virginia St., 206/838-7388, www.seriouspieseattle.com; 11am-11pm daily

South Lake Union   Map 2

SEAFOOD
Flying Fish $$$

While the raw halibut soar through the air at Pike Place Market, the dishes at Flying Fish arrive in a much calmer fashion. Seafood-first restaurants should be a dime a dozen in Seattle, but they're really not, and this is one of just a few in the neighborhood. But that's not its only claim to fame. After 18 years, a neighborhood move, and numerous accolades, the chef sold to a Chinese restaurant group and started incorporating Asian flavors into the menu—Thai crab cakes, cod served with Sichuan broth, and mussels with chili-lime dipping sauce. But the menu still emphasizes organic, wild ingredients, and the space has the same happy din. The interior colors are bright, with none of the all-shades-of-blue cliché found in so many sea-themed eateries.

MAP 2: 300 Westlake Ave. N, 206/728-8595, www.flyingfishrestaurant.com; 11am-10pm Mon.-Thurs., 11am-11pm Fri., 3pm-11pm Sat., 3pm-10pm Sun.

NEW AMERICAN
Re:public $$

Though the signage is weird—just pronounce it "republic"—this restaurant is straightforward new American fare, with a gourmet poutine and spicy tartare to start the meal and wild boar Bolognese to end it. The street-facing windows bring light and air into the dark, sophisticated space, and the starters and cocktails are so good that happy hour can bleed into a satisfying meal. The restaurant is 21 and over only, but even if Re:public accepted kids, it wouldn't feel particularly welcoming to the crayons-and-high chair set. Dinner reservations are accepted; while not required, they're not a bad idea in this rapidly growing neighborhood.

MAP 2: 429 Westlake Ave. N, 206/467-5300, http://republicseattle.com; 11am-2:30pm and 5pm-10pm Mon.-Thurs., 11am-2:30pm and 5pm-1am Fri., 5pm-1am Sat., 10am-2:30pm and 5pm-10pm Sun.

KOREAN
Revel $$

Once a highlight of the Fremont dining scene, this bright spot has moved to South Lake Union but hardly skipped a beat. Its Korean-inspired dishes include a pork belly pancake and lemongrass beef, and dumplings require an extra wait that's definitely worth it. The interior feel hasn't changed much: light wood, clean lines, and a bustling dining room. When there's a wait for a table, spend time with a house-infused soju or a cocktail made with Revel's own chili tincture or local ginger beer. Word is the restaurant will move back to Fremont in 2019, when a new building goes up in its original location. The restaurant hosts cooking classes on Sunday, and reservations fill up fast.

MAP 2: 513 Westlake Ave. N, 206/547-2040, www.revelseattle.com; 11am-2pm and 4pm-9pm Mon.-Thurs., 11am-2pm and 4pm-10pm Fri., 4pm-10pm Sat.

MEXICAN
Cactus $$

Because it's located right across the street from a popular location of Portage Bay Cafe, Cactus may be best known as a backup brunch location when its neighbor's lines are too intimidating. And the brunch is good, especially the rich *tres leches* French toast topped with caramelized bananas. But Cactus is also a hopping happy hour joint, where the guacamole and margaritas cheer up gray Seattle workdays. The local chain—there are several around the city—is known for serviceable Mexican fare in a brightly colored dining room, pulling from both Mexico and the Southwest, including Navajo fry bread. Prices are fairly cheap for the neighborhood. There are plenty of margarita variations, but the house classic, with agave nectar, is hard to improve upon.

MAP 2: 350 Terry Ave. N, 206/913-2250, www.cactusrestaurants.com; 11am-10pm Mon.-Thurs., 11am-11pm Fri., 10am-11pm Sat., 10am-10pm Sun.

BURGERS
Lunchbox Laboratory $$

The mad scientist who came up with Lunchbox Laboratory had some strange experiments—how else do you explain burgers made of churken (chicken and turkey) or dork (duck and pork)? For all the eccentric combos, this upbeat burger joint is a cheery place decorated in bright oranges and exposed ductwork, and each tasty offering is almost big enough to split. Lunchbox pays homage to the Dick's burger—a Seattle drive-in classic—and offers plenty of normal combinations as well. Sweet potato fries are the best side dish, and the milk shakes come either virgin or with alcohol. Weekly specials are billed as experiments and are even crazier than the regular menu. The bar takes up much of the 1st floor of the eatery, though there's more regular seating upstairs and some outdoor tables as well. The brightly colored spot is close to REI and makes a whimsical destination for grown-ups. Where else can you drink a beer while surrounded by old lunchboxes serving as decor?

MAP 2: 1253 Thomas St., 206/621-1090, www.lunchboxlaboratory.com; 11am-11pm daily

SANDWICHES AND QUICK BITES
Serious Biscuit $

Famed local chef Tom Douglas has restaurants all around town, but this location joins two under one roof—next to the Serious Biscuit counter are tables for one of his Serious Pie pizza joints. The airy Westlake space has more than enough room for both, and it's best to settle at a table with tall stools after ordering at the Serious Biscuit walk-up counter. The biscuit sandwiches are meals unto themselves and don't travel particularly well. The fried chicken with gravy sandwich is one of the best, though the softball-sized biscuits also come with simply jam or butter. A "serious brunch" combines the best of both eateries on weekends, with biscuit sandwiches and breakfast dishes made in the wood-fired pizza oven.

MAP 2: 401 Westlake Ave. N, 206/436-0050, www.seriouspieseattle.com; Biscuit 7am-3pm Mon.-Fri., 9am-3pm Sat.-Sun., Pizza 11am-10pm Sun.-Thurs., 11am-11pm Fri.-Sat.

Capitol Hill
Map 3

SEAFOOD
Coastal Kitchen $$

You're always at the seaside at Coastal Kitchen, even though the location of the coast changes. The seafood restaurant has a rotating focus that shifts every three months. The destinations are specific, like Veracruz, Mexico, or New Orleans, Louisiana. The regular menu includes seafood standbys, like fish-and-chips, oysters, and calamari, plus a few entrées other than seafood. The space is open late and has $6 and $8 drinks at its three "Don't Judge Me" happy hours (one is 8am-10am). Art pieces on the wall rotate with the changing menu, and humorous language lessons play in the bathroom. The large restaurant has several counters and bars, plus tables and a garage door that's open on nice days. On Mondays the restaurant hosts jazz performances.

MAP 3: 429 15th Ave. E, 206/322-1145, www.coastalkitchenseattle.com; 8am-midnight daily

Taylor Shellfish Farms $

At Taylor Shellfish Farms, local oysters and mussels are ready to be slurped and steamed. This gourmet shop with a wine bar abuts Melrose Market. Inside, freshly harvested shellfish are arranged in wet tanks under white subway tile walls. The menu also includes crab, poke, and geoduck, a local delicacy. There are a few stools for those who can't wait to get a little errant sand between their teeth with a good oyster.

MAP 3: 1521 Melrose Ave., 206/501-4321, www.taylorshellfishfarms.com; 11am-9pm Sun.-Thurs., 11am-10pm Fri.-Sat.

NEW AMERICAN
✪ Skillet Diner $$

Skillet Diner started as one of Seattle's most successful food trucks, and

Skillet Diner

Hill, is now open to all as a loud, very social eatery. Starting at brunch, chatter echoes off the brick walls and from the open kitchen while students and freelancers peck away at laptops. The menu tends toward healthy-sounding dishes like the kale and farro bowl and roasted free-range chicken, but there are also more indulgent options like a porchetta sandwich or, during brunch, brioche French toast. Expect a full restaurant long into the evening, as this spot is known for quality food and happens to be on one of the Hill's busiest streets.

MAP 3: 1525 10th Ave., 206/325-0807, www.oddfellowscafe.com; 8am-10pm Sun.-Thurs., 8am-11pm Fri.-Sat.

its brick-and-mortar outlet is like a diner reimagined by a hungry hipster. There's a long counter that has the swiveling chairs of a classic greasy spoon, but some of those seats face a bar with local beers and craft cocktails. The bar-going Capitol Hill crowd and Seattle University students comprise much of the clientele. Dishes are generous—the restaurant must go through leftover boxes like tissue paper—with mounds of gravy over biscuits and the kind of burger that takes squared shoulders and an ambitious bite. The weekend brunch scene—and wait times—can be intense, but breakfast dishes like tomatillo chilaquiles and a special scramble are served daily until dinnertime. Skillet's signature bacon jam, served on its burger, is sold in jars by the host stand.

MAP 3: 1400 E. Union St., 206/512-2001, www.skilletstreetfood.com; 7am-9pm Sun.-Thurs., 7am-10pm Fri.-Sat.

Oddfellows Café and Bar $$

The Odd Fellows are a social order akin to the Masons. Its former Seattle home, a century-old hall in Capitol

Oddfellows Café and Bar

Sitka & Spruce $$

Sitka & Spruce is the crown jewel of Melrose Market, a collection of food-based shops and eateries in Capitol Hill. Headed up by rising-star chef Matthew Dillon, the restaurant excels at Northwest cuisine. The menu is short but aggressively local: Seasonal veggies are served without unnecessary fanfare, and diners share flavorful chicken, salmon, chanterelles, mussels, or whatever's freshest that day. It's all prepared in a kitchen that isn't just open—it's an equal part of the small space, with cooks bustling around the chopping blocks and stoves with bundles of greenery. Diners sit at the windows, at small tables, or at a large, blocky communal table.

MAP 3: 1531 Melrose Ave., 206/324-0662, www.sitkaandspruce.com; 11:30am-2pm and 5pm-10pm Mon.-Thurs., 11:30am-2pm and 5pm-11pm Fri., 10am 2pm and 5pm-11pm Sat., 10am-2pm and 5pm-9pm Sun.

Tallulah's $$

Though most of Capitol Hill is a buzzy scene, the eastern end of the hill is a quiet, sleepier neighborhood, and the slow charm of Tallulah's reflects it. Inside it's modern but warm, with decor that tends toward vintage and plenty of greenery. Veggies get special attention on the menu, with small plates like beet hummus and caramelized cauliflower, though the lamb burger is a moist treat. The bar serves homemade sodas and kombucha on tap, and in summer service extends to an outdoor patio. For dessert, pop a few doors down to the cookie bakery Hello Robin, which specializes in handmade ice-cream sandwiches.

MAP 3: 550 19th Ave. E, 206/860-0077, www.aneighborhoodcafe.com; 4pm-11pm Mon.-Thurs., 4pm-midnight Fri., 9am-midnight Sat., 9am-9pm Sun.

GASTROPUBS

Quinn's Pub $$

Everybody goes to Quinn's Pub, a two-story restaurant that occupies a prime location on one of Capitol Hill's busiest streets. It's nice enough for a business meal (well, a casual, impress with the food kind of business meal), dim enough for a date, rowdy enough for dinner with friends, and flavorful enough for a special occasion. The burger is one of the most popular menu items, but this is no burger joint; the bistro fare includes a Scotch egg and grilled Vermont quail. Desserts are small and, at $3-4 each, meant to be ordered in multiples. The bar, with access to knowledgeable bartenders pouring Trappist ales, is prime seating but hard to score. Upstairs tables have less ambience, but can mean more elbow room. Besides the 14 beer taps, the alcohol offerings lean toward bourbons and whiskeys.

MAP 3: 1001 E. Pike St., 206/325-7711, www.quinnspubseattle.com; 3pm-midnight Sun.-Thurs., 3pm-2am Fri.-Sat.

Smith $$

Want some dead animals for company with your dinner? The taxidermy at Smith is the cute vintage kind, the mounted deer antlers and stuffed birds sharing wall space with framed portraits straight out of an English gentleman's club. Though the space is definitely a restaurant—the bar isn't big, so most people are at tables or booths—it's as dark and loud as a bar in the evenings, making it a popular date spot on Capitol Hill's growing 15th Avenue stretch. The meats spice up the menu, with brisket-topped poutine and roasted bone marrow among the offerings. The bar serves cocktails on tap, including a house tonic to mix with vodka or gin.

MAP 3: 332 15th Ave. E, 206/709-1900, www.smithseattle.com; 4pm-1am Mon.-Thurs., 4pm-2am Fri., 9am-3pm and 4pm-2am Sat., 9am-3pm and 4pm-1am Sun.

Grim's Provisions & Spirits $

Don't confuse this spot with Quinn's Pub just down the street; the two restaurants are a lot alike, though Grim's take on rustic gastropub is a little

Stateside

more relaxed. A brief menu focuses on spruced-up classics like grilled cheese with herbed leeks and macaroni and cheese drizzled with truffle oil. Drinks are served in quaint jam jars, and the beer selection is a little more worldly than the rest of the Hill—it has the local Manny's and some Oregon standbys, but it also pours English ale and Framboise lambic. Though the main floor houses a cozy eatery, the 2nd floor is a thumping dance club called The Woods, where DJs spin on weekends.

MAP 3: 1512 11th Ave., 206/324-7467, www.grimseattle.com; 4pm-midnight Thurs., 4pm-2am Fri., 6pm-2am Sat.

VIETNAMESE
✪ Stateside $$

Despite the name, there's not much to do with the States at one of Capitol Hill's best-regarded restaurants. Chef Eric Johnson pulled from his own international travels to create a menu of Vietnamese cuisine with French and Chinese influences, served in a white-walled space accented with palm frond wallpaper and teal trim that recalls colonial Asia. Standout dishes include chili-cumin pork ribs, best ordered very spicy, and a dreamy goat curry. For all the serious attention from foodies and critics, Stateside retains a sense of humor, its menu noting of the rum cocktail served in a fresh-cracked coconut, "Yes, there is an umbrella." Reservations are recommended.

MAP 3: 300 E. Pike St., 206/557-7273, www.statesideseattle.com; 5pm-10:30pm Mon.-Fri., 10am-2pm and 5pm-10:30pm Sat.-Sun.

Monsoon $$

Along with Tallulah's, Monsoon holds down the only active corner in a quiet end of Capitol Hill. The Vietnamese restaurant is an established favorite among locals drawn to the combination of sophisticated cocktails and modern cuisine. Saigon-inspired dishes are joined with fresh Northwest ingredients, like Alaskan black cod with mushrooms and prawns in a yellow curry, or the catfish clay pot that is served hot right out of the oven. Weekends bring a dim sum brunch where Bloody Marys are made with pho broth.

MAP 3: 615 19th Ave. E, 206/325-2111, www.monsoonrestaurants.com; 11:30am-3pm and 5pm-10pm Mon.-Thurs., 11:30am-3pm and 5pm-11pm Fri., 10am-3pm and 5pm-11pm Sat., 10am-3pm and 5pm-10pm Sun.

COFFEE

Caffe Ladro $

Though chain coffee was more or less born in Seattle, the city's independent coffee shops and mini-chains inspire the real devotion among locals. The handful of Caffe Ladro locations in the city are known for high-quality coffee and consistent service. The usual flock of laptop writers and students fill the wooden chairs, and there are only a few outdoor seats in summer. There's a reason so many residents pop by for one of the signature yellow cups on their way to work: Ladro is classic Seattle coffee.

MAP 3: 435 15th Ave. E, 206/267-0551, www.caffeladro.com; 5:30am-8pm Mon.-Fri., 6am-8pm Fri.-Sat.

Starbucks Reserve Roastery & Tasting Room $

Starbucks began as a modest coffee shop near Pike Place Market, and it has grown to include outposts on nearly every Seattle corner, plus a global headquarters south of the stadiums. But its pinnacle might be Capitol Hill's roastery, an airy space meant to show off the company's claim to high-end coffee mastery. It doesn't serve the normal Starbucks menu, but rather its limited Reserve line roasted here and brewed in a variety of methods—pour-over, Clover, French press, and more. The coffee show happens in a room filled with copper pipes and beans running through pneumatic tubes. Princi Bakery, an Italian café with high-end breads and pizzas, exists as a somewhat separate entity inside the space, and lounge seating is available near a fireplace. When it's too late for straight coffee, try a cocktail made with a cold brew or tea.

MAP 3: 1124 Pike St., 206/624-0173, http://roastery.starbucks.com; 7am-11pm daily

Victrola

Victrola $

Capitol Hill was once known for its coffee shops, but many have been forced out in recent years, unable to keep up with the skyrocketing rents in the hip neighborhood. One survivor is Victrola, where the usual bustle of baristas and students hums under a kind of gallery space for local artists. The venue has hosted radio events, movie nights, and even an insect safari. It also serves up standard café fare like sandwiches and salads. Victrola does its roasting at its second location, which is farther down Capitol Hill (310 E. Pike St.) along the neighborhood's former auto row; that location has free educational coffee tastings on Wednesdays at 11am.

MAP 3: 411 15th Ave. E, 206/325-6520, www.victrolacoffee.com; 6am-10pm Mon.-Sat., 6am-9pm Sun.

ITALIAN
Altura $$$

Broadway may bustle, but one of the city's best examples of classic fine dining is hidden in plain sight right in the middle. Much costlier than any food joint that surrounds it, the Italian restaurant stays quiet inside despite its open kitchen. The tasting menu is the only option, priced at $137 per person, and it changes daily to suit the chef's favorite local ingredients and seasonal offerings. Expect a leisurely parade of rich but rustic Italian flavors, served in a candlelit room that still feels casual. Make a reservation in advance, and leave plenty of time.

MAP 3: 617 Broadway E, 206/402-6749, http://alturarestaurant.com; 5:30pm-10pm Tues.-Thurs., 5pm-10pm Fri.-Sat.

Spinasse $$$

In a city where new American pub cuisine and creative seafood concepts get all the attention, Spinasse excels at Italian fare and a sophisticated atmosphere. The food is from northern Italy and relies on local ingredients and handmade pastas. Salads, antipasti, and meaty rabbit or pork belly are all delicious, but the *tajarin*—egg pasta served with ragu or butter—is the simple, delectable standout. It may be the single best dish in Seattle, so splurge for the bigger portion. If your table doesn't devour the shareable plates, it makes for killer leftovers. Some seats face the open kitchen. The sister bar next door, Artusi, also has small Italian

bites, plus expert bartenders and a sunny, modern space.

MAP 3: 1531 14th Ave., 206/251-7673, www.spinasse.com; 5pm-10pm Sun.-Thurs., 5pm-11pm Fri.-Sat.

Rione XIII $$

With sleek, polished wood tables under an exposed brick wall that feels fancy, not trendy, Rione XIII—from noted local restauranteur Ethan Stowell—from might be Capitol Hill's most grown-up restaurant. It features Roman-style pizza made in a wood-fired oven, along with hearty meat dishes and a slate of pastas. Unlike most restaurants nearby, the spot features patient, full service, rather than counters or bars that encourage more casual gatherings. Named for a district in Rome, Rione has a menu that feels specific to that city but approachable to any casual diner, especially one who wants to sit back with a glass of red wine. Two happy hours—one early, one late—offer excellent food specials in the bar area.

MAP 3: 401 15th Ave. E, 206/838-2878, www.ethanstowellrestaurants.com; 5pm-10pm Sun.-Thurs., 5pm-11pm Fri.-Sat.

MIDDLE EASTERN
Mamnoon $$

The white-tiled walls of Capitol Hill's best-loved Middle Eastern restaurant give the space a sleek sophistication and nod to the ceramic traditions of the region, but their best use may be in keeping the focus on the food. The menu draws from the owners' Syrian, Lebanese, and Iranian roots, with lamb wraps and lentil-filled small plates at lunch and grilled meats and stews at dinner. Dishes are rich and distinct, some made with herbs not seen on Western menus. Even the hummus, today a standby in every corner deli and supermarket, is memorable here.

MAP 3: 1508 Melrose Ave., 206/906-9606, www.mamnoonrestaurant.com; 11:30am-10pm Sun.-Thurs., 11am-10pm Fri.-Sat.

INTERNATIONAL
Cook Weaver $$

The cozy stone building that holds Cook Weaver looks like it belongs in an old English village, or maybe a fairy tale. But what's inside is hardly old fashioned; the restaurant bills itself as "Eurasian," combining international flavors in mostly sharable plates. The nori dumplings, served with kimchi, are a crowd-pleaser, and the smoked black cod with collard greens makes the most of the fish's rich flavor. Tables are cozy, and the walls are decorated with murals that date back to the 1930s, depicting the story of a tsar and a swan. In summer, the small space can get a bit too warm for comfort, but it's ideal the rest of the year.

MAP 3: 806 E. Roy St., 206/324-0599, www.cookweaver.com; 5pm-10pm Tues.-Sun.

Nue $

The foodie world's obsession with street food is nothing new, but Nue has taken it up a notch by featuring street food from every corner of the planet. There are East Indies Brussels sprouts, Malaysian curry *laksa,* and even South African Bunny Chow—not a rabbit dish at all, but chicken served in a bread bowl. Both the long communal tables and the small dishes encourage sharing plates, though be prepared to fight for your favorites. The Trinidad goat curry, served with coconut and pineapple corn bread, goes quickly. The drinks menu is just

Nue

as worldly, with cocktails made from a Hungarian aperitif or vodka infused with Thai water beetles (yes, the drink is called Beetle Juice).

MAP 3: 1519 14th Ave., 206/257-0312, www.nueseattle.com; 10am-10pm Sun.-Thurs., 10am-midnight Fri.-Sat.

INDIAN
Poppy $$$

The cheery Poppy is a less common take on Indian dining. The menu is based around *thali* platters of many small dishes, using local ingredients and traditional Indian spices. The *thalis,* which might include soup, salad, nigella-poppy naan, some kind of pickle, and a braised meat or fresh fish, change daily. The cocktails use fresh juices and flavors that match the complex *thalis.* The small garden out back has both outdoor seating and the restaurant's herb garden. Inside it's all exposed brick and bright-orange design accents.

MAP 3: 622 Broadway E, 206/324-1108, www.poppyseattle.com; 5pm-10:30pm Sun.-Thurs., 5:30pm-11:30pm Fri.-Sat.

MALAYSIAN
Kedai Makan $$

At first, you could only get Kedai Makan's Malaysian fare at a walk-up window on Olive Way, where it served as a de facto kitchen for the dive bar Montana next door. But the owners finally moved to a nearby spot to create a space almost as loud as the bar-filled street they left; with bright teal walls and lots of tall tables and bar seating, the vibe is lively. The food still has the hearty warmth of good takeout, including fried rice and noodles in rich duck broth. Chili *pan mee,* with pork and a side of broth, is becoming a favorite of the sit-down iteration of the restaurant. Fortunately, prices haven't gone too high with the introduction of table service.

MAP 3: 1802 Bellevue Ave., www. kedaimakansea.com; 5pm-11pm Wed.-Sat., 5pm-10pm Sun.

SOUTHERN
Witness $$

Praise the lord and pass the artisanal cocktail. The theme of this Broadway bar is a Southern house of worship, and the faithful do fill the pews that form the seats (a century old and from a real Southern church). The menu features Southern standards like beignets, fried green tomatoes, and chicken and waffles, with a few more adventurous offerings like Dixie poutine with pimento cheese and duck-and-green-bean casserole. The drink menu flings an even wider net with classic and modern cocktails; ask one of the talented bartenders for a Divine Intervention or a custom cocktail. Though the restaurant is popular at brunch, it's most alive late on Saturday nights. Sometimes the owner comes out to give a sermon in true revival-preacher form, though he's more likely to be praising the sins of the flesh than condemning them.

MAP 3: 410 Broadway E, 206/329-0248, http://witnessbar.com, 4pm-1am Mon.-Thurs., 4pm-2am Fri., 9am-2am Sat., 9am-1am Sun.

BURGERS
Dick's Drive-In $

There are many things Dick's is not. It's not a drive-in in the traditional sense, for one. The walk-up window doesn't have an extensive menu—it's pretty much just burgers, fries, and milk shakes. There are no substitutions or customizations on the slim burgers. And late at night, the greasy takeout joint isn't always a calm place to hang out, since it attracts folks who've hit the bars hard. But the restaurant, part of a local chain, is a Seattle classic—so much so that Macklemore used it as a set in one of his music videos. With a deluxe burger priced at $3.10 and milk shakes that are just $2.50, it's a cheap way to experience something every local has—the thrill of cheap grease and the unsettling realization, 10 minutes later, of how much grease you just ate.

MAP 3: 115 Broadway E, 206/323-1300, www.ddir.com; 10:30am-2am daily

Li'l Woody's $

Only one thing at Li'l Woody's is "li'l"—the quarter-pound burger that comes with Tillamook cheese and basic toppings. The rest of the burgers are a third of a pound and loaded with bacon and horseradish, or green chilies, or pickled figs with gorgonzola cheese. You can even load a burger with peanut butter. Skinny skin-on fries come plain, with house-made cheese, or with "crack," a small bowl of milk shake for dipping. With a few local beers on tap, a loft seating

Li'l Woody's

a late-night menu with cheap sandwiches and pork rillettes.

MAP 3: 1117 12th Ave., 206/709-7674, http://cafepresseseattle.com; 7am-2am daily

Volunteer Park Cafe $$

The welcoming yellow building that houses Volunteer Park Cafe reflects the cheerful, no-pretense dining inside. Breakfast and lunch means homey seasonal dishes ordered at the counter while hoping for a spot at the few chairs; favorites include the Reuben on house-made pastrami or brioche French toast with seasonal fruit. Dinner continues the down-home trend with mac and cheese or potpie, and a brisket is served with creamy polenta. Fresh pastries are available any time. About once a month, the restaurant hosts a fixed-price Sunday supper with a single seating; the chef makes a seasonal three-course meal, sometimes themed around a holiday.

MAP 3: 1501 17th Ave. E, 206/328-3155, http://alwaysfreshgoodness.com; 7am-4:30pm and 5:30pm-9pm Tues.-Fri., 8am-4:30pm and 5:30pm-9pm Sat., 8am-4:30pm Sun.

area, and a window-facing counter, the small restaurant manages to be an eat-in joint, not just a fast-food spot (though the service is pretty speedy). Head up the stairs for a more relaxed spot to eat, since the tall stools downstairs are close to the cooks shouting out orders. It's on the edge of Capitol Hill, just across the freeway from the convention center, making it the best burger close to downtown.

MAP 3: 1211 Pine St., 206/457-4148, www.lilwoodys.com; 11am-11pm Mon.-Thurs., 11am-3am Fri.-Sat., 11am-10pm Sun.

CAFÉS AND BISTROS

Café Presse $$

Capitol Hill's French bistro isn't trying too hard, but somehow it manages to radiate cool. The café and newsstand has a simple bar area and racks of magazines, and European sports are often on the TV. In the morning it's a place for coffee and croissants, and at night it's ideal for a glass of wine and perhaps a croque madame topped with a runny egg. Call ahead to order the roast chicken for two, which requires an hour of advance warning. After 11pm, there's

The Wandering Goose $$

The Wandering Goose sounds like a fairy-tale character, and indeed the owner has written a children's book based on the joint. The restaurant itself is sweet and comfortable, with counter service and wooden chairs at little wooden tables. The food is Southern and breakfast-inspired: biscuits, grits, ham, gravy, plus some salads for lunch and baked goods. The honey is house made and sourced from beehives on the roof. On Fridays, a special fried-chicken meal ($25) is served at 5pm: three pieces of buttermilk chicken, a biscuit, and three sides, like collard greens or coleslaw. If a farmhouse café was neatly blended with a Southern diner, it would look and feel—and taste—something like this.

MAP 3: 403 15th Ave. E, 206/323-9938, www.thewanderinggoose.com; 7am-4pm Sat.-Thurs., 7am-4pm and 5pm-9pm Fri.

Fremont

Map 4

SEAFOOD
RockCreek Seafood & Spirits $$$

Seattle may sit on Puget Sound, near the source of some of the best seafood in the world, but that's not the only fish to be found on local plates. Chef Eric Donnelly serves seafood of all kinds but named the restaurant after his favorite fly-fishing river in Montana; river fish are often a highlight of the menu. The two-story space has an airy cabin feel—it could be a high-end fishing resort in Montana—and the fin fish section of the menu may pull from spots as diverse as Hawaii, Iceland, and Washington's own Neah Bay. While there is a short list of meat and pasta offerings, come for the fish flavors, done in simple but meticulous preparations.

MAP 4: 4300 Fremont Ave N, 206/557-7532, http://rockcreekseattle.com; 4pm-11pm Mon.-Fri., 9am-11pm Sat.-Sun.

The Whale Wins $$$

There's a rustic farmhouse vibe inside famed chef Renee Erickson's Fremont eatery, thanks to white paneled walls and stacks of firewood around the wood-fired oven—but it's a little farmhouse by the sea, not on the prairie. A wall mural has the look of *Moby-Dick* as reimagined by Lewis Carroll, and seasonal seafood is prominent on the menu, from local clams to herring

butter. Don't shy away from dishes that make fresh veggies the star, and save room for the fruity, creamy Eton Mess for dessert.

MAP 4: 3506 Stone Way N, 206/632-9425, www.thewhalewins.com; 5pm-10pm Mon.-Sat., 5pm-9pm Sun.

✪ Manolin $$

The disco ball that hangs above this otherwise simple restaurant feels a bit out of place, since this Fremont eatery has a casual-chic feel. Start a meal with firm, brightly flavorful ceviche featuring avocado. Move on to the mains—seafood dishes like octopus right off the grill, smoked salmon, and albacore served with a bouquet of fruit—and a side of plantain chips, and leave room for creative cocktails made with shrubs and flavored liqueurs. Inside, diners get a view of the open kitchen, but atmospheric fire pits are outdoors.

MAP 4: 3621 Stone Way N, 206/294-3331, www.manolinseattle.com; 4pm-10pm Tues.-Sat., 4pm-9pm Sun.

NEW AMERICAN
Tarsan i Jane $$$

Yes, it's named for the king of the jungle Tarzan and his lady, spelled the way they do it in Valencia, Spain. The Spanish flavors are served in an elaborate prix fixe experience ($185) that's as much theater as dinner. Diners are seated together at a chef's table, and each course is introduced with a story. On Sundays, paella takes center stage. It's an unusual experience for Seattle, but the departure makes it all the more fascinating.

MAP 4: 4012 Leary Way NW, www. tarsanijane.com; 6pm-10pm Thurs.-Sat., 11am-2pm and 6pm-10pm Sun.

Tilth $$$

Organic isn't just a buzzword in the green house just east of Fremont, it's an ethos—Tilth's food is almost entirely organic, and much of it is gluten-free. Vegetarians will also find plenty to love from Maria Hines, a chef who worked at New York's vaunted Eleven Madison Park before making Seattle her home. The regular menu includes seared tuna and mini duck burgers, and the tasting menus have almost as much variety—there are vegetarian, gluten-free, and vegan options, all packed with locally sourced ingredients and available with wine pairings. There are just as many choices to make regarding seating in this craftsman house, including a patio with a backyard feel, bar seats in a sunroom overlooking the street, and a counter with a view of the kitchen.

MAP 4: 1411 N. 45th St., 206/633-0801, http://mariahinesrestaurants.com; 5pm-9pm Sun.-Thurs., 5pm-10pm Fri., 10am-1:30pm and 5pm-10pm Sat., 10am-1:30pm and 5pm-9pm Sun.

Brimmer & Heeltap $$

Tucked unobtrusively between Ballard and Fremont on an otherwise residential block, Brimmer & Heeltap is the very model of a neighborhood restaurant. White chairs and white plank walls give it a farmhouse vibe, but bright teal decor and a leafy patio keep it from feeling too modern—or bland. Buzzy and hip when it first opened in

2013, it now hums with a friendly local clientele. The menu is brief, changing the local grass-fed beef preparation and seafood dish with the season, and picky eaters might balk at the limited options. Still, the most memorable dish is the "bread" appetizer: one thick piece of hearty white toast, simply buttered and seasoned with salt and pepper. It's big as a plate, and surprisingly satisfying.

MAP 4: 425 NW Market St., 206/420-2534, www.brimmerandheeltap.com; 5pm-10pm Wed.-Sun.

GASTROPUB

Norm's Eatery & Alehouse $$

Welcome to a casual eatery that's literally gone to the dogs. Named for the owner's own pooch, Norm's is famous for its canine-friendly policy. On any given evening there may be a dozen dogs inside, and they have their own set of rules (leashes on, barking not allowed) and, of course, a menu. People eat wraps, burgers, and wings, while dogs choose from cod skins and marrow bones, leaving room for doggy desserts like peanut-butter cookies. It always feels a little active inside Norm's, with college students eating their filling meals and dogs eyeing them in case they drop a fry.

MAP 4: 460 N. 36th St., 206/547-1417, www.normseatery.com; 11am-11pm Mon.-Thurs., 11am-midnight Fri., 9am-midnight Sat., 9am-11pm Sun.

COFFEE

Fremont Coffee Company $

Fremont Coffee roasts its own fair trade beans and serves locally made pastries. The company is located in a house right on Fremont's main drag, and inside you'll find a series of small rooms. Like any classic Seattle coffeehouse, it displays local artwork on the walls and offers outdoor seating on the front porch.

MAP 4: 459 N. 36th St., 206/632-3633, www.fremontcoffee.net; 6am-8pm Mon.-Fri., 7am-8pm Sat.-Sun.

Lighthouse Roasters $

Tucked into the calm, low-key upper Fremont neighborhood, this corner coffee shop has the kind of local crowd that few downtown spots can boast; people come here to be part of the community, not merely grab caffeine on the way to work (though that happens too). Roasting since 1993, several other well-loved coffee shops around town serve its beans. The shop itself, with locals and their dogs at outside tables and lingering patrons inside, always has the requisite deep coffee smell in the air. Coffee snobs should be prepared to take some beans to go.

MAP 4: 400 N. 43rd St., 206/633-4775, http://lighthouseroasters.com; 6am-7pm Mon.-Fri., 6:30am-7pm Sat.-Sun.

ITALIAN
Agrodolce $$$

Intended as a salute to southern Italy and Sicily, this neighborhood restaurant seems to have borrowed a bit of that region's sunshine. A tall wall of windows lets light into the dining room, where creative midcentury modern light fixtures hang over an otherwise spare space. Veggie-heavy dishes and house-made pasta rule the day, and meats are roasted with local foraged ingredients. A family-style option, for $48 per person, is a three-course chef's choice experience, available daily but with a hyper-regional focus on Sundays and Mondays.

MAP 4: 709 N. 35th St., 206/547-9707, http://mariahinesrestaurants.com; 11:30am-2pm and 5pm-9pm Mon.-Thurs., 11:30am-2pm and 5pm-10pm Fri., 10am-2:30pm and 5pm-10pm Sat., 10am-2:30pm and 5pm-9pm Sun.

MIDDLE EASTERN
Café Turko $$

As colorful as Turkish tilework, this cozy Fremont joint is a casual and joyful spot. The hummus menu alone is a color wheel, with varieties made from beet, spinach, and yam; try the rainbow hummus plate for a taste of all, served with hot, soft pita. The menu is otherwise thorough, with salads and various traditional Turkish dishes, including shish kebabs. The outdoor patio has views of the underside of the Aurora Bridge (more scenic than it sounds).

MAP 4: 750 N. 34th St., 206/284-9954, http://cafe-turko.com; 10am-9:30pm Sun.-Fri., 10am-10pm Sat.

MEXICAN
Pecado Bueno $

When "I feel like Mexican food" really means "I want a margarita," the perky, casual Pecado Bueno (translation: "sin well") has you covered. The house marg is only $3.75 all day, served fast and furious from the walk-up counter. Tacos, tostadas, and nachos are nothing fancy, but for the young crowds at the outdoor fire pit tables, the speed and price make up for it. It's a definite step up from fast food, and it's on a busy block of Fremont favored by locals.

MAP 4: 4307 Fremont Ave. N, 206/457-8837, http://pecadobueno.com; 11am-11pm Mon.-Sat., 11am-10pm Sun.

CARIBBEAN
✪ Paseo $

In Seattle, Paseo isn't a sandwich shop, it's *the* sandwich shop. Famous for its out-the-door lines for two decades, the eatery inspired citywide panic when both its outposts closed in 2014 after falling into bankruptcy. A few months later, the main Fremont location opened its doors again under new management. But the cherry-red paneling and tin awning out front were the same, as was the famed Caribbean Roast sandwich—marinated pork shoulder on a baguette with aioli, giant chunks of cooked onion, and pickled jalapeños. The menu is long, with a slew of pork, prawn, and even tofu sandwiches, plus larger scallop and chicken entrées served with a side of roasted corn. Since there's little seating, a sandwich to go is the most popular order. A second restaurant opened in SoDo (1760 1st Ave. S; typically 11am-7pm Tues.-Sat., 11am-3pm Sun.-Mon., closing hours may vary based on local events), far south of the stadiums.

MAP 4: 4225 Fremont Ave. N, 206/545-7440, www.paseoseattle.com; 11am-9pm Tues.-Fri., 11am-8pm Sat., 11am-7pm Sun.

BURGERS
Uneeda Burger $

Head to this bustling block of upper Fremont when you need a sizable portion of meat topped with roasted chili relish, shallots, or, in the intimidating Madame, a combination of ham, a sunny-side egg, and truffle fries. The patio tables are a nice spot to wait for your order on a sunny day. Be prepared for a lot of food; you might need to choose between the fries or the ice-cream floats made with artisanal sodas.

MAP 4: 4302 Fremont Ave. N, 206/547-2600, www.uneedaburger.com; 11am-9pm daily

PIZZA
Frelard Pizza Company $

The name of this restaurant comes from the upstart neighborhood located between Ballard and Fremont, increasingly popular with casual, high-quality eateries and tiny breweries. Frelard's thin-crust pizzas are served by the slice or whole, and include the carbonara and a genius combination of pepperoni, pineapple, and jalapeño. Though only some of the tables are technically outside, surrounding a fire pit and decorative wood barrels, the whole place feels al fresco when the giant garage-door-style windows are open. There's a whole walled-off play area for kids, so the joint is popular with families. During "flour hour" (4pm-6pm and 10pm-11pm Sun.-Thurs.), slices are $2, best consumed with a local Northwest beer or Italian wine.

MAP 4: 4010 Leary Way NW, 206/946-9966, www.grubbbrospizza.com; 4pm-10pm Mon.-Thurs., 4pm-11pm Fri., 11am-11pm Sat., 11am-10pm Sun.

RESTAURANTS

BALLARD

SEAFOOD

Ray's Boathouse $$$

This pierside restaurant serves local seafood specialties in addition to Maine lobster and gulf prawns. Each of the restaurant's two floors has views of Shilshole Bay and the distant peaks of the Olympics. The downstairs bar faces the water and is topped with blown-glass light fixtures. The café upstairs is more casual (and cheaper), though the "fancier" restaurant on the lower floor is hardly black-tie— you can get away with jeans if they're your best pair.

MAP 5: 6049 Seaview Ave. NW, 206/789-3770, www.rays.com; restaurant 5pm-9pm daily, café 11:30am-9pm daily

✪ The Walrus and the Carpenter $$

An oyster bar named for the poem in *Through the Looking-Glass,* The Walrus and the Carpenter has wait times that are hard to believe—up to or surpassing two hours, even on a weeknight. The small space has a handful of tables and a bar, and all the seafood is locally sourced. A handful of veggie dishes complement the oysters and shellfish, the most noteworthy being the fried Brussels sprouts. Steak tartare and cheese plates complete the menu from celebrity chef Renee Erickson, but the spot isn't a good bet for anyone uninterested in seafood. And yes, the wait is worth it for a table

The Walrus and the Carpenter

in the sparkling white space and handfuls of sharable plates. To ease the pain of the line, leave a phone number at the door and head to another bar on Ballard Avenue for a drink—they'll call when you're next up for oysters.
MAP 5: 4743 Ballard Ave. NW,
206/395-9227, www.thewalrusbar.com;
4pm-10pm Sun.-Thurs., 4pm-11pm Fri.-Sat.

NEW AMERICAN
Bitterroot BBQ $$

The sleek Bitterroot doesn't look like most barbecue joints—no rustic chic or barn-like decor here. The restaurant offers a refined take on a messy food, right on Ballard's busiest block. Its subway tile and white brick make a crisp backdrop for smoked chicken, brisket, and ribs. Sides are classics like collard greens and black-eyed peas, and the hush puppies are made with smoked jalapeño. The whiskey selection is impressive, including dozens of rye whiskeys, and two happy hours per day offer discounts on bourbon cocktails.
MAP 5: 5239 Ballard Ave. NW,
206/588-1577, www.bitterrootbbq.com;
11am-2am daily

THAI
Pestle Rock $$

A long-loved treasure in the heart of Ballard, Pestle Rock offers generous portions and a warm, friendly atmosphere. Its cuisine hails from Thailand's Isan province; don't expect by-the-numbers pad Thai or the usual curries here. Spices are intense, and dishes incorporate fresh vegetables and charbroiled meat. For all the creative dishes on the menu, it's an accessible joint for diners in search of flavor. With neon lights and shutters on interior windows, the restaurant feels like a bit of a hodgepodge, a great

relief from the fussy interior design that can plague other Ballard eateries.
MAP 5: 2305 NW Market St.,
206/466-6671, http://pestlerock.com;
11:30am-9:30pm Mon. and Wed.-Thurs.,
11:30am-10pm Fri., noon-10pm Sat.,
noon-9pm Sun.

FRENCH
Bastille Café $$$

Bastille Café is a lovely, adult addition to a bar-heavy neighborhood that's matured in recent years. The walls are rustic exposed brick and gleaming white tiles, menus are scrawled on mirrors, and chandeliers hang from exposed beams. The outdoor patio and indoor fire hearth fill for weekend brunches and casual dinners; look for the Back Bar entrance when the main dining room is full. Sconces and other touches try to evoke a hip French bistro (or maybe a very fancy metro station). Honey is sourced from 50,000 honeybees living in hives up on the roof, and a jazz group plays on the terrace on Sunday nights in the summer.
MAP 5: 5307 Ballard Ave. NW,
206/453-5014, www.bastilleseattle.com;
5pm-10pm Mon.-Thurs., 5pm-11pm Fri.-Sat.,
10am-3pm and 5:30pm-8pm Sun.

Copine $$$

Located in an out-of-the-way corner of Ballard—mostly residential and about a 10-minute walk from the neighborhood center—Copine has quickly become a local favorite for fine dining. The French fare is carefully rendered, and the chef-manager couple who run the restaurant worked together at New York's Per Se. Rabbit confit, lamb dishes, a grilled rib eye—the menu is straightforward and often uses seasonal produce, particularly mushrooms. The quiet restaurant feels like something halfway between a simple

French farmhouse and a chic modern loft; not a place you need to dress up for, but where the food dresses up the diner.

MAP 5: 6460 24th Ave. NW, 206/258-2467, www.copineseattle.com; 5pm-9pm Tues.-Sat.

ITALIAN
Staple & Fancy $$$

With the buzzy, in-demand Walrus and the Carpenter on the back side of the building—and visible through interior glass windows in the back of the dining room—Staple & Fancy could be easily overshadowed. But with an open kitchen and the remnants of old warehouse signage on the brick walls, it's hardly a modest restaurant from Seattle culinary bigwig Ethan Stowell. The "staple" part of the menu is straightforward Italian dishes like pesto gnocchi and grilled pork chop, while the "fancy" is a chef's tasting menu served family-style, delicious but not too fussy or elegant. It may be where people end up when they can't stomach the Walrus wait, but the experience is memorable all on its own.

Staple & Fancy

MAP 5: 4739 Ballard Ave. NW, 206/789-1200, www. ethanstowellrestaurants.com; 5pm-11pm daily

MEXICAN
La Carta de Oaxaca $$

It's a long way from Seattle to the Mexican border, but La Carta de Oaxaca has authentic Mexican fare in a small, crowded space. The guacamole is made by hand, and the open kitchen proves that the mole is made here. A wall of framed photographs lightens the restaurant, but everyone is concentrating on shoveling in tortillas, tostadas, and *entomatadas*. Reservations are not accepted, and the spot's quality is well known, so expect a wait.

MAP 5: 5431 Ballard Ave. NW, 206/782-8722, www.lacartadeoaxaca. com; 5pm-11pm Mon., 11:30am-3pm and 5pm-11pm Tues.-Thurs., 11:30am-midnight Fri.-Sat.

CARIBBEAN
Un Bien $

If famed sandwich shop Paseo was an institution, Un Bien is its next iteration. When Paseo closed in 2014, the owner sold his original store, but his sons sought to carry on his legacy with their own walk-up eatery. Serving their own family twist on the original Paseo sandwich, they've inspired legions of roasted pork fans to hotly debate the merits of the two eateries. (Too bad it's almost impossible to eat both giant, messy sandwiches in one day.) The bright-pink shack has a few outdoor tables to one side, and customers scarf down their takeout sandwiches so fast that snagging one is usually possible. Fish, tofu, prawn, and chicken dishes are also available, and

PIZZA
✪ Stoneburner $$

The restaurant that sits below the Hotel Ballard is named after its founding chef, Jason Stoneburner, but it's the perfect name for an eatery that cooks pizza in a stone oven. The signature dish comes with a dusty char, topped with sausage, porchetta, or chanterelles. A rounded bar with comfy black stools sits under pressed tin and wood paneled ceilings, and the spot is surprisingly popular at brunch—perhaps explained by the best dish on the menu, a breakfast pizza with whole eggs and slices of bacon. The menu includes plenty beyond pizza, including meatballs and brick-pressed chicken.

MAP 5: 5214 Ballard Ave. NW, 206/695-2051, www.stoneburnerseattle. com; 3pm-10pm Mon.-Thurs., 3pm-11pm Fri., 10am-11pm Sat., 10am-10pm Sun.

Stoneburner

the fire-roasted corn comes doused in the house-made aioli. A second location opened near Shilshole Bay (6226 Seaview Ave. NW, 206/420-7545; 11am-8pm Wed.-Sun.), about halfway between the Ballard Locks and Golden Gardens Park.

MAP 5: 7302.5 15th Ave. NW, 206/588-2040, http://unbienseattle.com; 11am-9pm Wed.-Sat., 11am-8pm Sun.

University District   Map 6

ASIAN
✪ Din Tai Fung $$

This globe-spanning Taiwanese chain, famous for its dumplings, finally landed in Seattle near the university, in the city's nicest shopping center. The *xiao long bao*, or soup dumplings, are warm balls of pork and hearty liquid, served by the dozen (it's a good idea to bring the whole gang). Order from a long menu of dumpling, rice, noodle, and meat dishes; the green beans are especially buttery and decadent. This outpost features dark wood paneling and a window view into the kitchen, where bright lights illuminate white-clad cooks assembling dumplings. Another outpost quickly opened downtown on the heels of this one (600 Pine St., 206/682-9888; 11am-10pm Mon.-Fri., 10am-10pm Sat.-Sun.).

MAP 6: 2621 NE 46th St., 206/525-0958, http://dintaifungusa.com; 11am-9:30pm Mon.-Thurs., 11am-10pm Fri., 10am-10pm Sat., 10am-9:30pm Sun.

Thai Tom $

Any decent college town needs a joint with good Thai for broke and hungry students, and this restaurant is only steps from the sprawling University of Washington campus. Bring cash—no cards accepted here—for the pad Thai or spicy curries. The painted menu on the wall is just brief enough to make choosing a hot and cheap entrée easy. It's definitely not fancy, and eating near the open kitchen means smelling the strong scents of everyone's dishes. But the bubble tea is popular for a reason, and it's a reliable destination for something hot and delicious.

MAP 6: 4543 University Way NE, 206/548-9548; 11:30am-9pm Mon.-Thurs., 11:30am-10pm Fri.-Sat., noon-9pm Sun.

MEXICAN
Agua Verde Cafe $

You have two choices at Agua Verde Cafe, located on Portage Bay between Lake Washington and Lake Union: Eat Mexican food and then rent a kayak, or kayak first and then bliss out on tacos, Mexican beer, and margaritas. You can skip the boat rentals altogether, but the view and their proximity make them very tempting. Both the restaurant and paddle club are located in a funky two-story aqua building that looks more like a surfer's home in Baja than a Seattle institution. The restaurant has dishes with a Baja California vibe—empanadas, enchiladas, and open-face tacos, all ordered from a counter. The patio seats go first in nice weather. The attached Agua Verde Paddle Club (206/545-8570, $18-23 per hour) rents single and double kayaks and stand-up paddleboards.

MAP 6: 1303 NE Boat St., 206/545-8570, www.aguaverde.com; 7:30am-9pm Mon.-Fri., 9am-9pm Sat.

SOUTHERN
JuneBaby $$

Who knew that a Southern restaurant could make such a splash in this Pacific Northwest corner of the United States? Chef Edouardo Jordan opened JuneBaby in 2017 and was quickly overcome with praise. He puts creative spins on Southern American classics like fried pig ears and catfish. Cornbread, biscuits, and antebellum wheat buns start the meal, and sides of chitlins and collard greens are recommended. His adaption of his mother's bone-in oxtail recipe has been a standout from day one. The small, simple space gets crowded quickly, and ever since Jordan received a James Beard Award in 2018, the no-reservations restaurant (except for large groups) has seen lengthy wait times. Expect to dine an hour or two after you arrive and put your name on the list; the hosts will likely point you to a nearby bookstore while you wait.

MAP 6: 2122 NE 65th St., 206/257-4470, www.junebabyseattle.com; 5pm-10pm Wed.-Fri., 11am-3pm and 5pm-10pm Sat.-Sun.

BREAKFAST AND BRUNCH
✪ Portage Bay Cafe $$

Breakfast is no afterthought at one of the city's most popular restaurants: It's Portage Bay's whole reason for being, and this original location spawned three others throughout the city. Eggs Benedicts are made with Dungeness crab or wild mushrooms, and a farmer's hash uses local corned beef, sausage, or cold-smoked wild salmon. It's hard to skip a dish that includes a trip to the breakfast bar—order pancakes or French toast, then head to the

Portage Bay Cafe

bar for a dizzying mix of fruit, nuts, creams, and syrups. Tables are spread throughout two dining rooms, but that never seems to be enough. Service can be slow even when the kitchen is only dishing out piles of pancakes. This is a place to get energized by breakfast, not laze through a quiet, intimate brunch. Weekday lunch means more sandwiches on the menu, but there are still a few breakfast options. Expect a wait on weekends. There is another location in South Lake Union (391 Terry Ave. N, 206/462-6400; same hours). **MAP 6:** 4130 Roosevelt Way NE, 206/547-8230, www.portagebaycafe. com; 7am-2pm Mon.-Fri., 7:30am-2:30pm Sat.-Sun.

International District and SoDo

Map 7

CHINESE

Shanghai Garden $$

The hand-shaved noodles are popular at this bare-bones Chinese joint, which has glass-topped tables and a mirrored pillar in the middle of the dining room. The noodles come in a basic chow mein, but the barley green noodles are a more unusual take on a classic dish. The tender noodles are slick with oil but not overwhelming, bright with leafy flavor. Service is speedy, and the noodle devotees are a diverse crowd. The brightly lit space is popular with families.
MAP 7: 524 6th Ave. S, 206/625-1688; 10:30am-9:30pm daily

Canton Wonton House $

You don't go to Canton Wonton House for the fancy digs. The storefront is plain and the tables are the standard Formica found in cafeterias and company lunchrooms. Instead, you come for the steaming dishes: all varieties of noodle soup, noodles with meat and vegetables, and congee. The restaurant is family run, and customers are firm devotees of the more than two dozen varieties of noodle soup on the menu. The spot has the hole-in-the-wall feel that makes fancier furniture—or a floor that's not linoleum—unnecessary.
MAP 7: 608 S. Weller St., 206/682-5080; 11am-10pm Sun.-Thurs., 11am-11pm Fri.-Sat.

Jade Garden $

Dim sum is a beloved tradition, a chance to sample a variety of Chinese dishes as staff roll carts of options past your table. Weekends mean lines to get a table at this International District staple, though waits are almost always less than an hour. Doughy dumplings, *shumai* (a thin-skinned type of dumpling), fried tofu, and egg tarts are all popular choices. The food is tasty, but the space is minimally furnished, and service is known to be on the abrupt side. Satisfy your dim sum cravings during the week to get a calmer experience.
MAP 7: 24 7th Ave. S, 206/622-8181; 9am-2:30am Mon.-Thurs., 9am-3:30am Fri.-Sat., 9am-1am Sun.

VIETNAMESE

✪ Tamarind Tree $

It can be hard to locate this long-popular Vietnamese restaurant, so locals who frequent the space tend to feel like it's their own special secret. The modern, leafy design inside feels fully realized. The finished wood ceilings and a few tall tables with inset fire pits complete a well-considered layout. The restaurant serves provincial Vietnamese food, so casual diners may find new dishes to try. In a town that loves pho, it's no surprise that the specialty soup menu is so long, with bamboo duck noodles, fried fish tomato noodles, a lemongrass sausage rice soup, and much more—but there's also basic pho for anyone feeling overwhelmed by the options. The menu also includes a wide range of meat, noodle, and rice dishes. A long list of martinis offers plenty of reasons to linger over dinner. To find the restaurant, look for the rust-colored awning in the Asian Plaza shop complex.

MAP 7: 1036 S. Jackson St., 206/860-1404, www.tamarindtreerestaurant.com; 10am-10pm Sun.-Thurs., 10am-11pm Fri.-Sat.

Green Leaf $

The Vietnamese fare is straightforward and cheap at this unassuming hole-in-the-wall favorite, tucked behind a small awning but crowded with bamboo decor inside. Portions are substantial, and the pho, a Vietnamese soup that's long been a Seattle favorite, is made with meat options like seafood, brisket, and meatballs. The delicate Vietnamese crepes are crisp, made with shrimp and bean sprouts. The restaurant has a good reputation, and the service lives up to it. This International District location is smaller than its downtown branch, which makes it feel busier and livelier, especially around dinnertime.

MAP 7: 418 8th Ave. S, 206/340-1388, http://greenleaftaste.com; 11am-10pm daily

JAPANESE

Tsukushinbo $

There isn't really a sign for this restaurant, though the lines that form outside the office building that holds it are a dead giveaway on ramen Fridays—yes, the ramen is only served on Friday in limited quantities, and it's famously tender and flavorful. At other times, the menu includes sushi and a variety of home-style Japanese dishes. A Japanese-language menu is on the wall, but there are printed English versions. Service can be slow and erratic, but the food is generally worth the bother.

MAP 7: 515 S. Main St., 206/467-4004; 5:30pm-10pm Mon., 11:45am-2pm and 5:30pm-10pm Tues.-Thurs., 11:45am-2pm and 5:30pm-11pm Fri., 5:30pm-11pm Sat., 11am-2pm and 5:30pm-9:30pm Sun.

ASIAN

Red Lantern $

Red Lantern delivers both ambience and flavor, in a space that stays simple with wood tables and sleek red light fixtures. The food hails from northern China and Korea, which means familiar bites like pot stickers and sweet and sour beef, plus brown-braised pig feet and duck cooked in Shaoxing wine. Certain house specialties, like Sichuan peppercorn crab and steamed ginger fish, require calling ahead. The dessert menu has red tea tiramisu and black tea crème brûlée. Service can be touch and go, but it's welcoming to folks who don't have much Asian dining experience.

MAP 7: 520 S. Jackson St., 206/682-7211, www.redlanternseattle.com; 11am-2:30pm and 5pm-9:30pm Mon.-Fri., noon-3pm and 5pm-9:30pm Sat.

BAKERIES
✪ Fuji Bakery $

This bakery may specialize in Japanese products, but it also sources vanilla beans from France and cultivates its own yeast in-house. Filled croissants and long almond sticks fill the display cases, and doughnuts filled with azuki bean paste are large and fluffy. The Matcha Melon Pan are round and bright green, while the smoked salmon brioche are baked into neat, doughy cubes. It's a small space, little more than a curved pastry case and a big coffee machine, with attendants smiling behind the tall glass. There's no place to eat, so it's a quick stop while on the go. With a combination of the best of France and Japan on offer, expect to take extras for later.

MAP 7: 526 S. King St., 206/623-4050, http://fujibakeryinc.com; 7am-5pm Mon.-Fri., 7am-3pm Sat.-Sun.

Macrina Bakery $

There's a reason that restaurants around town call special attention to the fact that they serve Macrina's breads: The artisan loafs are perfectly baked and the baguettes famous for just the right amount of crispy crust. Though there are storefronts around town, the SoDo location sits outside the bread bakery, with windows open to the magicians working inside. Loaves and rolls are best purchased to be part of a picnic or meal, while the sweet pastries, sandwiches full of fresh greens and meats, and mac and cheese made with salami are best consumed at the small tables on-site.

MAP 7: 1943 1st Ave. S, 206/623-0919, www.macrinabakery.com; 7am-6pm Mon.-Fri., 7am-5pm Sat., 8am-5pm Sun.

NIGHTLIFE

It's been a long time since the city was known just for grunge music. The music scene in Seattle ranges from a strong jazz tradition to emerging indie artists.

a cocktail at Canon

Seattle's quirky sensibilities are still found in bars, clubs, and music venues, and its cocktail culture is nationally recognized.

Craft beer is gaining popularity across the country, but the Pacific Northwest, with its hops farms, has always been at the forefront of beer trends. Expect even basic offerings to include hoppy IPAs and creative porters, with plenty of seasonal beers and brewery collaborations. Take care when ordering specialty beers at places like Chuck's Hop Shop or Pine Box: The (higher than usual) alcohol percentages are listed on the menu for a reason.

Capitol Hill is the city's nightlife hub, and the streets are packed on weekend nights. Creative bartenders mix new versions of classic cocktails. The scene is dominated by gay clubs, all of which are welcoming to anyone who wants to throw back shots or just dance. Downtown bars tend to be attached to a hotel and often double as restaurants.

Head here for classic cocktails and good wine; expect a decent beer selection almost everywhere.

Visit Ballard for creative drinking holes and the University District for a classic college dive like The Blue Moon Tavern. Spots like The Triple Door attract crowds for live music.

Many bars are open past midnight, with Capitol Hill's staying open until 2am and its clubs even later.

HIGHLIGHTS

✪ **BEST DINNER AND A SHOW: The Triple Door** pairs intimate, acoustic performances with food from Asian fusion restaurant Wild Ginger (page 128).

✪ **BEST COZY TIPPLE:** The British-inspired **White Horse Trading Company** has comfy seats and old-timey decor behind a quaint half-door in Pike Place Market (page 130).

✪ **BEST HIDEAWAY:** The speakeasy-inspired **Bathtub Gin and Co.** isn't easy to find—and after a few cocktails in its cozy environs, it won't be easy to leave (page 132).

✪ **BEST CLASSIC COCKTAILS:** With experienced bartenders and specialty ice, **Rob Roy** is the ideal spot for an old-fashioned (page 132).

✪ **BEST BEER:** Though it's more bottle shop than bar, **Chuck's Hop Shop** has an unmatched selection of craft beers—expect rare pours and themed flights (page 136).

✪ **BEST SHAKE, STIR, AND POUR:** With an encyclopedic whiskey library and world-class talent behind the bar, **Canon** is the best in a city filled with great cocktail bars (page 136).

✪ **BEST THREE-RING CIRCUS:** Proving that a dive bar doesn't have to be dark and dank, **Unicorn** puts a carnival spin on a raucous drinking hole (page 141).

✪ **BEST NEIGHBORHOOD BREWERY:** At **Fremont Brewing,** you can sip away the day in a popular beer garden (page 144).

✪ **BEST HANGOUT: King's Hardware** offers plenty of room to spread out, as well as a youthful, joyful crowd that will make you want to stay all night (page 147).

✪ **BEST WILDERNESS TAVERN:** You can plan your next adventure with the books and maps at **Noble Fir,** though you may never want to leave the posh indoors (page 147).

✪ **MOST BOOKISH BAR: The Blue Moon Tavern** has hosted the city's literary stars for years and hosts open-mic readings nearly every night (page 148).

Seattle's skyline

Downtown and Pioneer Square

Map 1

LIVE MUSIC

✪ The Triple Door

Intimate performances take place at downtown's The Triple Door main stage, which offers plush booth seating and an Asian fusion menu. Located across the street from the symphony hall and below the restaurant Wild Ginger, it combines flavorful food (the two eateries share a kitchen) with unusual music. The stage was a vaudeville theater nearly a century ago, but now it's more likely to host acoustic acts, jazz, burlesque, or a novelty cabaret cooking show. There's no cover charge to hear the acts that play The Triple Door's MQ lounge, where the full menu is served. Showtimes vary, but usually start between 7pm and 9pm.

MAP 1: 216 Union St., 206/838-4333, www.thetripledoor.net; hours vary by performance; $20-90

Showbox

The art deco styling of the downtown Showbox doesn't lie. The theater has been around since the 1930s and once hosted burlesque superstar Gypsy Rose Lee here in her hometown. Today the space creates intimacy by spreading the audience over several levels, making it a popular stop for rock, indie, and R&B acts. In 2018 the building's new owner announced plans to raze the theater to build apartments, and protests ignited discussion on declaring the theater a landmark; the issue has been hotly contested since.

MAP 1: 1426 1st Ave., 206/628-3151, www.showboxpresents.com; hours and ticket prices vary by performance

CRAFT BEER

Pike Brewing Company

Inspired by the beers of Europe, Charles and Rose Ann Finkel opened the city's third microbrewery in 1989 in a space near Pike Place Market. It started brewing an IPA—today the Pacific Northwest's signature beer style—way back in 1990, but today the brewery is best known for a Scotch ale called the Kilt Lifter. Watch the brewers at work in the pub, which serves pizzas, salads, and chowder alongside beers and samplers. Accessed from 1st Avenue near the market (and therefore more overrun with tourists than most Seattle breweries), Pike Brewing has the cluttered charm of an old bar that never tried to be cool—vintage tin plates are glued to the ceiling and framed black-and-white photos and tchotchkes coat nearly every other surface between the booths and low-hanging lights. An addition opened in 2017 incorporates a restaurant section, an oyster bar, and a view of the brewing facilities.

MAP 1: 1415 1st Ave., 206/622-6044, http://pikebrewing.com; 11am-midnight daily

Tap House Grill

There are bars with impressive beer options, and then there's the Tap House. A curved wall behind the bar is sprinkled with 160 taps, what Tap House claims is the largest selection

LIVE MUSIC

Seattle's storied live music scene attracts talent from around the world and across genres. This is the city that Jimi Hendrix called home, where Kurt Cobain found fame before his tragic end, and where Macklemore became an independent rap sensation.

Back in the beginning of the 20th century, Seattle was known for jazz, folk, and burlesque acts. The dancer Gypsy Rose Lee got famous here. Later, Ray Charles came to the city as he built his career. Jimi Hendrix and Quincy Jones were both raised in the area before gaining international stature.

In the late 1980s, a new sound emerged from Seattle, a mix of hard rock and punk, from bands that cared more about delivering emotional power and soulful energy than polished tunes. It became known as grunge, and several local bands became overnight

The Triple Door

sensations: Alice in Chains, Soundgarden, Pearl Jam, and Nirvana brought their unwashed, loud chic to the masses. Local label Sub Pop became known for representing the Seattle sound (look for a store from the still-active label in Sea-Tac Airport).

The era of grunge eventually passed, but it left the city with a reputation for awe-inspiring live music performances. In the early 2000s, bands like Death Cab for Cutie, Band of Horses, and Modest Mouse carried the alternative banner for Seattle. A rapper long known around town, Macklemore, made a record outside the traditional label system and released it himself; it became one of the best-selling independent records ever. Previous to Macklemore, Sir Mix-a-Lot was Seattle's best-known rapper.

Today, rock, soul, and pop acts are drawn to stages at the likes of Neumos, Tractor Tavern, The Triple Door, and even the busking corners in Pike Place Market. The Seattle Symphony balances traditional symphonic works with exciting new ones; the "Become Ocean" piece it commissioned earned a Pulitzer Prize in 2014. The Seattle sound is always evolving and diversifying, but is still internationally known.

- **The Triple Door:** This intimate venue showcases acoustic and other acts and has the chill vibe of a basement hideaway, with flavorful food to boot (page 128).

- **Dimitriou's Jazz Alley:** Enjoy some jazz in this stately, decades-old two-story performance space (page 131).

- **Neumos:** Listen to artsy, quirky pop and folk at this hip Capitol Hill classic (page 136).

- **Tractor Tavern:** Home of rollicking country acts, this is the closest you'll get to a honky-tonk in Seattle (page 145).

- **Seattle Symphony:** A world-class orchestra balances classic works with daring new compositions (page 153).

in the region. They include international styles like Belgians and bitters, but this being the hoppy Pacific Northwest, there are almost two dozen IPAs. Nearly all the local breweries are represented, including the ubiquitous Georgetown Brewing Company and Fremont Brewing, plus Olympia's Fish Tale organic ales and crowd-pleasers from Bellingham's Boundary Bay. Bartenders will offer tastes to help customers find their perfect choice.

The Tap House is otherwise a large, corporate-style restaurant in a basement space, but the happy hour flatbreads topped with chicken sausage or bacon and pineapple are a great deal. The rest of the menu is broad, encompassing nearly as many food styles as beer varieties: jambalaya, prime rib, pad Thai, and more.

MAP 1: 1506 6th Ave., 206/816-3314, http://taphousegrill.com; 11am-1am Sun.-Fri., 11am-2am Sat.

COCKTAIL BARS
The Nest

Indoors or out, the Thompson Hotel's rooftop bar boasts the best drinking views in the city, plus excellent cocktails to sip while watching ferry boats inch across Elliott Bay. Intricate wallpaper decorates the interior where bartenders mix drinks behind piles of fresh fruit and long, glassy shelves of liquor. The midcentury furniture feels a little on the formal side, but patrons are casually dressed. It's a special occasion spot; there's even a $150 punch bowl made with cognac and champagne for groups of at least four.

MAP 1: 110 Stewart St., 206/512-1096, www.thompsonhotels.com, 3pm-midnight Mon.-Tues., 1pm-midnight Wed.-Sun.

Zig Zag Café

Downhill from Pike Place Market is the quintessential Seattle cocktail bar, Zig Zag Café. Bartenders in neat black vests take pride in crafting memorable cocktails and remembering customers' faces, making it a local's favorite even as tourists wander up the steps outside. The space is sparsely lit and cave-like, so it always feels like late evening inside, even when the sun is still blazing outside—though a handful of patio tables are here as well. To find it, look for the steps that go down the hill from the market to the waterfront.

MAP 1: 1501 Western Ave., No. 202, 206/625-1146, www.zigzagseattle.com; 5pm-2am daily

WHISKEY BARS
Bookstore Bar & Café

Head here for a literary quaff: Bookstore Bar sits under rows of books for sale. Any tome is $5, and happy hour dishes aren't much more. The best reading in the house, however, is the menu of 70 single-malt Scotch whiskies and almost as many American whiskeys. During the day it has a café vibe, serving a wide range of breakfast dishes to hotel patrons.

MAP 1: Alexis Hotel, 1007 1st Ave., 206/624-3646, www.bookstorebar.com; 7am-midnight Mon.-Fri., 8am-midnight Sat., 8am-10pm Sun.

Bookstore Bar & Café

PUBS
✪ White Horse Trading Company

Stroll down the alley that runs just uphill from Pike Place Market and look for a half-open Dutch door; that's White Horse Trading Company, a snug British pub crowded with old-time golf clubs, bookshelves, and paintings of red-coated fox hunters. Besides British ales, the bar serves

Pimm's Cup highballs, a drink that's to Brits at Wimbledon what a mint julep is to southerners at the Kentucky Derby.

MAP 1: 1908 Post Alley, 206/441-7767; 5pm- 2am daily

Kells Irish Restaurant and Pub

Almost hidden in one of Pike Place Market's alleys, Kells is a traditional Irish bar—with all the crowds and revelry that implies. Its two stories fill during Seattle Sounders games, and it's the most popular spot in town on St. Patrick's Day. Otherwise it's a friendly joint serving Guinness and steak and kidney pie amid wood floors and wood-paneled walls. There's live Irish music every night, and the energy never flags in the market's busiest bar.

MAP 1: 1916 Post Alley, 206/728-1916, www.kellsirish.com/seattle; 11:30am-2am daily

Queen Anne and Belltown

Map 2

LIVE MUSIC

The Crocodile

The Croc is what passes for a historic music venue in Seattle. It opened its doors back in 1991 as Crocodile Cafe, when grunge was still making its way out of Northwest garages, and the owner ended up marrying one of the members of REM. Nirvana, Pearl Jam, and Yoko Ono have played the small venue, which closed briefly in the early 2000s. It reopened as The Crocodile and these days hosts emerging rock, indie, folk, and hip-hop acts. The on-site Back Bar hosts Liquid Courage Karaoke, burlesque, and other small-scale shows, and it has a menu of wood-fired pizzas. Look for the green scales on the sign.

MAP 2: 2200 2nd Ave., 206/441-4618, www.thecrocodile.com; 4pm-2am daily; prices vary by performance

Dimitriou's Jazz Alley

Dimitriou's Jazz Alley has been a jazz spot for decades, earning a reputation as one of the West Coast's best. The range of performances here is international, including blues performers, African and South American singers, and crossover artists. The stage is surrounded by two levels of tables that fill with upscale diners. For the 7:30pm set, choose a seat at a dinner or cocktail table; dinner tables have better views, but diners must order one entrée per person. The cocktail tables also have access to the whole menu. (There are no requirements for the 9:30pm set.) The venue is all-ages, save for the bar area, and there are two sets per night.

MAP 2: 2033 6th Ave., 206/441-9729, www.jazzalley.com; 7:30pm and 9:30pm Tues.-Sun.; $26-102

CRAFT BEER

Hilltop Ale House

The top of Queen Anne Hill is mostly residential, with little for the Seattle tourist besides the view from Kerry Park. But this beer-centric bar has the advantage of elbow room and a chill vibe among the many tables and few fixed-position stools. The menu lists hot sandwiches, but the beer list is the real draw: There's a rotating IPA tap and collaborations with local breweries that bring unique brews you can't get anywhere else. There's usually at least one beer each from the big Seattle craft names (Georgetown Brewing Company, Fremont Brewing, Mac & Jack's Brewery, and Hale's Brewery). Serious aficionados will gravitate to the occasional nitro option, where a beer is served with added nitrogen (instead of carbon dioxide), resulting in a creamier taste.

MAP 2: 2129 Queen Anne Ave. N, 206/285-3877, www.seattlealehouses.com; 11am-11pm Sun.-Thurs., 11am-midnight Fri.-Sat.

Holy Mountain Brewing

Holy Mountain is truly a beer nerd's brewery. There's no crowd-pleasing signature beer that's always on tap; instead, the experienced brewers like to rotate new experiments and unusual beers. The taproom, located in an industrial section east of Queen Anne called Interbay, is plenty welcoming to neophytes, and its crisp white walls and minimalist black stools make sure that the beers get center stage. Expect to find sour beers or saisons, and often at least one pale ale with plenty of hops. There's no food, but food trucks sometimes park by the rear door on weekends.

MAP 2: 1421 Elliott Ave. W, http://holymountainbrewing.com; 3pm-9pm Mon.-Thurs., noon-10pm Fri.-Sat., noon-9pm Sun.

COCKTAIL BARS
✪ Bathtub Gin and Co.

Peek down an alleyway and look for a metal placard marking the entrance to neo-speakeasy Bathtub Gin and Co., a thin, multilevel establishment that does more than trade on its twee theme. Great dates take place in the bar's intimate nooks, but it's worth sitting at the small bar to have the talented bartenders create you an original cocktail. When it comes time to pay, request a receipt—they'll usually handwrite one, complete with doodles of beer bottles or cocktail glasses.

MAP 2: 2205 2nd Ave., 206/728-6069, www.bathtubginseattle.com; 5pm-2am daily

✪ Rob Roy

For fancy cocktails downtown, head to Rob Roy. The space is dark, thanks to few windows, stonework on the wall, and black leather furnishings. But a little golden light gives it a warm feel, and it manages to welcome some of the neighborhood's young, enthusiastic drinkers while mostly catering to mature customers with opinions about the vinyl spinning in the background. Even the classic cocktails here are on the obscure side (ever heard of a Jungle Bird?). If you're lucky, a bartender will chop ice by hand for your drink. The original creations are even more eyebrow raising—the Gunpowder Punch includes rum, gin, spices, and actual gunpowder. Just a little, though.

MAP 2: 2332 2nd Ave., 206/956-8423, www.robroyseattle.com; 4pm-2am daily

Pennyroyal

From its position in the bottom of the Palladian hotel, Pennyroyal has the respectable, even staid feel of an after-work stop for business travelers. That's no criticism: It's a spacious, uncomplicated drinking spot in a neighborhood crowded with tourists and rowdy bars. The house cocktails, complicated confections using bitters, egg whites, and obscure liquors, have names like Lovers Are Liars or Hymn of Confession.

The long bar has comfy high-backed stools, plus there are plenty of small tables scattered throughout the space. While you're there, wander into the Palladian's lobby to see the hotel's signature portraits of famous Seattle figures painted to look like 18th-century dukes and lords.

MAP 2: 2000 2nd Ave., 206/826-1700, www.pennyroyalbar.com; 2pm-midnight daily

The Sitting Room

Though it's only a few blocks from Seattle Center and just around the corner from the busy part of Queen Anne, The Sitting Room feels like a calm neighborhood joint far removed from the bustle of the well-touristed neighborhood. The small chairs and vintage couch give it a coffee shop feel, with a European twist thanks to an extensive wine list. It's dark, warm, and cozy in the winter, but on warm nights the front wall of windows opens to patio seating. Many cocktails use fresh herbs and fruits, and there are two happy hours on most days (5pm-7pm and 9pm-10pm Mon.-Wed., 5pm-7pm and 10pm-11pm Thurs.-Sat., 5pm-10pm Sun.). The proximity to the ballet and Seattle Center's theaters make it the perfect pre- or post-show destination.

MAP 2: 108 W. Roy St., 206/285-2830, www.the-sitting-room.com; 5pm-11pm Sun.-Wed., 5pm-2am Thurs.-Sat.

Some Random Bar

Yes, the name is a joke; the exposed brick wall and mason jar lights feel very specifically Seattle, and the blackboards on the wall are as likely to feature a snarky observation about the cocktail scene as the daily specials. Cocktails tend toward the sweet, like a key lime pie martini or moonshine lemonade. The seasonal menu can include straightforward bites like tacos or pork loin or a more unusual selection like a spicy elk chili dog.

MAP 2: 2604 1st Ave., 206/745-2185, http://somerandombar.com; 4pm-midnight Mon.-Thurs., 4pm-1am Fri.-Sat., 10am-midnight Sun.

Tin Lizzie Lounge

The cocktail bar at the MarQueen Hotel is a total throwback, starting with the name—it was a nickname for the Model T car that ruled the streets in the early 1900s, when Seattle was a newborn city. It's billed as a speakeasy, but it's not terribly hidden—it's easily accessed from the hotel lobby and has windows that face the street. The tin ceilings and white leather couches look ready to receive partying flapper girls, and the menu is filled with Prohibition puns and boozy classics. There's live blues or jazz music on some nights, and the small lounge is a nice respite from the crowded bars across the street.

MAP 2: 600 Queen Anne Ave. N, 206/282-7407, http://thetinlizzielounge. com; 3pm-2am Mon.-Sat., 3pm-midnight Sun.

WHISKEY BARS
The Whisky Bar

There are a few things essential to any good whiskey bar, like a long wooden bar top, cushy stools, and bartenders who respond to a request for "something peaty, but not really." The menu is divided into the many kinds of scotch, plus sections for Tennessee and American whiskeys and even Indian, Welsh, and corn varieties. There is also an impressive list of local draft beers if you're merely accompanying a whiskey fanatic.

MAP 2: 2122 2nd Ave., 206/443-4490, http://thewhiskybar.com; noon-2am daily

WINE BARS
Triumph Bar

With its location close to Seattle Center, Triumph is the bar most likely to serve as a meeting spot prior to a theater, ballet, or opera performance. Though in a fairly new building with lots of windows, after dark it feels like a cozy spot. It's primarily a wine bar that focuses on Italian pours, though the drink menu also includes some local wines and craft cocktails. After grabbing a seat at one of the small tables, pair your drinks with meat and cheese plates, or a select few cooked veggies and seafood bites. Large parties can make reservations.

MAP 2: 114 Republican St., 206/420-1791, http://triumphbar.com; 3pm-1am daily

DIVE BARS
Buckley's

When you want to watch sports, even at 9am on a Saturday morning, there's one place in town that's happy to pour you a beer. Flags from dozens of colleges hang from the ceiling of the large main room at Buckley's, appropriate because alumni clubs gather here for football and basketball games. The din can be overwhelming when a rivalry takes over the screens, and the tater tots and fried chicken burgers could stop a heart before halftime, but there's nothing slick or corporate about this sports bar. Games play on moderate-sized flat-screens, unless it's a big event, in which case the pull-down projection screen comes out.

MAP 2: 2331 2nd Ave., 206/588-8879; 11:30am-2am Mon.-Fri., 9am-2am Sat.-Sun.

Mecca Café and Bar

Though the big neon sign outside calls this joint a café, this is more of a hard-living diner and bar where the motto is "alcoholics serving alcoholics since 1929." The long, skinny booths don't seat more than four people at a time, and it somehow always feels like both 10am and 10pm inside. Sodas come in a pitcher-sized glass, and a full pound of fries can be smothered in chili and cheese. The menu also points out that a single cup of tea only gives you the table for an hour. Breakfast, including fluffy meal-sized pancakes, is served all day, though the tableside waffle iron shuts down at 2pm.

MAP 2: 526 Queen Anne Ave. N, 206/285-9728, http://mecca-cafe.com; 7am-2am Sun.-Thurs., 7am-3am Fri.-Sat.

Shorty's

If you could get inside the head of a circus clown, it would probably look something like Shorty's: rows of pinball machines and red-and-white-striped lamps, gaudy neon, and painted walls at every turn. It's one of Belltown's most beloved dive bars, serving hot dogs (Seattle style with cream cheese or smothered in chili) and a no-frills beer list. Inside, the Trophy Room is like a bar within a bar. Its teal upholstered chairs and dark walls make it a slightly more somber space for serious conversations over cocktails. The young crowd loves the cheap prices and irreverence, while older Seattleites have nostalgic affection for the goofy bar.

MAP 2: 2222 2nd Ave., 206/441-5449, www.shortydog.com; noon-2am daily

PUBS

Brave Horse Tavern

Watch out when happy hour hits: This Tom Douglas joint abuts one of the biggest Amazon office buildings, and after work the long wooden tables fill with Amazon workers looking to shed their badges and the company's famously stressful work environment for 30-plus local beers on tap and giant pretzels. Fortunately there's lots of room around the bar and the indoor shuffleboard tables, plus outside patios. On a sunny day, you'll likely end up sharing a table; there's no room for privacy at this popular spot. The beer list focuses on West Coast pours and includes a few ciders, and there's a house-made sangria for anyone tired of brews. It's the kind of place that convinces customers to turn a quick drink into a long hangout with a few rounds of food to balance the IPAs. The burgers are meaty satisfaction, and the wood-fired pretzels come with an assortment of dips. It can get boisterous during the hours when one might conceivably order a platter of tater tots and shots—it's on the menu—but is otherwise a good spot for a sociable meal. The bar is adults-only at all times.

MAP 2: 310 Terry Ave. N, 206/971-0717, www.bravehorsetavern.com; 11am-10pm Mon.-Thurs., 11am-midnight Fri., 10am-midnight Sat., 10am-10pm Sun.

Feierabend

In a town devoted to the American beer, especially the Northwest favorite IPA, it's harder to find German beer bars. This one, on an otherwise quiet South Lake Union street, isn't particularly easy to find, but once you're close the big open windows are likely to share the quiet roar of happy hour drinkers enjoying 18 draft beers from Germany. The German owner doesn't eschew the Pacific Northwest totally, however, and the food menu includes some fresh local veggies alongside hearty brats and pommes frites with curry ketchup.

MAP 2: 422 Yale Ave. N, 206/340-2528, www.feierabendseattle.com; 11:30am-1am daily

DANCE CLUBS

Lo-Fi Performance Gallery

Despite its location as a lonely club on a somewhat quiet street, Lo-Fi Performance Gallery is best known as a dance club, especially on its most popular theme nights. A '60s soul night steers away from overplayed hits, while the massively popular monthly '90s dance party is full of chart toppers. Small indie-rock bands play on other nights, and DJs spin modern and eclectic dance tunes. The two dance floors aren't huge, which means it gets comfortably crowded early in the night. Look for a vintage working photo booth in one of the dark corners and vintage video games in a side room.

MAP 2: 429 Eastlake Ave., 206/254-2824, www.thelofi.net; 9pm-2am daily; cover free-$10

LIVE MUSIC
Neumos

Neumos got its name because it's the "New Moe's," the resurrection of a '90s club that welcomed Radiohead, Pearl Jam, and Neil Young. Even President Bill Clinton popped in for a show when he was in town. The performance space is the center of a complex that includes a fish fry eatery, a casual bar, and a more intimate stage. Today the acts are more artsy pop, folk, and quirky cover bands, but it's still dark and loud.

MAP 3: 925 E. Pike St., 206/709-9442, www.neumos.com; cover $5-20

CRAFT BEER
✪ Chuck's Hop Shop

The Central District is a mostly residential neighborhood just behind Capitol Hill, but its beer store might be one of the area's best hangouts. The walls are lined with coolers displaying beers from around the world for sale, but most people come for pints and growler fills from the 50 taps. Though Chuck's itself sells chips and a few food items, most comers eat from food trucks that park out front on a rotating basis. Around the indoor and outdoor tables, it's more like a neighborhood center than a bar, with trivia nights and tons of dogs and babies—especially on a weekend afternoon. Beer nerds will appreciate the diversity of brews and ability to make flights of any kind.

MAP 3: 2001 E. Union St., 206/538-0743, www.chuckscd.com; 11am-midnight daily

Pine Box

The idea of a beer bar in a mortuary sounds grim, but in practice it's a perfect fit. With its giant curved windows and high molded ceilings, this space feels like a warm church dedicated to the worship of beer and hanging out. The bar has a few dozen beers on tap, and the food menu is split between "less," "more," and pizza dishes, all the kind of spicy, saucy eats that pair well with a high-alcohol specialty beer. For all the grandeur of the former place of mourning, including a semi-covered outdoor space and a loft overlooking the whole bar, it's a loud and crowded beer hall.

MAP 3: 1600 Melrose Ave., 206/588-0375, www.pineboxbar.com; 3pm-2am Mon.-Fri., 11am-2am Sat.-Sun.

Canon

COCKTAIL BARS
✪ Canon

The area's cocktail cathedral is the prim and proper Canon, where the bartenders, whiskeys, and bitters are the stars. No one is let inside unless a seat is available, so there's no throwing elbows to reach the bar. Not that there isn't a sense of humor here: Page 63 of the massive menu is labeled "hard-core porn," for bottles like a $1,225 Canoe Club whiskey from 1898 or a Maker's Mark named for the Triple Crown-winning horse Seattle Slew.

MAP 3: 928 12th Ave., 206/552-9755, www.canonseattle.com; 5pm-2am daily

Bait Shop

Take to the seas in this small bar on Broadway that embraces Seattle's nautical history with sea creatures painted on the walls and wooden boat steering wheels hung for decoration. There are a couple of cocktails on tap at the bar, including a Dark and Stormy made with ginger beer and rum, plus lots of tropical mixed and frozen drinks on the menu. The food is snacky and unhealthy—fish-and-chips, Dungeness crab fritters—and you can add pineapple to any dish or drink. The space isn't large, with the booths going quickly and a lively atmosphere on most evenings.

MAP 3: 606 Broadway E, 206/420-8742, www.baitshopseattle.com; 4pm-2am daily

Knee High Stocking Co.

Speakeasy bars may be trendy, but they are exciting when they serve quality drinks like this hidden joint, which could be named for the buzzer that sits just above knee height. Despite a tiny plaque, the door is hard to find; look for the narrow corner where Olive Way and Olive Place meet. Reservations are recommended and are available by texting the bar directly, though the lighter crowds of recent years have allowed for more walk-ins. Inside the establishment, bigger since a basement level was added, most tables are intimate and candlelit, but the best seats are at the bar, where you can converse with the artists creating the cocktails. As with any joint with talented bartenders, it's easier to chat with them

than to decipher the giant cocktail menu. The Filipino food served here is flavorful, also sold as takeout at the window outside.

MAP 3: 1356 E. Olive Way, 206/979-7049, www.kneehighstocking.com; 5pm-midnight Mon.-Thurs., 6pm-2am Fri.-Sat., 6pm-midnight Sun.

Liberty

Liberty

Sushi and cocktails—they're a natural pairing, both heavily dependent on creativity, quality ingredients, and careful combinations of flavors. The delicacy of sushi won't overwhelm a good cocktail like a plate of fried jalapeños or poutine might. You can enjoy both at the few low couches and tables inside this dark Capitol Hill den, which is almost always crowded, even when it's more of a café during daylight hours. Liberty never takes a day off—ever—so it's a popular joint on major holidays. The bar is so well stocked that it's usually best to ask the bartenders to suggest something; if they don't have your favorite, they welcome suggestions of what else to add to their stores. The names of the bar's many whiskeys hang from large signs on the wall. Check behind the mirrored door for a bonus room of seating, and try the Seattle Sour, which comes with coffee liqueur and Manny's Pale Ale foam.

MAP 3: 517 15th Ave. E, 206/323-9898, www.libertybars.com; 9am-2am daily

Single Shot

The shot in this bar's name could mean a single, dignified shot of liquor, which is the only kind that would feel right in the glistening white space decorated with black furniture and posh globe lights. But it more likely refers to what would come out of the vintage 12-foot replica rifle hanging above the bar, a piece of whimsy in an otherwise sophisticated spot. There's a full cocktail and wine list, and the food menu, while short, is full of well-prepared seasonal vegetables and a few serious meat and fish dishes, with brunch offerings composed of mostly egg dishes. There are very few beer taps; the creative cocktails are the real draw.

MAP 3: 611 Summit Ave. E, 206/420-2238, www.singleshotseattle.com; 5pm-10pm Mon.-Fri., 10am-2pm and 5pm-10pm Sat.-Sun.

Sol Liquor

Sol Liquor was one of the first bars to capture cocktail cool in Seattle, even opening a distillery outpost a few blocks away. The original bar is tucked into a mostly residential neighborhood and recently changed its name from "Sun" to "Sol," but it continues to serve drinks made from house-made syrups and its own gin and vodka. Small tables are pushed together, and the few bar seats are usually filled with first-daters and neighborhood locals. Strings of lights keep the small bar festive, and there are always plenty of tiki and tropical drink options, albeit ones mixed by expert bartenders.

MAP 3: 607 Summit Ave. E, 206/860-1130, www.solliquor.com; 5pm-2am daily

LGBT BARS AND CLUBS

C. C. Attle's

It's a chill scene at C. C. Attle's, a bear bar with pool tables and more sunlight than many other drinking holes on Capitol Hill. The smoking corner outside is very social, and during Pride the crowds spill out into the streets. The rest of the time it's quiet enough for conversation, and there's never a cover.

MAP 3: 1701 E. Olive Way, 206/726-0565, www.ccattles.net; 3pm-2am Mon.-Fri., 2pm-2am Sat.-Sun.; no cover

Cuff Complex

Cuff Complex is unapologetically a gay bar. It's popular among the leather, bear, and fetish crowds, but the dance floor draws a diverse mix of men, and the spot's disco ball has hung in local gay bars since the 1970s. In a bar this dark and loud, there's no point in starting a philosophical discussion. Come here to dance, drink, or seek out a like-minded fetishist.

MAP 3: 1533 13th Ave., 206/323-1525, www.cuffcomplex.com; 2pm-2am daily

Neighbours

The music is thumping, the floor's a little sticky, and the only palatable drinks are straight shots—must be a weekend night at Neighbours, the city's best-known gay dance club, still well loved despite its faults. Accessed through an alley door (go just west of Broadway on East Pike Street and look for the crowds), there's something a little seedy about the institution, though it's perfectly welcoming to anyone who'll shell out the cover. The club holds more than a thousand people over its two floors, and the people-watching from the 2nd-floor balcony is classic—you'll see great dancers and

SMOKING IN SEATTLE: CANNABIS CULTURE

a legal marijuana store

Seattle is the marijuana frontier. When Washington State legalized recreational marijuana in 2012, at the same time as Colorado, it became part of a grand experiment. Could legal drugs work? The answer is still a big "maybe"—though recreational stores popped up and money from the steep taxes came rolling in, there are still occasional protests outside the biggest pot stores and use of marijuana in public is still strictly verboten, even if the smell is commonplace on Seattle's sidewalks. The city is no Amsterdam . . . at least not yet.

Though there are dozens of kinds of marijuana for sale in the newly opened stores, there's also been a big rise in edibles: hard candies and pastries filled with various amounts of mind-bending cannabis products. Like the smokables, they can only be bought with cash from a licensed store (most have ATMs handy)—although some of the larger stores now accept credit cards—and the prices are steep. Patrons must be over 21, with valid ID, to enter. Anyone unused to the effects of the drug should proceed carefully.

Every summer the weed celebration Hempfest descends on Seattle, and local cops have been known to pass out bags of Doritos stickered with gentle reminders about public smoking, rather than run around handing out tickets. Illegal, on-the-street drug sales are still targeted, though, and the city is still dealing with its share of dangerous illegal drugs.

As the novelty of legal marijuana has worn off, the pot stores now blend into the background just like the medical marijuana dispensaries. Notable dispensaries include:

- **Uncle Ike's** (2310 E. Union St., 800/438-3784, http://ikes.com; 8am-11:45pm daily) is a continuously growing Seattle weed empire, and this flagship set the tone for local shops with its cheery decor, super-helpful staff, and a separate glass and goods store for paraphernalia. Prices are among the cheapest in town.

- Belltown's **Have a Heart** (115 Blanchard St., 206/588-2436, http://haveaheartcc.com; 8am-11:45pm daily) has a bright green exterior that makes it easy to find, and it carries a ton of locally grown product.

- Don't know anything about weed? SoDo's **Dockside** (1728 4th Ave. S, 844/362-5420, www.docksidecannabis.com; 9am-11pm Mon.-Sat., 9am-10pm Sun.), near the stadiums, has a series of cannabis exhibits on display that show the history behind the plant and its uses, including a smelling station.

awkward hookups galore. The club has been the heart of the Capitol Hill gay dance scene for more than 30 years, and it shows no signs of slowing.

MAP 3: 1509 Broadway, 206/324-5358, www.neighboursnightclub.com; 9pm-2am Tues.-Thurs., 9pm-4am Fri.-Sat., 10pm-2am Sun.; cover $10

Q

With its white walls and floor, sleek surfaces, and high-concept lighting, Q can feel more like an Apple Store than a dance club. But then the music kicks up and drinks start flowing, featuring house-made infused vodkas in hickory bacon or choco-mint flavors. Young, energetic gay men make up the core of the clientele, but the club's central location draws a variety of dancers and students from nearby Seattle University.

MAP 3: 1426 Broadway, www.qnightclub. com; 9pm-2am Wed.-Thurs., 10am-3am Fri.-Sat.; cover $10-20

R Place

There's a little bit of everything at R Place (yes, it's a pun), one of the older gay bars in Capitol Hill. There's a drag show on Thursdays, upstairs has a dance floor pumping hip-hop and pop, and karaoke is on three days a week—plus there's a seating area with pool tables for actual conversation. All three floors get packed on weekends, with a majority of male patrons, but it's a welcoming club (albeit one that often has a cover charge). The neon lights and black walls have a timeless feel, so the whole effect is of a comfortable place where no one's trying too hard.

MAP 3: 619 E. Pine St., 206/322-8828, www.rplaceseattle.com; 4pm-2am Mon.-Fri., 2pm-2am Sat.-Sun.; cover $3 and up

ART BARS
The Hideout

To call The Hideout an art bar is a vast understatement—nearly every inch of the 16-foot-high walls is plastered with canvases, with a thoughtful still life next to a frantic modern collage. The signage outside is modest, perhaps to fit in with the surrounding hospitals in First Hill (or "Pill Hill"). Be sure to swing by the art vending machine in the bar's dark corner before ordering from the bar. You can get a beer, a decent cocktail, or an artwork price list and flashlight to shop the gallery around you.

MAP 3: 1005 Boren Ave., 206/903-8480, www.hideoutseattle.com; 4pm-2am Mon.-Fri., 6pm-2am Sat.-Sun.

PUBS
Canterbury Ale House

After years as a well-worn dive with a light medieval theme, this locals' bar received a makeover with giant TV screens and tidy corners. Now, the cavernous space, with its wood-accented walls, fills to the brim during big sports events, and on nice days one section of wall rolls open like a garage door. The long bar offers a glimpse at the tap lineup—a respectable mix of local beers—while nooks off to the side of the dining room are ideal for groups of six or eight looking for a little privacy. The fare is basic pub food; mostly fried and good with beer. Kids are welcome until 9pm.

MAP 3: 534 15th Ave. E, 206/325-3110, http://thecanterburyalehouse.com; 2pm-midnight Mon.-Thurs., 2pm-2am Fri., 10am-2am Sat., 10am-midnight Sun.

Rhein Haus

The barn-like Rhein Haus is a German theme park unto itself, with multiple bars, indoor bocce courts, a fireplace,

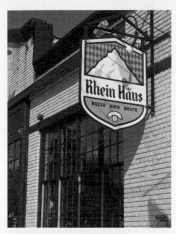

Rhein Haus

and long beer-hall tables popular with students from Seattle University across the street. Beer comes in glasses that range from a two-ounce taster to a full-liter mug, and most pours hail from Germany and Austria. A special machine spirals potatoes thin, so they can be fried on a stick like a never-ending potato chip.

MAP 3: 912 12th Ave., 206/325-5409, www.rheinhausseattle.com; 4pm-2am Mon.-Fri., 11am-2am Sat., 9am-2am Sun.

Stumbling Monk

Local beer is crucial to the Pacific Northwest drinking scene; since most of the nation's hops are grown here, the bitter IPA practically flows from the local water taps, and every week there's a new local brewery putting out IBUs from a suburban garage or Ballard bike shed. Stumbling Monk, a fixture that sits between two busy hubs of Capitol Hill, takes a different approach to beer appreciation by specializing in Belgians and other imports. It's as dark as a European pub, with high-backed booths and wooden tables that look like they have as much history as the

Hapsburgs. Though the bottle menu attracts aficionados, the selection of board games is a clear sign that the joint isn't about beer snobbery.

MAP 3: 1635 E. Olive Way, 206/860-0916; 6pm-2am daily

DIVE BARS

✪ Unicorn

Every pattern under the sun is represented at Unicorn, a veritable assault on the senses. Decorated like a circus seen through an acid trip, it even has horned beasts mounted on the walls—real stuffed ones, not unicorns. Downstairs is even wilder: a basement bar called the Narwhal, named for the unicorns of the sea. Pinball machines, a photo booth, and sticky floors are a good match for the cheap cocktails and bowls of popcorn.

MAP 3: 1118 E. Pike St., 206/325-6492, www.unicornseattle.com; noon-2am Mon.-Fri., 11am-2am Sat.-Sun.

Kessler's

Sports bar? Gay bar? Dive bar? Kessler's is a little of each. Located next to an unambiguously LGBT-first establishment, C. C. Attle's, Kessler's gets some of its weekend night overflow. Most of the time, though, it's a chill neighborhood sports joint with plenty of TVs and, usually, a darts game happening in the corner. During football season the clientele is more Midwestern than usual—this is the place in Seattle to watch the Green Bay Packers—but service is friendly and familiar year-round.

MAP 3: 1703 E. Olive Way, 206/457-4453; 4pm-11pm Mon.-Thurs., 4pm-2am Fri.-Sat., 10am-9pm Sun.

Linda's Tavern

How can you tell that this is an older Capitol Hill bar? It doesn't really have a theme beyond "drinking." Sure, there's a stuffed bison head over the bar and a few other pieces of Western memorabilia, but the exposed roof beams read more "unfinished" than "artisanal." Linda's has been around long enough that it was the last place Kurt Cobain was seen in public before his 1994 suicide. It's a very casual drinking hole with a hardware store-style neon sign in the window (no, Linda's doesn't actually carry "Tools, Radio, Tackle"). There are local beers on tap, and the Bloody Marys are strong and famous, topped with a whole garden of garnishes. Head out to the back patio to share french fries or a big greasy brunch plate on weekends.

MAP 3: 707 E. Pine St., 206/325-1220, www.lindastavern.com; 4pm-2am Mon.-Fri., 10am-2am Sat.-Sun.

Montana

There's an obvious Western theme at Montana, where specials are scrawled on a blackboard. Bearded young men in flannel shirts fill the wooden booths, and even the women here are likely to be wearing plaid. Montana fits in well with the party atmosphere of Capitol Hill; the interior graffiti and fake log cabin walls are a good fit for the neighborhood's irreverence.

MAP 3: 1506 E. Olive Way, 206/422-4647, www.montanainseattle.com; 4pm-2am daily

DANCE CLUBS
The Baltic Room

Though located in Capitol Hill, The Baltic Room is just a bridge away from downtown, so it pulls scenesters from both neighborhoods. It hosts a wide range of DJs and the usual mix of pop, R&B, and house-music nights, but you can also find odder things taking place on the dance floor, like a live painting event in which speakers thump dance music as artists work.

MAP 3: 1207 Pine St., 206/625-4444, www.balticroom.com; 9pm-midnight Sun.-Tues. and Thurs., 6pm-midnight Wed., 8pm-2am Fri.-Sat.; cover $5 and up

Fremont   Map 4

LIVE MUSIC
High Dive

You can't miss this Fremont mainstay; the giant sign features a woman mid-dive. Live music shows here are very intimate, with an eager crowd pressed right up to the small stage; acts tend to be modern and eclectic rock. Mondays feature karaoke. You can also order barbecue here; it comes from a nearby eatery and is a step above normal club fare.

MAP 4: 513 N. 36th St., 206/632-0212, www.highdiveseattle.com; hours vary by performance; $5-20

Nectar Lounge

Having hosted hip-hop, funk, and dance acts since 2004, the Nectar has figured out how to pack a club. Its three bars serve the kind of drinks and shots that go well with loud music—in other words, easy to make and easily forgettable—and a

CRAFT BEER

To explain the craft beer scene in Seattle, it's important to know one thing: This is hops country. Of course, not every signature Seattle beer is a hop-heavy pale ale, like the India pale ale (IPA) that seems ubiquitous in the city's bars. But the fact that 75 percent of the country's hops—a major ingredient in such ales—are grown in the nearby Yakima Valley means that IPAs dominate.

Until the late 1990s, beer in Seattle was all about Rainier. The lager was simple, light, and local, and it had catchy commercials and a history dating back to the late 19th century, making it even older than Washington's statehood. The brewery, located in Georgetown next to I-5, was topped with a giant neon "R" (today the sign has a place in the Museum of History and Industry). There was also Olympia, another lager brewed an hour south of Seattle and known for the "It's the Water" slogan.

Fremont Brewing

In the 1980s a new beer paradigm began to emerge: the microbrewery. Pike Brewing Company and Redhook appeared, tweaking recipes and using the hops crop from just east of the Cascade Mountains to create lively, flavor-forward ales. Breweries like Pyramid and Elysian established themselves, many selling to larger corporations once they had a decade or two of success.

Today, the closest beer to Rainier's onetime ubiquity is Manny's, a pale ale made by Georgetown Brewing (located very close to where the Rainier brewery stood). You'll find the beer on tap in many of the city's bars, though never canned or bottled. Brewers are stretching beyond IPAs into new specialty areas, including porters, sour beers, and session ales. Bars like Tap House Grill and Noble Fir offer a chance to taste the wide variety of Pacific Northwest beers.

- **Tap House Grill:** Compare and contrast craft beer styles at this downtown bar boasting 160 taps (page 128).

- **Holy Mountain Brewing:** Unusual brews are perfected at this out-of-the-way spot for serious beer geeks (page 132).

- **Chuck's Hop Shop:** There are so many taps at this bottle shop and all-ages hangout that no beer nerd will fail to find a favorite (page 136).

- **Fremont Brewing:** Enjoy offerings from the popular brewery at its large outdoor beer garden (page 144).

- **Brouwer's Cafe:** At this two-level space you can imbibe Belgian and European as well as Pacific Northwest brews (page 144).

mezzanine overlooks the main floor. Music spills out to the outdoor patio on most nights. College students love the place, but its Fremont location means that the crowded floor fills with more than just undergrads.

MAP 4: 412 N. 36th St., 206/632-2020, www.nectarlounge.com; 11am-5pm and 8pm-2am Mon.-Fri., 8pm-2am Sat.-Sun.; cover up to $30

CRAFT BEER
✪ Fremont Brewing

You'd be hard-pressed to find a Seattle beer drinker who doesn't enjoy Fremont, a widely available brand despite only starting in its funky namesake neighborhood in 2009. Today the brewery has a large outdoor beer garden on Fremont's main drag and picnic tables that fill up as fast as the bike racks during sunny afternoons. Expect to find the signature Interurban IPA on tap, along with the Universale Pale and, during the warmest months, the popular Summer Ale with a touch of citrus. There's plenty of indoor space for when it rains, though many folks will tough it out under the white tents that protect the outdoor tables. Free pretzels are the only munchies available, so anyone who walks in with takeout grub gets plenty of jealous looks. Bring a picnic and a deck of cards, and make friends.

MAP 4: 1050 N. 34th St., 206/420-2407, www.fremontbrewing.com; 11am-9pm daily

Brouwer's Cafe

Don't be fooled by the name: Brouwer's is not a café, but a large Belgian beer bar with two levels of seating. There's nothing small or quaint about the 64 beers on draft or hundreds of bottled beers available. Despite the dozens of Belgian and European beers, there are even more Pacific Northwest craft varieties, most of which are helpfully served in multiple sizes. Besides stocking beers from the nearby Fremont Brewing, Brouwer's also sources from small brewers like Arlington's Skookum Brewery and Dru Bru, made in the mountains at Snoqualmie Pass. Though the 2nd-level balcony seating looks down on the spacious open floor, the lighting is just dim enough to make the big joint feel cozy. The food served is heavy, satisfying fare, like pommes frites and Belgian stew. Dessert means a beer float: a stout or framboise served with vanilla ice cream. For those who aren't fans of ale, there are also 60 kinds of scotch on the menu.

MAP 4: 400 N. 35th St., 206/267-2437, http://brouwerscafe.blogspot.com; 11am-midnight Sun.-Thurs., 11am-2am Fri.-Sat.

Hale's Ales

In a city full of craft breweries, Hale's has grown since 1983 (back when they were called "microbreweries") to be a stalwart of Seattle beer. The brewpub, open since 1995, is no hole-in-the-wall taproom but a full-on restaurant with hearty salads, calzones, and shepherd's pie. The Supergoose IPA, a Northwest classic using Yakima hops that impart citrus and pine flavors, is its best-known beer, but the brewpub also offers its nitrogen-conditioned Cream Ale—America's first—and Leary Way Limited beers that arise from brewer experimentation. Inside, you can look at the brew equipment as you drink, but outdoor seating is popular during summer months.

MAP 4: 4301 Leary Way NW, 206/782-0737, http://halesbrewery.com; 11am-10pm Sun.-Thurs., 11am-11pm Fri.-Sat.

COCKTAIL BARS
The BackDoor

Though the joint is known more formally as "The Backdoor at Roxy's," located behind a diner that faces Fremont's main drag, the bar is no afterthought. It operates as its own sizable bar with a statement chandelier, bright murals, sculptures, and mirrors on the wall. The fanciness is all in fun, and the cocktails have fun names even when they combine unusual liquors with muddled fresh ingredients.

MAP 4: 462 N. 36th St., 206/632-7322, www.backdooratroxys.com; 5pm-2am daily

The Barrel Thief

Focusing on wine and whiskey, this dark den of drinking caters to the finer things in life. With more than 175 wines by the glass and almost twice that in whiskeys, bourbons, ryes, and scotches, making a decision is near impossible. Fortunately the bartenders are attentive and helpful under the Tiffany-style lamps that light the cozy, calm bar.

MAP 4: 3417 Evanston Ave. N, #102, 206/402-5492, http://bthief.com, 2pm-11pm Sun., 4pm-11pm Tues.-Wed., 4pm-midnight Thurs., 3pm-1am Fri., 2pm-1am Sat.

PUBS
George & Dragon Pub

English Premier League soccer fans use this classic pub as a gathering point, even when games start annoyingly early. Other sports light up the TV around the clock, and the menu ranges from classic British offerings like shepherd's pie and fish-and-chips to regular bar staples like onion rings. The dark wood inside almost captures the feel of an authentic British pub.

MAP 4: 206 N. 36th St., 206/545-6864, http://theegeorge.com, 11am-2am daily

Ballard Map 5

LIVE MUSIC
Sunset Tavern

The divey Sunset isn't trying to be anything fancy, a fact that's obvious from the dated decor left over from a previous iteration as an Asian restaurant. But the back stage gathers groups of sweaty, enthusiastic music fans for indie folk, rock, dance, and lots of alt rock. The bar even once hosted a

Tractor Tavern

competition to find the worst band in Seattle—and it had plenty of entrants. Open since 2000, the Sunset knows exactly what it is: a grungy, unpretentious venue that's small enough to make any music performance feel intimate and exciting. Betty's Room, the bar in the front half of the joint, is free to enter and has a photo booth in one corner. Cover is charged to access the performance space.

MAP 5: 5433 Ballard Ave. NW, 206/784-4880, http://sunsettavern.com; 5pm-2am daily; no cover for front bar, $8-20 cover for stage

Tractor Tavern

As the name might suggest, the Tractor gets plenty of country acts, mostly alt-country and singer-songwriters, in addition to hosting regular square-dancing nights. The venue also stacks its bills with plenty of rock, soul, and indie acts, and even a few tribute bands. Shows featuring national acts tend to sell out in advance, mostly because it's a great place to see live music—lots of energy, a few booths and seats near the back, and a bar that's just far enough out of the way to be accessible during the show, but close enough to feel part of it.

MAP 5: 5213 Ballard Ave. NW, 206/789-3599, www.tractortavern.com; 8pm-2am daily; cover $10-30

CRAFT BEER
Maritime Pacific Brewing Company

The Jolly Roger Tap Room, the drinking arm of this brewery that dates back to 1990, keeps the nautical flair of the operation going with some pirate flags and a map painted on the floor. Otherwise, it's a staid, dated pub serving thick soups and crisp hush puppies, the whole place exuding comfort. It's the kind of drinking hole that suits Ballard and its long history with the fishing industry. The 14 taps of Maritime brews include three on English beer engines (devices for pumping beer from a cask) and one reserved for its Old Seattle Lager. The light beer is no heavy, hoppy IPA, but rather a crisp pour more like Seattle's old signature drink, Rainier (a beer that still exists, but is no longer brewed locally).

MAP 5: 1111 NW Ballard Way, 206/782-6181, http://maritimebrewery. com; noon-10pm Mon.-Thurs., noon-11pm Fri.-Sat., noon-9pm Sun.

Stoup Brewing

In a neighborhood full of breweries, Stoup is a local's favorite. It's just far enough off the main path to be well loved by Ballard's beer-smart 20-, 30-,

and 40-somethings, but not so far as to be difficult to find. It's a relative newcomer to the Seattle beer scene, open only since 2013, but has drawn attention for its citrusy IPAs. The head brewer's chemistry degree is evident in the brand's devotion to the science of brewing. The brewery's taproom opens to the outside when the garage door is up, and picnic tables sit next to a brightly painted shipping container. Except on weekends, when it gets too crowded for canines, there are usually dogs accompanying their owners. The taproom doesn't serve much food, but there's often a local food truck parked just outside.

MAP 5: 1108 NW 52nd St., 206/457-5524, www.stoupbrewing.com; 4pm-10pm Mon.-Tues., noon-10pm Wed.-Thurs., noon-11pm Fri.-Sat., noon-9pm Sun.

COCKTAIL BARS
The Gerald

Cocktail culture may be a growing trend, but The Gerald is not chasing fads; it's a grown-up bar and restaurant with mod decor—the light fixtures and polished wood statement wall fairly scream *Mad Men*. Even the mac and cheese is sophisticated, made with a blend of Northwest cheeses and varied daily as a special. The cocktail menu includes mixes barrel-aged on the premises, Moscow mules on tap, and separate sections for citrus-first and spirit-first drinks.

MAP 5: 5210 Ballard Ave. NW, 206/432-9280, http://thegeraldseattle.com; 4pm-midnight Mon.-Thurs., 4pm-2am Fri., 10am-2am Sat., 10am-10pm Sun.

Hazlewood

What Hazlewood lacks in size it makes up for in straightforward quality. The bar has only a handful of stools, making it feel private despite its location on one of Ballard's biggest streets, but a loft upstairs has more comfortable seating and the classic draperies-and-chandeliers decor of a gentleman's club (the kind with cigars, not dancers). Not that it's the kind of place to dress up: The clientele is a little older than other local joints but definitely casual. Go for Prohibition-era classics or champagne cocktails and keep an eye out for the bar's hidden peephole.

MAP 5: 2311 NW Market St., 206/783-0478; 4pm-2am Mon.-Sat., 4pm-midnight Sun.

Percy's & Co.

The decorative entry and gold lettering in the front window at Percy's suggest a fussy speakeasy-style joint, and the bartenders just might be wearing suspenders. But the atmosphere is friendlier than it looks, drawing after-work groups of fashionable young Ballardites. The patio out back has views of the industrial waterfront, and a great happy hour is the best time to combine cocktails with chili-lime popcorn or steamed clams. The drinks are "apothecary-style," meaning they infuse bourbon with sage and vodka with lemongrass, and they'll mix in tinctures meant to improve libido, complexion, or brain power for free.

Percy's & Co.

King's Hardware

You have to give them points for creativity, even if it can end up feeling a bit silly.

MAP 5: 5233 Ballard Ave. NW, 206/420-3750, www.percysseattle.com; 4pm-2am Mon.-Fri., 10am-2am Sat.-Sun.

BARS AND PUBS

☆ King's Hardware

The spacious King's Hardware isn't the only bar in Seattle with Skee-Ball, but it's probably the best. Linda Derschang, Seattle's expert on great casual hangouts, helped create the bar in an old hardware space, taking care to include must-haves like an outdoor patio, a vintage Donkey Kong game, burgers, and a jukebox. One wall is blanketed with black-and-white snapshots, another with mounted animals. Though there's a wall of liquor, the draft beer and pitchers are just as popular. House-made bottled cocktails use infusions made on-site.

MAP 5: 5225 Ballard Ave. NW, 206/782-0027, www.kingsballard.com; 3pm-2am Mon.-Fri., noon-2am Sat.-Sun.

☆ Noble Fir

The upscale Noble Fir is a sleek establishment that gets more natural light than most firs in the forest. The beer menu shows evidence of fastidious selection, mostly from the Pacific Northwest, but there are also some Scandinavian choices and a number of ciders. Pours come from well-known craft brewers like Seattle's Georgetown Brewing Company and Eugene's Ninkasi Brewing Company, as well as smaller outlets like the Olympic Peninsula's Finnriver Cidery. One corner has a library nook lined with shelves of travel books, hiking guides, and maps, perfect for planning an adventure.

MAP 5: 5316 Ballard Ave. NW, 206/420-7425, www.thenoblefir.com; 4pm-11pm Wed.-Thurs., 4pm-1am Fri., 1pm-1am Sat., noon-6:30pm Sun.

Conor Byrne Pub

A good Irish bar has lots of seating and at least one piece of decoration on the wall that says "Guinness," and Conor Byrne definitely accomplishes both. It gets plenty crowded, thanks to the frequent live shows on the corner stage in back. A giant chalkboard "Calendar of Awesome" notes which nights are open mics and when the bar is taken over by dance parties or bluegrass. The

cocktail menu leans rather Irish—a Jameson Ginger is exactly what you think—but this is the kind of place to enjoy a Harp, Smithwicks, or yes, a Guinness.

MAP 5: 5140 Ballard Ave. NW, 206/784-3640, www.conorbyrnepub.com; 4pm-midnight Mon.-Thurs., 4pm-2am Fri.-Sun.; cover up to $15

Lock & Keel

Lock & Keel is overwhelmingly themed, with maritime signifiers scattered throughout. It's a solid pub on a busy street, with a clientele that's had tattoos since before they were trendy. Wings are cheap during sporting events, and the Sunday breakfast menu includes homemade corned beef hash and oversize biscuits and gravy. There are a few local ales on tap, but it's no beer snob's bar; it's the place for mid-priced whiskey or a Guinness, enjoyed while hunched over a barstool or while playing at one of the pool tables in back.

MAP 5: 5144 Ballard Ave. NW, 206/781-8023; 4pm-2am Mon.-Fri., 2pm-2am Sat., 10am-2am Sun.

University District   Map 6

DIVE BARS
✪ The Blue Moon Tavern

The Blue Moon has literary cred in spades. This dive bar has been open, reportedly, since the repeal of Prohibition and is known for having hosted readings by Northwest greats like Tom Robbins, Ken Kesey, and poet Theodore Roethke. Allen Ginsberg and Dylan Thomas were known to pop in when they were in town, and it's now officially recognized as a

Seattle landmark. The space has the well-worn furniture and barstools you'd expect from a longtime college-area dive, plus live music or open-mic readings almost every night. Don't be surprised if you feel like spouting your own poetry after a few local brews from the taps.

MAP 6: 712 NE 45th St., 206/675-9116, http://bluemoonseattle.wordpress.com; 2pm-2am Mon.-Fri., noon-2am Sat.-Sun.; cover $7 Thurs.-Sat.

The Monkey Pub

The decor in this University District favorite can best be described as eclectic. There are a few sports logos, some old posters, and some kegs hanging from the wall. It's an old-fashioned kind of joint that gets people to socialize the classic ways, with busy pool tables and a thrice-weekly karaoke night. Trivia, followed by karaoke, is on Friday nights. Drink selections are modest but sufficient for the beer-smart undergraduates that make up much of the crowd, but it's not strictly a student scene.

MAP 6: 5305 Roosevelt Way NE, 206/523-6457, http://themonkeypub.com; 5pm-1:45am daily

International District and SoDo

Map 7

LIVE MUSIC
Showbox SoDo

Though not as central as its sister space next to Pike Place Market, the Sodo version of the Showbox draws similar national musical acts, mainly of the rock, independent, and hip-hop variety. Fans who like an uncomplicated space for appreciating and dancing to their favorite bands flock to this warehouse-style space, though the flat, square shape means there are few spots to see over the crowd.

MAP 7: 1700 1st Ave. S, 206/652-0444, www.showboxpresents.com; hours vary by performance; tickets from $25

DIVE BARS
Hooverville

Featuring a mishmash of vintage touches—an arcade corner, formica tables, and green pleather stools—as well as a blackboard beer list and peanut shells on the floor, Hooverville feels much less corporate than most sports bars. Located near CenturyLink and Safeco Fields, the faithful not attending the games gather in their blue-and-green Sounders, Mariners, or Seahawks gear to toast the teams.

MAP 7: 1721 1st Ave. S, 206/264-2428, www.hoovervillebar.com; 2pm-2am daily

DANCE CLUBS
Aston Manor

In a city not known for its expansive nightclubs—Seattle is really more of a beer bar or cocktail club place—this SoDo location delivers a dance scene worth dressing up for. The decor celebrates the opulent 1920s with soft banquettes, gilded mirrors, and chandeliers, and there are quirky bookshelves that open to become doors. The whole place plays off a story about a bootlegger who created a speakeasy-turned-dance club, a fun aesthetic that doesn't get in the way of the booming dance, EDM, and top 40 music on weekends.

MAP 7: 2946 1st Ave. S, 206/382-7866, www.astonmanorsea.com; 10pm-2am Fri.-Sat.; cover $10-30

ARTS AND CULTURE

Though Seattle is known for its tech industry, its coffee, and its outdoorsy activities, the art scene hardly takes a backseat. This is the city that birthed grunge music and the world's most famous glass artist, and sends musicals straight to Broadway.

public art in Seattle

It might surprise you to know that beyond its classical productions, the Seattle Symphony also commissions groundbreaking new works on a regular basis. At the city's jazz, rock, and indie venues, only the biggest national acts sell out immediately, meaning there's almost always a place to find live tunes. Try not to think too hard about what category a musical act belongs to; indie, alternative, punk, dance, rap, grunge, rock, and even jazz genres blend together on Seattle's stages.

You only have to witness the crowded streets of the monthly art walk to see how much visual art is appreciated here. Take an evening stroll in Pioneer Square on the first Thursday of the month, or pop by a gallery any time. The Seattle Museum of Art's gallery, located behind the gift shop, has affordable art ready to be taken home.

Though there's plenty of culture throughout the year, the city comes alive whenever there's a big festival to be celebrated—whether it's the Americana focus of Folklife, Bumbershoot's salute to all music and arts, or Comic Con or PAX to embrace nerd culture. Even local neighborhood events like the Capitol Hill Block Party are becoming institutions. There's no shortage of imagination in the city, and plenty of places to see that creativity on display.

HIGHLIGHTS

✪ **BEST AFFORDABLE ART:** The works on sale at the **Seattle Art Museum (SAM) Gallery** are a little cheaper than the pieces in the actual museum—and represent the same Pacific Northwest creative spirit (page 152).

✪ **BEST OUT-OF-TOWN TRYOUT:** So many shows from **5th Avenue Theatre** have transferred to Broadway that it's become a musical theater legend (page 152).

✪ **BEST STAGE PRESENCE:** From its location in Seattle Center, **Seattle Repertory Theatre** sets the standard for high-quality stage performances (page 155).

✪ **BEST TOE-TAPPING:** The nationally known **Pacific Northwest Ballet** balances classic works with cutting edge choreography (page 155).

✪ **BEST BIG SCREEN:** You won't see a curved movie screen like the one at **Cinerama** anywhere else; neither will you find popcorn as good (page 155).

✪ **COOLEST ART SPACE:** Located on the University of Washington campus, the **Henry Art Gallery** is not only a museum for art lovers but a lively cultural hub (page 158).

✪ **BEST POP CULTURAL CONVERGENCE:** At **Emerald City Comicon,** movie and TV stars appear alongside gaming enthusiasts, literature lovers, and, of course, comic book collectors (page 159).

✪ **BEST CANNABIS-CENTRIC WEEKEND:** The annual **Hempfest** is the largest of its kind in the world, occupying several of the city's parks for a weekend every summer (page 161).

✪ **MOST POPULAR GAMING EVENT:** The Seattle iteration of the Penny Arcade Expo, **PAX West,** originated in nearby Bellevue. It sells out tens of thousands of tickets nearly instantaneously each year (page 162).

Hempfest

Downtown and Pioneer Square

Map 1

GALLERIES

✪ Seattle Art Museum (SAM) Gallery

Tucked behind the Seattle Art Museum's gift shop—just keep walking past the counter—this small gallery features artwork much more accessible than the priceless works on display in the museum galleries upstairs. Offering rentals and payment plans, the gallery introduces local artists to local art aficionados through their collections. Pieces often reflect Seattle life, such as rainy views of local traffic, rendered in oil paints to be more beautiful than reality.

MAP 1: 1300 1st Ave., 206/343-1101, www.seattleartmuseum.org; 10am-5pm Wed. and Fri.-Sun., 10am-9pm Thurs.

Foster/White Gallery

One of the city's oldest and best-known galleries, Foster/White has been around since 1968, though it has moved around Seattle since its opening. Pillars and original wood beams fill the current space in a century-old building in Pioneer Square, but the artwork is often much more contemporary. Mediums include painting, sculpture, and glass art.

MAP 1: 220 3rd Ave. S, 206/622-2833, www.fosterwhite.com; 10am-6pm Tues.-Sat.

Greg Kucera Gallery

Opened in 1983, this Seattle gallery first operated out of a shabby storefront, and by the late 1990s it owned a fancy building in Pioneer Square, more than 4,000 square feet that includes an outdoor sculpture garden. While it started off featuring regional and emerging artists, today it sells contemporary paintings, prints, and sculptures from artists from around the world.

MAP 1: 212 3rd Ave. S, 206/624-0770, www.gregkucera.com; 10:30am-5:30pm Tues.-Sat.

THEATER

✪ 5th Avenue Theatre

It may be more than 3,000 miles from 5th Avenue Theatre to Broadway, but several musicals produced here have gone on to successful Broadway runs—including two Tony Award winners for Best Musical. Besides blockbusters like *Memphis* and *Hairspray*, the theater also hosts touring productions. The theater's interior has Asian-influenced decor, with designs of dragons, gold birds, and orange blossoms on the ceiling. Look up before you walk in to see the elaborate detail in the exterior panels painted in green, blue, and gold, and then do so again when you're inside to examine the giant chandelier.

Foster/White Gallery

ART ON THE MOVE

On the first Thursday of each month, rain or shine, the galleries of Pioneer Square and downtown open their doors and invite the public in for the **First Thursday Art Walk** (www.pioneersquare.org), during which most galleries stay open until 8pm or later. The streets fill with pedestrians wandering from gallery to gallery, having a free glass of wine here or nibbling on a cheese plate there, sometimes even shelling out for the art on the walls. Started in 1981, it was the first event of its kind in the United States, though the concept has since traveled to nearly every city in the country. Three Pioneer Square garages offer free parking during the monthly event—find participating spots online, then grab a voucher from a gallery participating in the Art Walk. During the walk, local bars and restaurants fill to the brim. Look online for schedules and exhibit descriptions, or simply wander the neighborhood and duck into any Victorian-fronted building with its lights on.

MAP 1: 1308 5th Ave., 206/625-1900, www.5thavenue.org; showtimes vary by production; $45-140

ACT

Located near the convention center, the ACT brings a bit of culture to an otherwise business-oriented downtown district. The theater has five stages in a 1925 Fraternal Order of Eagles building with an ornate white exterior. Inside, the art is newer: ACT stands for A Contemporary Theatre. Plays and musical theater pieces that debut here often move to New York.

MAP 1: 700 Union St., 206/292-7676, www.acttheatre.org; showtimes vary by production; $20-60

MUSIC

Seattle Symphony

From its home stage at Benaroya Hall, Seattle Symphony performances are an electric highlight of the city's cultural life. The group gained international attention in the 2010s under the direction of rising star conductor Ludovic Morlot; he oversaw the world premiere of a commissioned piece by John Luther Adams that won a Grammy Award and a Pulitzer Prize. He was succeeded by Thomas Dausgaard, a Danish conductor who'd already served as the group's principal guest conductor. Though the symphony does often look to new composers and cutting-edge performances, it also has a repertoire of symphonic classics, and a pops conductor swings in regularly to lead the group through movie scores or holiday classics. The symphony's season runs from early fall to late spring, and throughout the year the Benaroya stage also hosts talks and even film screenings. A giant Dale Chihuly sculpture decorates the main hall, and tall windows open to a downtown view.

MAP 1: 200 University St., 206/215-4800, www.seattlesymphony.org/benaroya; showtimes and tickets prices vary by performance

Benaroya Hall, home to the Seattle Symphony

PERFORMANCE VENUES

Moore Theatre

The city's oldest theater that's still hosting live performances has been open since 1907, and was the first home of two city institutions, the Seattle Symphony and the Seattle International Film Festival. The Moore is so old that its second balcony was built specifically for segregated seating. The ornate ceiling, stage, and balconies have long since been renovated. It largely welcomes midsize pop/rock music acts, comedians, and dance troupes. Tom Douglas's catering wing provides the concessions, including chocolate cookies from much-loved Dahlia Bakery.

MAP 1: 1932 2nd Ave., 206/682-1414, www.stgpresents.org/moore; showtimes and tickets prices vary by performance

Paramount Theatre

Paramount Theatre

Born as a beaux arts vaudeville and movie theater in the 1920s, the Paramount Theatre now welcomes traveling Broadway shows, big-name headlining musicians, and massive political rallies. The old dame of a theater was renovated in the 1990s by Microsoft executive Ida Cole with a flair for the dramatic; she donated the theater to a nonprofit group to manage it. The theater has been restored to the rococo style it had in its early days: gold leaf and chandeliers, with molding on the walls and ceiling. The theater hosts classic silent movie nights throughout the year, with accompaniment by its original Wurlitzer organ.

MAP 1: 911 Pine St., 206/902-5500, www.stgpresents.org/paramount; showtimes and tickets prices vary by performance

Queen Anne and Belltown

Map 2

THEATER
✪ Seattle Repertory Theatre

Seattle Repertory Theatre dates back to the arts enthusiasm that arose after the 1962 World's Fair left the city with a number of performance spaces. The group has premiered plays by big-name playwrights like August Wilson and Neil Simon, and its theater in Seattle Center is recognized as the city's foremost nonmusical theater stage.

MAP 2: 155 Mercer St., 206/443-2222, www.seattlerep.org; showtimes and tickets prices vary by performance

BALLET
✪ Pacific Northwest Ballet

Seattle's professional ballet company has won national acclaim. The company's repertoire includes everything from Balanchine classics to new ballets, and the city supports the group with a healthy subscription base. Its annual *Nutcracker*, which used to famously feature sets designed by Maurice Sendak, has undergone a rebirth in recent years, and is now a more traditional version of the holiday classic. Most performances take place at McCaw Hall in Seattle Center.

MAP 2: 321 Mercer St., 206/441-2424, www.pnb.org; showtimes and ticket prices vary by performance

OPERA
Seattle Opera

The city's opera company has been around for more than 50 years, emphasizing the work of Richard Wagner; it once performed *The Ring* every year for nine seasons in a row. The slate of productions is still varied, however, featuring classics with technologically advanced stagings. The company produces podcasts, artist interviews, and videos to start the audience immersion before the performances even begin. Operas take the stage at Seattle Center's McCaw Hall.

MAP 2: 321 Mercer St., 206/389-7676, www.seattleopera.org; showtimes and ticket prices vary by performance

CINEMA
✪ Cinerama

Harking back to the 1960s, when both Seattle and Hollywood dreamed of a hip Technicolor future, Cinerama represents a historic kind of movie viewing. The theater fell into disrepair as a second-run theater in the 1990s. Former patron and Microsoft cofounder Paul Allen bought Cinerama and its kicky red-and-blue sign before it could be demolished and has since renovated it into a high quality destination. The big curved screen is served by a unique three-projector system, and seats are assigned at the time of

Pacific Northwest Ballet

Cinerama

purchase, making it popular for big sci-fi releases, though it also regularly shows classics like *Lawrence of Arabia* and *2001: A Space Odyssey*—it even has its own specially made print of the Kubrick classic.

MAP 2: 2100 4th Ave., 206/448-6680, www.cinerama.com; $17 general admission

Big Picture

Even though Big Picture is both an adorable movie theater and a bar, it isn't big. Located underneath the palatial El Gaucho restaurant, it's merely a screening room with only a few dozen seats and tiny anteroom of a bar where the walls are decorated with musical instruments and cushy couches. Bring your martini or prosecco-based Bond Girl cocktail into the screening of a first-run flick. Popcorn comes in champagne buckets, and the bar and theater are both open only to adults 21 and over.

MAP 2: 2505 1st Ave., 206/256-0566, www.thebigpicture.net; $13.25 adults, $11.25 seniors, matinee, and happy hour

SIFF Uptown

One of Seattle's classic old movie theaters was rescued by the Seattle International Film Festival in 2011, and it now devotes almost as much time to festival flicks and special engagements as it does to small-release first runs. The inside of the three-screen theater is nothing special, but the proximity to restaurants and bars makes it popular.

MAP 2: 511 Queen Anne Ave. N, 206/324-9996, www.siff.net; $14 adults, $13 children and seniors, $11 matinee

Capitol Hill

Map 3

CINEMA
Egyptian Theatre

Housed in a building that used to be a Masonic temple, the Egyptian has one screen and a lot of historical charm. When it closed as an independent theater in 2013, it was a blow to a buzzy, active neighborhood that needed this kind of funky movie house. Fortunately, the Seattle International Film Festival arranged to take over the space, making it just one of the city's movie theaters saved from the wrecking ball by a festival that remains active all year. Now it screens both independent and mainstream films, and is part of the intense early-summer SIFF festival.

MAP 3: 805 E. Pine St., 206/324-9996, www.siff.net/egyptian-theatre; ticket prices vary by film

Egyptian Theatre

Fremont

Map 4

PERFORMANCE VENUES
Fremont Abbey Arts Center

Don't expect singing nuns at this abbey; this performance space may have been born as St. Paul's Lutheran Church in 1914, but its offerings are much more secular now. It became a community arts center in the 2000s and got a full renovation, leaving a long, beautiful hall with curved wooden beams and domed windows. Now it hosts open mic nights, storytelling events, live music, and a monthly production called The Round that joins slam poets, musical acts, and visual artists.

MAP 4: 4272 Fremont Ave N, 206/414-8325, www.fremontabbey.org; showtimes and tickets prices vary

ARTS AND CULTURE

UNIVERSITY DISTRICT

GALLERIES
Venue

This combination of store, gallery, and work studio represents the artsy side of Ballard, a side that's only grown since the neighborhood became known for its street life instead of its fishing catch. Venue displays works from local sculptors, painters, and jewelry makers in a space that's been open since 2005. Many products on sale have either overt Seattle symbols—like Space Needle paintings or baby onesies featuring the cityscape—or, even more popular, a certain Seattle aesthetic, like concrete jewelry, letterpress products, and blown-glass housewares.

MAP 5: 5408 22nd Ave. NW, 206/789-3335, www.venueballard.com; 11am-6pm Tues.-Fri., 10am-5pm Sat., 10am-4pm Sun.

CINEMA
Majestic Bay Theatres

Though it plays first-run movies like the bigger movie theaters in town, the Majestic Bay has a bit more character than a megaplex. Near the smaller screening rooms upstairs is a line of posters representing the theater's top-grossing movies, plus signed broadsheets from well-loved flicks. Look for the pig statue (part of a citywide series that honors Pike Place Market) and the hand-blown glass light fixtures.

MAP 5: 2044 NW Market St., 206/781-2229, www.majesticbay.com; $10.50-13.50

MUSEUMS
✪ Henry Art Gallery

The University of Washington's Henry Art Gallery is located in the middle of campus, close to Red Square, in a building that combines classic brick architecture with modern glass additions. Thanks to its proximity to the undergraduate population, the museum never feels old or stuffy. Founded by a local philanthropist as the first public art museum in the state, it began with 19th- and 20th-century paintings but later grew its now-substantial collection to include photography and new-media installations. There are also textiles from around the world, including rugs from central Asia and costumes from eastern Europe. And it's not only a repository for art but one of the school's hubs for cultural events, from lectures to dance parties and musical performances. The gallery's café, Molly's at the Henry (8am-4pm Tues.-Fri., 10:30am-2pm Sat.-Sun.), has salads, sandwiches, and Stumptown Coffee, plus pies from a local bakery.

MAP 6: 15th Ave. NE at NE 41st St., 206/543-2820, www.henryart.org; 11am-4pm Wed. and Sat.-Sun., 11am-9am Thurs.-Fri.; $10 adults, $6 seniors, students and children under 14 free

PERFORMANCE VENUES

Neptune Theatre

Opened in the early 1920s, the Neptune was renovated in 2011 and now serves as a modern venue for music and comedy acts. It was a movie house for years and still has its original stage, along with ornate ceilings and moldings. Now run by the same theater group that operates the bigger Paramount and Moore Theatres, the Neptune tends to host acts that appeal to a younger college audience. There's a free tour on the third Saturday of the month, comprising a 90-minute walk behind the scenes where you'll hear how the theater has remained under the ownership of the family that founded it. Though it was designed for silent films, the Neptune has blossomed as a live music venue, hosting such artists as Ani DiFranco, Animal Collective, and George Clinton.

MAP 6: 1303 NE 45th St., 206/682-1414, www.stgpresents.org/Neptune; showtimes and ticket prices vary

Festivals and Events

WINTER

Winterfest

During the month of December, Seattle Center erupts into holiday cheer during Winterfest, with a temporary ice rink, ice sculpture competitions, twinkling lights, live performances, and hot chocolate for sale.

Queen Anne and Belltown: Seattle Center, 305 Harrison St., www.seattlecenter. com/winterfest; end of Nov.-end of Dec.; prices vary by event

SPRING

Northwest Flower & Garden Show

Spring hits early in this region: In late February, with snow still falling in the mountains, sea-level Seattle is starting to sprout and bloom. The Northwest Flower & Garden Show fills the Washington State Convention Center downtown with show gardens, shops, and seminars about bringing plants to life.

Downtown: Washington State Convention Center, 705 Pike St., 800/343-6973, www.gardenshow.com; last week of Feb.; $17-22 adults, $5 children 13-17, children under 13 free

✪ Emerald City Comicon

Emerald City Comicon takes place in the spring at the Washington State Convention Center downtown and has quickly grown to become one of the country's signature versions of Comic Con, with pop-culture stars signing autographs and acres of conference center displays. It's more than just comics—it encompasses movie, literary, TV, and gaming enthusiasts.

Downtown: Washington State Convention Center, 705 Pike St., 888/372-3976, www.emeraldcitycomicon. com; first week of Mar.; tickets $30 and up

Moisture Festival

The four-week-long Moisture Festival claims to be the world's largest comedy/variety festival. It includes acts like jugglers, comedians, and aerialists, as well as burlesque. Most performances last about two hours and take place in various venues across the city. **Various locations:** 206/297-1405, www.moisturefestival.com; mid-Mar.-early Apr.; showtimes and ticket prices vary

Taste Washington

Washington is one of the biggest wine producers in the country, so it's no surprise that Taste Washington is a massive food and drink festival. Hundreds of wineries from across the state and dozens of local restaurants come together over several days to show off Northwest flavors in multiple locations across the city. The Grand Tasting, held at CenturyLink Field, is the headline event. **Various locations:** http://tastewashington.org; first weekend of Apr.; ticket prices vary by event

Northwest Folklife Festival

The Seattle Center grounds host this arts, dance, and music festival that celebrates long-standing Pacific Northwest traditions and the worldwide cultures that contribute to the city's diverse population. **Queen Anne and Belltown:** Seattle Center, 305 Harrison St., www.nwfolklife.org; Memorial Day weekend; free, $10 suggested donation

Seattle International Film Festival

Held for a month in late spring in movie theaters around the city, SIFF features both large-scale films and small productions, and is one of the most popular film festivals in the country. The organization supports Seattle filmmaking throughout the year and operates several small movie theaters. **Citywide:** 206/324-9996, www.siff.net; mid-May-mid-June; showtimes and ticket prices vary

SUMMER

Seafair

The city's sprawling summerlong festival includes parades, fairs, and performances, but it is best known for the hydroplane boat races held on Lake Washington and air shows put on by the Blue Angels jet squadron and other trick aircraft. **Various locations:** 206/728-0123, www.seafair.com; mid-June-mid-Aug.; ticket prices vary by event

Fremont Solstice

On the longest day of the year, when it officially becomes summer, Fremont comes alive for the Fremont Solstice, a celebration of all things free and expressive. Activities include a three-day music festival and a parade, a kind of mini Burning Man with wildly artistic floats and a good amount of free-living nudity. **Fremont:** http://fremontsolstice.com; weekend of summer solstice; free

Seattle PrideFest

Billed as the largest free Pride festival in the country, Seattle PrideFest puts on a month's worth of events celebrating the city's queer communities. The culminating jubilee, which occurs on the same day as the Pride Parade, fills Seattle Center with vendors and performers. **Queen Anne and Belltown:** Seattle Center, 305 Harrison St., www.seattlepridefest.org; June; free

Seattle Pride

Seattle's annual Pride Parade now celebrates the legalization of same-sex marriage in Washington. The parade usually starts at 11am and runs north down 4th Avenue to Denny Way.

Downtown: 4th Ave., 206/322-9561, www.seattlepride.org; last Sun. of June; free

Seattle International Beerfest

The three days of Seattle International Beerfest are a celebration of one of the city's favorite products and pastimes. The beer booths are spread across the venues and grounds of Seattle Center, with more than 200 ales, lagers, ciders, and barley wines available for sampling. The event is cash only, unless you purchase beer tickets in advance online.

Queen Anne and Belltown: Seattle Center, 305 Harrison St., www. seattlebeerfest.com; second weekend of July; $30-50

Capitol Hill Block Party

Once an upstart neighborhood event, July's Capitol Hill Block Party has grown into a raucous weekend music festival. Indie musicians appear on stages throughout the hipster enclave of South Capitol Hill, though the festival's growth has meant more and more recognizable names on the bill.

Capitol Hill: http://capitolhillblockparty. com; weekend in late July; ticket and pass prices vary

✪ Hempfest

Even before Washington legalized recreational marijuana use in 2012, Hempfest was the largest pot-themed gathering in the world. Bands, bong sales, and activists fill the now three-day festival held the third weekend in August. The festival, which takes place in a few of the city's waterfront parks, is always free and always 100 percent volunteer-run.

The Blue Angels perform during Seafair.

Various locations: www.hempfest.org; third weekend of Aug.; free

Bumbershoot

Named for the British slang word for umbrella—an accessory that's rarely needed over the event's Labor Day weekend dates—Bumbershoot is a music festival held at Seattle Center that regularly features nationally famous music acts and comedians. Past acts have included Death Cab for Cutie, The Weeknd, and Neko Case. Three-day passes go on sale well in advance, while one-day passes go on sale closer to the festival dates—but they are very popular and tend to sell out.

Queen Anne and Belltown: Seattle Center, 305 Harrison St., www. bumbershoot.com; Labor Day weekend; pass prices vary

❂ PAX West

The Labor Day weekend PAX, or Penny Arcade Expo, began in Bellevue in 2004 as a gaming exposition. It has since become a nationwide phenomenon with editions on the East Coast and even Australia. The Seattle version, or PAX West, sells out tens of thousands of tickets almost immediately every year, filling the street with costumed attendees on their way to gaming demonstrations and tournaments, panel discussions, and booths at the Washington State Convention Center downtown.

Downtown and Pioneer Square: Washington State Convention Center, 705 Pike St., http://west.paxsite.com; Labor Day weekend; badges $45-50.75 per day

FALL

Fremont Oktoberfest

Aping the fall celebrations that originated in Bavaria but are now a worldwide phenomenon, Fremont hosts a late-September beer fete in outdoor tents with hundreds of creative brews—many flavored with seasonal bounty like pumpkin—and themed food. Beer tokens come with admission, and no kids are allowed.

Fremont: 3503 Phinney Ave., 206/633-0422, http://fremontoktoberfest. com; last weekend of Sept.; $25-40

Earshot Jazz Festival

Seattle's biggest jazz event is held in performance spaces around the city including Benaroya Hall, the usual home for the symphony. The month-long festival makes a point to recognize local acts and bring in highly regarded groups for performances.

Citywide: 206/547-6763, www.earshot. org; early Oct.-early Nov.; showtimes and ticket prices vary

RECREATION

Seattle loves to get out and play. Even when the weather is iffy, there are plenty of places to enjoy the Pacific Northwest's famously fresh air. And it's an active city, so many of the city's outdoor spaces are devoted to sports.

The Burke-Gilman Trail is a paved route that cuts across Seattle, inviting cyclists to travel from Puget Sound to Lake Washington. Tucked under the interstate, I-5 Colonnade Park is a hidden web of mountain bike trails. The city's many waterways are popular for playtime, with kayakers and stand-up paddleboarders shoving off from the Ship Canal between Lake Union and Lake Washington.

Discovery Park, a former military site north of downtown Seattle, is now a 534-acre park full of walking trails, beachfront, and hidden stashes of wild berry bushes. Up on Capitol Hill, Volunteer Park takes a completely different angle on park space: It boasts manicured lawns, a museum, and an old water tower with a great view on top.

Burke-Gilman Trail

Of course, sometimes the best play is watching someone else be active. Just south of downtown, the city's two stadiums host crowds for baseball, soccer, and famously loud football games. It's not uncommon to hear the cheers through the evening air.

HIGHLIGHTS

✪ **BEST WATER-BASED TOUR:** Head out onto Elliott Bay or through the Hiram M. Chittenden Locks with **Argosy Cruises** to experience the essence of Seattle (page 165).

✪ **BEST PEEK INTO HISTORY:** The famous **Underground Tour** leads history buffs through the buried first floor of the Pioneer Square neighborhood (page 165).

✪ **BEST SHARED BACKYARD:** Somehow **Volunteer Park** manages to pack a museum, a conservatory, historic buildings, ponds, a playground, lawns, and a stage into a small urban space (page 169).

✪ **BEST URBAN BIKING:** The trails at **I-5 Colonnade Park** are short but steep, a playground for mountain bikers underneath a freeway overpass (page 169).

✪ **MOST SCENIC BIKING:** The paved **Burke-Gilman Trail** winds past marinas, parks, and historic residential blocks (page 170).

✪ **BEST FANS:** Seattle Seahawks fans set records for the loudest stadium at **CenturyLink Field,** where the fandom of "The 12s" is basically a citywide religion (page 173).

Volunteer Park

Downtown and Pioneer Square

Map 1

RECREATION

DOWNTOWN AND PIONEER SQUARE

BIKING

Seattle Cycling Tours

Hilly Seattle is rough on beginning bike riders, so this downtown-based tour company recommends a moderate skill level for most of its tours. The basic tour visits Pioneer Square, the waterfront, and South Lake Union in about 2.5 hours. It also offers longer trips to Capitol Hill (be ready for serious uphill riding) and Bainbridge Island. The tour price includes a bike and headgear (Seattle has a mandatory helmet law). The shop docs offer some bike rentals independent of its guided tours, but advanced booking is mandatory because staff often shut down the storefront, located near the Washington State Convention Center downtown, while they're out leading rides. Days and hours for tours change regularly and are listed on its website. MAP 1: 714 Pike St., 206/356-5803, www.seattle-cycling-tours.com; $59-89

TOURS

✪ Argosy Cruises

Though there are many ways to get on the water in Seattle, Argosy is the best way to get a tour by boat. The vessels travel around Elliott Bay on the Harbor Cruise and up to the Hiram M. Chittenden Locks on the Locks Cruise. There are also several other sightseeing trips on the city's lakes. A guide narrates for tour passengers, who can number in the hundreds on Argosy's larger boats. Guides supply tidbits of trivia and history, pointing out areas of interest along the waterfront. Boats go out in all weather, with multiple sailings daily. Most of the ships have a bar with snacks available for purchase. Look for a ticket booth at Pier 55. MAP 1: 1101 Alaskan Way, 206/623-1445, www.argosycruises.com; Harbor Cruise: $30.50 adults, $25.50 seniors, $16.50 children 4-12, children under 4 free

Underground Tour

✪ Underground Tour

If someone tells you a separate city exists underneath the streets of Seattle, they're not pulling your leg. The Underground Tour began in the 1960s when renovation of the Pioneer Square area revealed that the original

Argosy Cruises

165

GET OUT ON THE WATER

Seattle at times almost feels like an island, bounded as it is between Puget Sound and Lake Washington, and with Lake Union cutting a swath through the city. Fingers of water appear everywhere and bridges soar over the maritime channels that link recreational bays and industrial ports. Locals and visitors alike enjoy taking advantage of this waterfront bounty. Don't miss the chance to get out on Seattle's bodies of water somehow—from this vantage you'll get some of the best views of the city and the surrounding mountains.

Center for Wooden Boats

- **Do It All at the Center for Wooden Boats:** Here you can walk the floating docks; rent a rowboat, pedal boat, or sailboat; examine or take a free public ride on a historical schooner, steamboat, or yacht; or rent a model boat to float on a nearby pond (page 74).

- **Take a Water Taxi to West Seattle:** Commuters take Seattle's passenger-only ferries to West Seattle to bypass traffic during rush hour, but the water taxis are also a fun, cheap way for visitors to sightsee on a boat with classic city skyline views and an excuse for an excursion to this neighborhood across the bay (page 84).

- **Cruise Elliott Bay:** Argosy Cruises offers the best boat tours in town, with cruises around Elliott Bay as well as an option to add on a trip through the Hiram M. Chittenden Locks (page 165).

- **Kayak or Stand-Up Paddleboard:** Rent your own seafaring vessel at **Agua Verde Paddle Club** to explore Lake Union's placid waters, and follow up your paddle with margaritas from the club's attached café (page 171).

- **Hop a Ferry to Bainbridge Island:** It's easy to walk on this commuter ferry from downtown to take the short trip to Bainbridge Island across Puget Sound, during which you'll be treated to city views and maybe even some marinelife. And while you're here, check out the area around the ferry terminal, including some local art at the free **Bainbridge Island Museum of Art** (page 210).

first story of many buildings had been buried to stabilize the marshy tidal area. A *Seattle Times* reporter began leading people down dark stairways to the buried sidewalks and edifices. Now the tour is incredibly popular and even has an occasional adult-oriented version that points out old opium dens and red-light districts. The walking tour is fascinating, even if the underground spaces are a bit more cramped than one would imagine when they hear the phrase "buried city."

MAP 1: 608 1st Ave., 206/682-4646, www.undergroundtour.com; 9am-7pm daily; $22 adults, $20 seniors and students, $10 children 7-12, children under 7 free

Seattle Free Walking Tours

Reservations (but not payment) are required for these daily one-hour tours of Pike Place Market. Snag a ticket online ahead of time, then follow a guide who points out historic sites and tells stories about the changing downtown core of Seattle. The company recommends (but doesn't require) that customers tip, as tips are what comprise guide paychecks. The Market Experience tour comes with a few food samples and introductions to Pike Place Market vendors. It is mostly under cover and operates in most weather conditions.

MAP 1: Meeting point at Victor Steinbrueck Park, 2000 Western Ave., 425/770-6928, http://seattlefreewalkingtours.org; daily; free, tips encouraged

Queen Anne and Belltown

Map 2

PARKS

Kerry Park

For the absolute best view of the Space Needle, head to Kerry Park on Queen Anne Hill. This tiny space is known primarily for how it looms over the landmark. It fills quickly on New Year's Eve, when fireworks shoot from the top of the tower.

MAP 2: 211 W. Highland Dr., 206/684-4075, www.seattle.gov/parks; daily 24 hours

TOURS

Ride the Ducks

At one point the amphibious Duck boats were simply a goofy sight around Seattle's downtown, filled with boisterous tourists getting a look at landmarks on land before the vessels took a dip in Lake Union to see houseboats and Gas Works Park. In 2015 they became associated with a deadly crash that shut down the tour for months, but the company has quietly begun running the trips again, now with an extra staff member aboard and avoiding the busy Aurora Bridge where the accident occurred. The World War II-era vehicles are operated by drivers who are both sea captains and tour guides, and the ride is filled with jokes, props, songs, and kazoos shaped like duck lips. There's also a boarding location downtown at Westlake Center (4th Ave. and Pine St., 11am-3pm daily) with shorter operating hours. In winter, tours can wrap up for the day as early as 3pm.

MAP 2: 516 Broad St., 206/441-3825, www.ridetheducksofseattle.com; 10am-6pm Mon.-Thurs., 9:30am-6pm Fri.-Sun.; $35 adults, $32 seniors, $20 children 4-12, $5 children under 4

Ride the Ducks

South Lake Union

Map 2

PARKS

Lake Union Park

In a city of water, Lake Union is the most urban. The lake connects to the Ship Canal on its north end, linking Lake Washington to Puget Sound. Down here on its southern end, however, it's a placid bay where floatplanes take off (Kenmore Air's Lake Union terminal is just west of the park) and boats bob around the city's famous houseboat communities. Though Lake Union Park can be overrun with geese—and goose poop—it's a vibrant little green space around MOHAI and the Center for Wooden Boats. Its 12 acres, curved around the lake's narrow south end, are well landscaped with plenty of places to sit on a pretty day. However, the park doesn't have restrooms—they're only available at MOHAI during business hours. Historic boats are docked at the wharf next to the museum, and small spray fountains cool down kids on hot afternoons. The Center for Wooden Boats rents model sailboats to put on the pond built just for sailing them; the rentals are models of a real boat tied up at the center.

MAP 2: 860 Terry Ave. N, 206/684-4075, www.atlakeunionpark.org; 4am-11:30pm daily

Lake Union

Capitol Hill

Map 3

RECREATION

PARKS

✪ Volunteer Park

Green-space impresarios the Olmsted Brothers (one of whom designed Central Park, among other spaces) designed Capitol Hill's Volunteer Park—less than 50 acres, but with a little bit of everything. A stately brick water tower offers panoramic views from the top, and a glass conservatory blooms even when the weather is at its worst outside. Lawns dot the space around the Seattle Asian Art Museum, guarded by twin camel statues, and the Isamu Noguchi sculpture *Black Sun* has a keyhole view of the Space Needle.

MAP 3: 1247 15th Ave. E, 206/684-4075, www.seattle.gov/parks; 6am-10pm daily

Volunteer Park

Cal Anderson Park

The large lawns of Capitol Hill's central park are often filled with dog walkers and studying students, and the sports fields that make up its southern end usually host pickup soccer and rowdy kickball leagues. The 7.5-acre park is also crammed with paved courts (home to bike polo players and locals shooting hoops), a bathroom, a small playground, giant chess sets, and a long reflecting pool fed by a volcano-shaped fountain. Pedestrians crisscross the space, making it more of a neighborhood crossroads than a retreat. Named for a state legislator, it's often the site where students and activists gather for protests. It's well lit and busy enough to be safe into the evening, but it's generally best to avoid it in the late evening hours and especially after it closes—though there are no gates and pedestrians continue to wander through all night.

MAP 3: 1635 11th Ave., 206/684-4075, www.seattle.gov; 4am-11:30pm daily

BIKING

✪ I-5 Colonnade Park

This area under the interstate could be a total waste, but Seattle turned it into an adventure park. Billed as the first urban mountain bike skills park, it has trails for jumping and turning tricks on mountain bikes, with features including short switchbacks, a suspension bridge, and a rock chute. The area under I-5 is surprisingly airy, and the cover means the trails stay dry. The terraces and trails are beautifully made, and it's a shame the park isn't used more. After dark, the underpass becomes a lot less comfortable.

MAP 3: 1701 Lakeview Blvd. E, 206/684-4075, www.seattle.gov/parks; 4am-11:30pm daily

BIKING, BRIEFLY

What if you could rent a bike by the minute—and drop it off anywhere? Unlike many bike share programs, **LimeBike** (www.li.me) and Uber's **JUMP** (http://jump.com) aren't located at specific docking stations but literally left along sidewalks. Setting up an account is required to rent and ride. For either service, you'll need to download the app. Locate the nearest bike on the app's map, then unlock/activate it using your cell phone. Lime-Bike offers both standard ($1 per 30 min.) and electric bikes ($1 fee and $0.15 per min.), while JUMP bikes are all electric ($1 fee plus $0.10 per minute and sales tax). The downside to the convenience is that while Seattle has a bicycle helmet requirement, there are no helmet rentals available via this bike share. Users are expected to provide their own, or you can buy one from sports stores like REI. And while you may see people riding without a helmet, it's not legal and not recommended.

Ballard   Map 5

BIKING
⊗ Burke-Gilman Trail

Cars have the freeway—and every other road in Seattle—but bikes have the lengthy Burke-Gilman Trail, a paved route that stretches almost 19 miles from Ballard to Bothell. It's separate from the street except for a few select spots. Enter the trailhead at NW 45th Street and 11th Avenue NW; when it reaches Fremont it travels right along the Ship Canal, then snakes toward the University District. Eventually the trail turns into the Sammamish River Trail around NE Bothell Way and 73rd Avenue NE, in Bothell. Hardy cyclists can pedal all the way to the wineries of Woodinville, enjoying the views of Lake Washington and the culinary delights at the other end. Commuting bikers are known to buzz leisurely walkers on the path if they don't pay attention to lane markings, and children could find the trail overwhelmingly busy on summer weekends.

MAP 5: Trailhead at NW 45th St. and 11th Ave. NW, 206/684-7583, www.seattle.gov/parks; 24 hours daily

Ascent Cycles

Part of Ascent Outdoors, the Ballard Avenue biking shop has rental ($40) and demo ($120) options by the day, plus plenty of two-wheelers for sale in front of its exposed brick walls. The shop also has a good selection of cycling apparel and gear, plus a service center that does tune-ups and repair. It's one of the closest rental shops you'll find near the Burke-Gilman Trail.

MAP 5: 5221 Ballard Ave. NW, 206/403-1824, www.ascentcycles.com; 11am-7pm Mon.-Fri., 10am-6pm Sat.-Sun.; $40-120

ROCK CLIMBING
Stone Gardens

The climbing never stops at Ballard's Stone Gardens, located next to the entrance to the Hiram M. Chittenden Locks—it's open every day of the year, including Christmas and Thanksgiving. Inside, the walls go up to 65 feet high; outside walls are as much as 40 feet high. Though climbers must pass a free test to belay for each other, there are also professional belay staff for hire. Even better, the bouldering walls

forgo the need for ropes altogether. The space is a tiny maze of walls jutting every direction, and it gets busy after work and on weekends. Toward the back, a weight room fills with climbers working on specific training, and classes for every level are held throughout the week. Shoes, harnesses, and helmets are available to rent ($13).

MAP 5: 2839 NW Market St., 206/781-9828, www.stonegardens.com; 6am-11pm Mon.-Fri., 8am-10pm Sat.-Sun.; $19 adults, $14 children under 13

Stone Gardens

University District   Map 6

BIKING
Recycled Cycles

Taking the environmental side of cycling all the way, this shop has specialized in renting used bikes since 1994. That means lower prices and a relaxed atmosphere in the University District location (its Fremont shop does not rent cycles). Rentals start at $40 per day for a cruiser that's perfect on the Burke-Gilman Trail, then go up to $60 per day for a mountain bike or battery-powered pedal-assist bike, or $90 per day for a road bike. The shop also offers trailers for towing kids, and all bikes come with lock, helmet, and flat-repair kit.

MAP 6: 1007 NE Boat St., 206/547-4491, www.recycledcycles.com; 10am-7pm Mon.-Fri., 10am-6pm Sat.-Sun.; $40-90

KAYAKING AND STAND-UP PADDLEBOARDING
Agua Verde Paddle Club

Located under the waterfront Mexican restaurant of the same name, Agua Verde rents the toys you need to get out on the waters of Lake Union. Kayaks start at $18 per hour, with doubles available, and stand-up paddleboards are $23 per hour. Both are beginner-friendly ways to ride the calm waters here; the wake from a slow motorboat is the only likely disturbance you'll encounter if you stay close to shore, though Lake Washington can be a bit choppier. The club also offers occasional guided kayak tours ($55-65) of the arboretum or houseboat areas of Lake Union; these must be reserved in advance on the club's website.

THE CITY'S OUTER PARKS

the lighthouse at Discovery Park

Though downtown Seattle doesn't have any major parks, the city's favorite outdoor spaces aren't far away.

DISCOVERY PARK

Located in the Magnolia neighborhood northwest of the central core, **Discovery Park** (3801 Discovery Park Blvd., 206/386-4236, www.seattle.gov/parks; 4am-11:30pm daily) occupies a sprawling 534 acres on the former grounds of the Fort Lawton army base. Miles of trails traverse giant lawns and sections of thick forest, a favorite for the abundant blackberry bushes during summer. Bluffs overlook Puget Sound, and there are two miles of beachfront strewn with driftwood. A **visitors center** (8:30am-5pm Tues.-Sun.) has information on how to explore the area. Don't miss the picturesque, squat West Point lighthouse that dates back to 1881.

GREEN LAKE PARK

Green Lake Park (7201 E. Greenlake Dr. N, 206/684-4075, www.seattle.gov/parks; 24 hours daily), located in a neighborhood also called Green Lake, is a recreation hub. A path almost three miles long loops around the urban lake and is incredibly popular with walkers, joggers, baby stroller-pushers, and dog walkers. There are basketball courts and a wading pool, even a place to rent kayaks and stand-up paddleboards. Though the water looks crisp and clean, the lake is known for its algae blooms—check for signs that note closures. On sunny days, expect the green lawns and shady spots around the lake to be chock-full of relaxing locals.

GOLDEN GARDENS

Located on the northwest side of Ballard, **Golden Gardens** (8498 Seaview Pl. NW, 206/684-4075, www.seattle.gov/parks; 6am-11:30pm daily) is barbecue central, and on summer evenings the smell of hot dogs and hamburgers drifts from every picnic shelter and table. The beach offers a beautiful view of Puget Sound, and orcas have been known to pop up just offshore. The water is cold year-round, and swimmers also battle sound currents and boat traffic—so most visitors just hang on the beach. However, the sand isn't kind to bare feet—between fire cinders and the occasional cigarette, it's more a shoes-on kind of beach. Fire pits are located at the north end of the park, near the renovated bathhouse that hosts many a wedding in summer months. There's also a small snack bar and an off-leash area for pets.

CARKEEK PARK

Though located deep in a residential area, waterfront **Carkeek Park** (950 NW Carkeek Park Rd., 206/684-0877, www.seattle.gov/parks; 6am-10pm daily) appeals to every kind of kid. Train-loving youngsters enjoy the footbridge that crosses the railroad tracks and cargo trains that often lumber by. On one side of the crossing is a stretch of beach for rock-throwing and exploring, while uphill is the oldest orchard in Seattle, a number of short trails through the woods and wetlands, and an elaborate playground. One play structure is a salmon-shaped slide that begins in the fish's mouth.

MAP 6: 1303 NE Boat St., 206/545-8570, www.aguaverde.com; 11am-7pm Mon.-Fri., 10am-7pm Sat., 10am-6pm Sun.; $18-23

SPORTS ARENAS
Husky Stadium

The University of Washington's football team is so popular that during home games, street parking is taken for miles around. Parts of the 70,000-person-capacity stadium date back to 1920, but the entire structure was renovated in 2012. It opens on one side to Lake Washington, allowing boaters and kayakers to inch up close to the games. Some seats are partially covered, but it hosts a lot of wet fans during the fall football season. Single-game tickets go on sale in August, but the high number of season ticket holders means that they're not cheap and sell out quickly. The light rail, which now ends close by, is the best way to reach the stadium for events.

MAP 6: 3800 Montlake Blvd. NE, 206/543-2200, www.gohuskies.com; $25-320

International District and SoDo
Map 7

SPORTS ARENAS
✪ CenturyLink Field

Otherwise known as "The Clink," this open-topped stadium can seat 67,000 fans for a Seattle Seahawks (www.seahawks.com) football game—generating noise so intense that it registers on the Richter scale. Getting tickets to watch the Super Bowl-winning team is no easy task; the waiting list for season tickets is long and individual game seats don't come cheap (from $120). But during the spring, summer, and even into fall, The Clink is also home to the Seattle Sounders soccer club (www.soundersfc.com), a relatively new team in Major League Soccer that is quite beloved by its many rabid fans (and its games are easier to attend). An enthusiastic marching band leads a mini parade into the stadium before the match begins, drawing attendees out of the surrounding sports bars so they can stream into the stands. Tours (daily summer, Fri.-Sun. fall-spring; $14 adults, $10 seniors, $8 children 5-11, children under 5 free) are 90 minutes long and offer a history of Seattle sports and visits to several scenic viewpoints around the stadium.

MAP 7: 800 Occidental Ave. S, http://centurylinkfield.com

Safeco Field

The Seattle Mariners are a scrappy baseball team, long loved by their city despite never having won a World Series. They play in a stadium with a retractable roof, meaning it's fairly dry when it rains and glorious when the sun comes out. Safeco's food and drink selection is well known to be top-shelf, with elegant salmon dishes, signature garlic fries served with apple slices, and food stands from celebrity chefs. The beers are mostly local craft brews, though no less expensive than what

CenturyLink Field

you'll find at any other major league ballpark. During the game, look for the signature hydroplane boat race animation on the big screen. Tickets are often available at the walk-up window on game days and start around $25. Hour-long tours ($12 adults, $11 seniors, $10 children) are available most days when there isn't a day game; they include a visit to the press box and owner's suite, among other locations.

MAP 7: 1250 1st Ave. S, http://seattle. mariners.mlb.com

SHOPS

Who says Seattle doesn't have style? It's a common joke, what with all the polar fleece and hiking boots worn on the street. But there is also a quirky sophistication on display, with local designers incorporating outdoorsiness into attractive pieces.

Fran's Chocolates

Most boutiques feature makers from around the Pacific Northwest, embracing artisans who repurpose natural or recycled materials into jewelry or decor. Chat with staff about their relationship to the brands; you might learn the story of how a piece was created. Gifts and clothes don't come cheap, but these stores offer quality goods that support local labor.

The city's two favorite things to buy are outdoor gear and books. The flagship REI store is merely one of many places to indulge in down jackets and portable kayaks. A number of local brands cater to the hiking, camping, running, and fishing demographic, including Outdoor Research, Brooks, and Evo. Don't be intimidated—you can wear their technical clothing on the street in Seattle and fit in perfectly.

The city is also dotted with bookstores: places to stock up on old-fashioned paper books and magazines as well as hang out and connect with the community. The aisles of The Elliott Bay Book Company represent Capitol Hill's artsy, political character, while the family hangout vibe of Third Place Books fits the quieter Ravenna neighborhood near the University of Washington. At Amazon's brick-and-mortar bookstore, there are books on the shelves but tech-first e-readers on display, too.

HIGHLIGHTS

✪ **BEST SHOPPING DISTRICT:** Wander the boutiques of **Ballard Avenue** for eclectic gifts and Pacific Northwest-chic clothing (page 177).

✪ **BEST PLACE TO GET LOST:** Old-fashioned paper maps might seem quaint, but **Metsker Maps** bookshop reminds shoppers how artful a simple map can be (page 177).

✪ **BEST DRESSED:** All the clothing at **Endless Knot** has a slightly vintage vibe though every piece is brand new (page 183).

✪ **BEST PLACE TO EMBRACE THE OUTDOORS:** Find down jackets, technical gear, and friendly service aplenty at South Lake Union's **Feathered Friends,** a quintessential Seattle store (page 184).

✪ **BEST SCIENTIFIC DISCOVERY:** The airy, lovely decor of **Ada's Technical Books and Café** proves that science can be beautiful (page 185).

✪ **MOST INDEPENDENT SPIRIT: The Elliott Bay Book Company** exemplifies the neighborhood bookstore with events, thorough stock, and the best recommendation shelf in the city (page 185).

✪ **BEST MALL FOR MALL-HATERS:** The artsy gifts and artisanal foods for sale at **Melrose Market** make shopping feel like a local adventure (page 187).

✪ **BEST SHOP TO FIND YOUR INNER CHILD:** A gag is always afoot at Fremont's famous joke shop, **Archie McPhee,** a celebration of the kid in all of us (page 188).

✪ **BEST FARMERS MARKET:** At the weekly **Ballard Farmers Market,** crowds come to buy produce, meat, prepared foods, and crafts (page 190).

✪ **MOST MUSICAL TREASURES:** Find a gem of an album from the half-million records in stock at **Bop Street Records** (page 191).

✪ **MOST SPECIFIC STORE:** There's only one thing sold at **Glassybaby**—a votive glass candleholder made in a multitude of colors (page 193).

✪ **BEST HIGH-END MALL:** At the outdoor **University Village,** splash out at such retailers as Apple, Jonathan Adler, and Room & Board (page 194).

✪ **BIGGEST ASIAN MARKETPLACE:** In the International District is **Uwajimaya,** where the proprietors stock more than just standard groceries—browse the selection of spices, sakes, gifts, and books (page 194).

SHOPPING DISTRICTS

Pioneer Square

Head down 1st Avenue where it transitions from downtown proper to Pioneer Square. You'll find gift and home design stores scattered among art galleries and restaurants.

MAP 1: 1st Ave. between Spring St. and S. Jackson St.

Pike-Pine Corridor

Though there are indie shops scattered all over Capitol Hill, the greatest concentration is just south of Cal Anderson Park, anchored by The Elliott Bay Book Company. High fashion and earthy home design shops populate the blocks around this area, known as the Pike-Pine Corridor, plus a record store for good measure.

MAP 3: 10th Ave. between Pike St. and Pine St.

✪ Ballard Avenue

There is no better collection of boutiques and small-scale retail than Ballard Avenue, where the ethos of the Ballard Farmers Market (handmade, local, and sustainable) is present for the entire week.

MAP 5: Ballard Ave. between NW Market St. and 17th Ave. NW

Downtown and Pioneer Square Map 1

BOOKS

✪ Metsker Maps

It's worth getting lost in Metsker Maps, a travel store with enough inspiration for several trips around the world. Besides a selection of travel books and folded maps representing every corner of the globe, the store specializes in map art, including gorgeous woodcut charts of the Salish Sea. It's one of the few places in town to buy a detailed topographical map for outdoor adventures, and the store also sells the parking passes needed for state and national park and forest access. The bookshelves include a significant local section, and it's an ideal spot for finding books tailored to, say, traveling the Pacific Northwest with a dog or by bicycle. One corner of the midsize store is devoted to map and globe art, with prints that turn any run-of-the-mill office into a distinguished study.

MAP 1: 1511 1st Ave., 206/623-8747, www.metskers.com; 9am-8pm Mon.-Fri., 10am-8pm Sat., 10am-6pm Sun.

Arundel Bookstore

The charming Arundel Bookstore is a sweet store in Pioneer Square that is dedicated to the printed word. It specializes in art and rare books and also runs a publishing operation so

Metsker Maps

small that it uses a hand-cranked press (not visible in the store, unfortunately). Unlike the city's bigger independent booksellers, there aren't usually crowds in the small spot, though the space marked by exposed brick walls and two-story bookshelves fills during occasional evening music or poetry performances.

MAP 1: 212 1st Ave. S, 206/624-4442, www.arundelbookstores.com; 11am-7pm daily

Barnes & Noble

Though it doesn't have the indie spirit of local bookstores, downtown's chain bookstore offers a large selection in a basement space (though there's one entrance on the street level). It's one of the only spots to buy DVDs and CDs in downtown Seattle, and it has both a café and large children's section. Tables on the street level display local travel books and guides, and the store hosts regular readings and story time.

MAP 1: 600 Pine St., 206/264-0156, http://barnesandnoble.com; 9am-9pm Mon.-Thurs., 9am-10pm Fri.-Sat., 10am-9pm Sun.

Globe Bookstore

In what's slowly become a kind of bookstore district in Pioneer Square, the Globe is a cozy little hole-in-the-wall lined with shelves of new and used books, and up a steep staircase there are vintage trade paperbacks on the 2nd floor. There's also a well-curated but small children's section. It's a tiny shop, but a good place to pass a little time on a rainy day or pick up a postcard to send home.

MAP 1: 218 1st Ave. S, 206/682-6882, www.seattlemystery.com; 11am-6pm daily

CLOTHING
Baby & Company

Downtown boutique Baby & Company has carried the torch for Seattle women's fashion since the 1970s, stocking quirky brands that defy the city's fleece-and-hiking boots reputation. The name is a bit misleading: This is style for the mature, cutting-edge woman (though there are some men's styles, too). The feel is one part bohemian, one part urban chic, all brought together in a glistening white space decorated with palm fronds.

MAP 1: 1936 1st Ave., 206/448-4077, www.babyandco.us; 10am-6pm Mon.-Sat., noon-5pm Sun.

Diva Dollz

Diva Dollz

Diva Dollz, in Pioneer Square, is a different kind of throwback, where pinup and rockabilly-style dresses create '60s silhouettes. Here, the clothes are new, but the aesthetic is vintage. The crowded store is an explosion of cherry patterns and polka dots, and the attentive salespeople have retro shoes handy to bring out the full effect of the dresses. It's not hard to imagine Bettie Page rocking these frocks—when she wore clothes at all, that is.

MAP 1: 624 1st Ave., 206/652-2299, www.divadollz.com; noon-6pm daily

ACCESSORIES
Goorin Brothers Hat Shop

There may not be many occasions in Seattle that call for a fancy chapeau from Goorin Brothers Hat Shop, but the staff specializes in personal service and fittings. There's a range of toppers, from deerstalkers straight out of Sherlock Holmes to packable straw summer hats. The store has the cozy feel of a Victorian haberdasher. Learn the difference between a cloche and a fedora, or pick up feathered pins to add flair to your favorite hat.

MAP 1: 1610 1st Ave., 206/443-8082, www.goorin.com; 10am-7pm Mon.-Thurs., 10am-8pm Fri.-Sat., 11am-7pm Sun.

GIFT AND HOME
Fireworks Gallery

If this store looks familiar, it might be because there's an outpost of the chain in Sea-Tac Airport. The windows here in the Westlake Mall location are lit with the paper lamps stocked by the store, the light reflecting on the exposed brick and piles of playful home items inside. Originally an art gallery that featured work from local artists, Fireworks leans toward the colorful and the quirky, with plenty of purses and statement jewelry pieces alongside clever notecards and goofy gag gifts. There's a good-sized children's section, including lots of baby onesies in animal prints and several Seahawks-themed outfits. It's nearly impossible to enter any of the seven locations without finding a gift for someone, and there's a persistent sense of fun that makes it an ideal browsing shop.

MAP 1: 400 Pine St., 206/682-6462, www.fireworksgallery.net, 10am-8pm Mon.-Sat., 11am-6pm Sun.

Sur La Table

With all the great food for sale in Pike Place Market, it's no surprise a cooking store opened up here. Born in an old speakeasy space downtown in 1972, Sur La Table moved into the market in 1980 and has since grown to a chain of more than 100 stores. This flagship shop is crammed with kitchenware from lowly spatulas to state-of-the-art mixers. In-store demos show off just how to use all the fancy tools, a coffee bar allows tastes from the espresso machines, and an in-store knife sharpening station keeps cleavers at their best.

MAP 1: 84 Pine St., 206/448-2244, www.surlatable.com; 9am-6:30pm daily

Tenzing Momo

Rich smells waft out of this herbal market next to Pike Place Market, leading shoppers to shelves of incense, herbs, and oils. The wares kept in the rows of glass jars come from Western, Chinese, and ayurvedic traditions. The store carries more than just the raw materials for herbalists; it has natural beauty products like lotions and soaps, plus books, Eastern prayer flags and materials, and gifts. The store has been open for more than four decades and regularly hosts tarot readers instore, who'll do a reading for a fee.

MAP 1: 93 Pike St., No. 203, 206/623-9837, www.tenzingmomo.com; 10am-6pm Mon.-Sat., 10am-5pm Sun.

Watson Kennedy Fine Home

There are gifts galore in Watson Kennedy Fine Home, but you'll likely be tempted to shop for yourself among the vintage-style glassware, framed art, and fine treats. Local touches can be seen in the variety of Fran's

Watson Kennedy Fine Home

Chocolates (a Seattle brand favored by President Obama) and weathered signs listing ferry destinations around Puget Sound. Everything smells good inside the store, thanks to the number of fragrant home products sold here. Service is slow but thorough: Don't be in a hurry when you ask for your purchase to be gift wrapped. The shop attracts a mix of tourists and locals on their lunch breaks looking to buy the perfect housewarming gift. Look for a smaller shop that focuses on body and bath products inside the market, at 86 Pine Street.

MAP 1: 1022 1st Ave., 206/652-8350, www.watsonkennedy.com; 10am-6pm Mon.-Sat., noon-5pm Sun.

HANDICRAFTS
Glasshouse Studio

Seattle is known for its glassblowing art scene, with Dale Chihuly as its most famous hometown artist. Pioneer Square's Glasshouse Studio, open since 1971, is the oldest spot for glass art in the region, and here you can watch experts heat glass to a molten state before manipulating it into shapes. The gallery displays finished platters, chandeliers, paperweights, vases, and other pieces, while the hot shop next door sees the artists give regular demonstrations Monday-Saturday and occasionally on Sundays.

MAP 1: 311 Occidental Ave. S, 206/682-9939, www.glasshouse-studio.com; 10am-5pm Mon.-Sat., 11am-4pm Sun.

GOURMET GOODIES
Beecher's

At Pike Place Market, local cheesemonger Beecher's offers a glimpse at its curds, whey, and giant metal mixers in the flagship store's signature cheddar assembly line. The Seattle brand has lately grown to have national reach, with stores opening in New York City and Wisconsin. The triangular wedges of cheddar are by far the most popular, though a Jamaican jack cheese named "No Woman" after the famous Bob Marley song is also a big seller. Though the cheese displays are large, the lines for prepared foods—mac and cheese especially—take up more space. If you're just looking for something to go, you can likely bypass the hordes of market tourists that wind through the store.

MAP 1: Pike Place Market, 1600 Pike Pl., 206/956-1964, www.beechershandmadecheese.com; 9am-7pm daily

Beecher's

DeLaurenti

As one corner of the mighty Pike Place Market, DeLaurenti has a prime location for its fine-food wares. A long cheese and meat counter sits toward the back, while prepared deli foods up front cause out-the-door lines to form at lunchtime. The shelves of the gourmet grocery are lined with European and global products, with an emphasis on the tastes of Italy—picture tons of high-end chocolate bars next to stacks of canned tomatoes, in a store where olive oil gets its own wall. It's hard to resist buying something to eat immediately. Head up the steps to a wine room that hosts tastings.

MAP 1: 1435 1st Ave., 206/622-0141, www.delaurenti.com; 9am-6pm Mon.-Sat., 10am-5pm Sun.

Fran's Chocolates

President Obama is reportedly a fan of this chocolate shop, having once ordered boxes for himself (or Michelle). Its downtown store, occupying a prime position across from the Seattle Art Museum, is a sparse, modern space where shopping for chocolates feels akin to buying art from an exclusive gallery. The signature pieces are salted caramels topped with gray or smoked salt, and truffles made with smooth, rich chocolate. The chocolates come in elegant boxes and serve well as gifts. The price point is high—boxes of caramels are as high as $220, and a seven-piece box starts at $15.

MAP 1: 1325 1st Ave., 206/682-0168, www.franschocolates.com; 9:30am-7:30pm Mon.-Sat., 11am-6pm Sun.

Pure Food Fish Market

The flying fish at Pike Fish Market aren't the only marine life in town. The Pure Food stand, located just a few steps south inside Pike Place Market, has many of the same favorites for sale—Alaskan salmon and halibut, Dungeness crab legs, and plump shrimp. The smoked salmon comes in alderwood, garlic-pepper, candied, and teriyaki varieties. This market stall, with the requisite bins of ice lined with open-mouthed fish and piles of shellfish, is almost always less crowded than the stall with the flying fish, with staff who have a little more time to answer questions about shipping the fish overnight or turning them into summertime barbecue skewers. They sell canned fish and boxed smoked salmon for easy travel.

MAP 1: 1511 Pike Pl., 206/622-5765, www.freshseafood.com; 7am-6pm Mon.-Sat., 7am-5pm Sun.

BEST SOUVENIRS

You can expect to come home from Seattle with tired feet from all your explorations, a million photos, and plans to return. But for physical souvenirs, look for the region's signature foods, or hunt down a unique piece of art.

COFFEE

Coffee culture was born in the Emerald City, and you can bring ground or whole beans home by the pound from many cafés. The Pike Place Special Reserve blend is sold only at the Pike Place Market's "original" **Starbucks** (page 61), not at any other of the chain's 27,000-plus locations. But you can also find special offerings to take home from small, local coffee roasters like **Cherry Street Coffee** (page 94) and **Fremont Coffee Company** (page 115).

GLASSWORKS

The Pacific Northwest is a great place to find glass treasures. Find hand-blown items in the museum gift shop at **Chihuly Garden and Glass** (page 71) or in Pioneer Square's **Glasshouse Studio** (page 180). Look to Fremont's **Glassybaby** (page 193) for a perfectly travel-sized votive holder made of sparkling glass. (Forget to make the trip to the shop? Sea-Tac Airport has a Glassybaby outpost on Concourse A.)

SMOKED SALMON

While the salmon may soar at Pike Place Market, packing fresh fish in your suitcase is not advised. To bring a taste of Seattle seafood home, look for packaged smoked salmon in the souvenir shops that surround Pike Place Market. Several are near the intersection of 1st Avenue and Pike Street, including **Pure Food Fish Market** (page 181). Smoked salmon is shelf-stable and easy to transport.

DEPARTMENT STORES

Nordstrom

The downtown Nordstrom serves as both the shopping chain's flagship and the city's retail anchor. The store's roots are in shoe sales: Back in the 19th century, Swedish immigrant John Nordstrom made his fortune in the Alaska gold rush and used the proceeds to open a shoe store in downtown Seattle. The giant has since grown to include high-end clothing, jewelry, and makeup. Some days a piano player serenades shoppers as they glide up and down the store's escalators. A lounge offers small gourmet bites and cocktails, and a recent remodel to the historic downtown building increased the amount of sunlight that reaches the sales floors; the owners aimed for an impressive experience like what you'd find in Paris's Galeries Lafayette. Anyone priced out of the main store can head underground next door to **Nordstrom Rack** (400 Pine St., 206/448-8522, 9:30am-9pm Mon.-Fri., 10am-9pm Sat., 10am-7pm Sun.). The outlet for the department chain has heavily discounted high fashion and rows of shoes on sale.

MAP 1: 500 Pine St., 206/628-2111, http://shop.nordstrom.com; 9:30am-9pm Mon.-Fri., 10am-9pm Sat., 10:30am-7pm Sun.

Queen Anne and Belltown

Map 2

SHOPS

QUEEN ANNE AND BELLTOWN

CLOTHING
✪ Endless Knot
Though this women's wear boutique isn't big, it offers plenty of vintage-style and colorful print dresses that serve as both attire and souvenir of a fashionable vacation. The store also sells an array of jewelry and purses, plus high-end hooded sweatshirts from Prairie Underground, a local company.
MAP 2: 2300 1st Ave., 206/448-0355, www.endlessknotseattle.com; 10am-7pm Mon.-Sat., 10am-6pm Sun.

Endless Knot

Alhambra
This women's clothing boutique is all about mature style, but not in the boring sense of the word. There's a boho feeling to the loose blouses and flowered prints, though the high quality of materials in the casual wear leads to high price tags. The store itself, with its palm decor and carved wooden displays, feels like a tropical retreat, and the staff greets customers with hot tea. On Saturdays, the shop brings in jazz musicians to give the boutique an even livelier feel.
MAP 2: 2127 1st Ave., 206/621-9571, www.alhambrastyle.com; 10am-6:30pm Mon.-Sat., 11:30am-5pm Sun.

BOOKS
Mercer Street Books
This small used bookstore has all the charm of an indie seller, right down to the walls crowded with framed posters and bookshelves topped with tchotchkes. There's no real specialty, just secondhand books and the chance to trade in a finished read for a new one. Service is non-cloying, a welcome style for a tiny shop, and it's an easy walk from Seattle Center.
MAP 2: 7 Mercer St., 206/282-7687, www.mercerstreetusedbooks.com; noon-8pm Mon.-Sat., 11am-7pm Sun.

MUSIC
Singles Going Steady
Look for the blue-and-red neon sign to find this small punk-first record shop, where knowledgeable salespeople jump at the chance to chat with music fiends looking for something specific—like, say, the Buzzcocks album from whence the store takes its name. Anyone not already well versed in the world of used vinyl and local bands might find it a little too niche.
MAP 2: 2219 2nd Ave., 206/441-7396; noon-6pm Sun.-Mon., noon-7pm Tues.-Thurs., noon-8pm Fri.-Sat.

South Lake Union

Map 2

OUTDOOR EQUIPMENT

✪ Feathered Friends

Though just a fraction of the size of REI across the street, this local shop is much more traditionally Seattle than its behemoth neighbor, beloved by a subset of Seattle outdoorspeople, particularly ones who venture to very cold spots. The company produces down blankets, down jackets, and down sleeping bags, even custom making down suits for explorers venturing up K2 or Mount Everest. The shop is also a retailer for outdoor clothing, backpacks, and some climbing gear, and the staff is reliably friendly and knowledgeable.

the REI flagship store

MAP 2: 263 Yale Ave. N, 206/292-2210, www.featheredfriends.com; 9am-7pm Mon.-Wed., 9am-8pm Thurs.-Fri., 10am-6pm Sat., 11am-5pm Sun.

REI

The outdoor store whose official name is Recreational Equipment, Inc. is still a co-op, as it was when it was founded by a group of Seattle hikers trying to get a decent price on imported climbing gear—only now it's supersized, with locations around the country. The flagship store's rock climbing wall, stone fireplace, and mini outdoor bike route allow customers to really test the merchandise, and counters within the store sell recreation passes, tune skis, fit backpacks, and rent equipment. You don't have to be a member to purchase something, though anyone who pays the one-time membership fee will get a 10 percent rebate—the "dividend"—back at the end of the year. The store is largely dedicated to lifestyle clothing and camping equipment that doubles as backyard picnic gear, but it is still the city's bigger outdoor outfitter. Head to the 2nd floor to find a trove of cheaper used gear, and check out the online schedule for free and fee-based workshops on hiking, biking, and camping.

MAP 2: 222 Yale Ave. N, 206/223-1944, www.rei.com; 9am-9pm Mon.-Sat., 10am-7pm Sun.

BOOKS

✪ Ada's Technical Books and Café

Walking into the old house that holds Ada's, it's hard to imagine anyone could find science anything but beautiful. The store was named for Ada Lovelace, the daughter of Lord Byron and a pioneer in computing; the space seems to marry the best of their poetic and mathematic genes. In a space that used to be a shabby used bookstore, there are shelves of fiction, nonfiction, science fiction, kids, and programming books, a café with surprisingly hearty offerings (and wine), cool model and experimentation kits and gifts, and displays explaining the store's many book clubs.

MAP 3: 425 15th Ave. E, 206/322-1058, www.seattletechnicalbooks.com; 8am-9pm daily

Ada's Technical Books and Cafe

✪ The Elliott Bay Book Company

In literate Seattle, The Elliott Bay Book Company is practically a church. Readers gather among bookshelves, in the café, or in a basement reading room that fills almost daily for names big and small. This is the kind of indie bookstore where the staff recommendations are spot-on and the café seats are a hot commodity. Dogs are welcome inside.

MAP 3: 1521 10th Ave., 206/624-6600, www.elliottbaybook.com; 10am-10pm Mon.-Thurs., 10am-11pm Fri.-Sat., 10am-9pm Sun.

GIFT AND HOME

Isla House + Flower

The fresh smell of flowers coming from this small shop, next to an ice cream parlor, is a sign of how delightful it is inside. Though flower arrangements are the main draw, the shop's shelves also feature gifts, cards, and darling receptacles and vessels for potted plants. Garden and plant lovers will be charmed by this sunny little store.

MAP 3: 919 E. Pine St., 206/618-5999, http://islahouseandflower.com; 11am-7pm Mon. and Wed.-Sat., 11am-5pm Sun.

ADULT

Babeland

Seattle is known for progressive politics, including some of the first same-sex marriage and legal marijuana laws in the country, and its shopping has the same reputation. The open-minded, sex-positive Babeland purports to be a sex toy shop without sleaze, one that resembles a high-end clothing boutique. Opened in 1993 to address the need for women-centered sex stores, it still has bubblegum-pink touches that stress the ladies-first attitude. The store's staff pride themselves on being nonjudgmental, friendly, and knowledgeable about the merchandise, and there are regular workshops to teach the basics of bondage or "sexy manicures."

MAP 3: 707 E. Pike St., 206/328-2914, www.babeland.com; 11am-10pm Mon.-Thurs., 11am-11pm Fri.-Sat., noon-8pm Sun.

CLOTHING
Freeman
Though this men's store is located on Broadway, it's part of a block where the street transitions from being the main thoroughfare to just another small neighborhood street. The owners, the Freemans, started their line of rain jackets in 2010 with a vintage-style slicker with a plaid lining that comes in bright primary colors. They've since expanded to make flannel shirts, vests, and T-shirts, some with retro pennant designs. The store also carries a number of American-made brands, all high-end men's products with a simple but throwback feel. To find the shop, look along a cottage-style row of small boutiques.

MAP 3: 713 Broadway E, 206/327-9932, www.freemanseattle.com; 11am-6pm Mon. and Wed.-Sat., 11am-5pm Sun.

Totokaelo
In a stylish, vast space, the wares of Totokaelo get a chance to breathe. The menswear, women's wear, and home furnishings are so fashionable that the local store has more customers in New York City than in Seattle. Clothing is mostly monochromatic, draping

The Elliott Bay Book Company

customers in bold and modern styles crafted from high-end black or white fabrics. The store peddles big-name designers not often seen elsewhere in Seattle, like Maison Margiela and Jil Sander.

MAP 3: 1523 10th Ave., 206/623-3582, www.totokaelo.com; 11am-6pm Mon.-Thurs., 11am-7pm Fri.-Sat., 11am-5pm Sun.

GOURMET GOODIES
✪ Melrose Market

There are two options at Melrose Market: Buy meats and cheeses for a picnic or meal at home, or order food from the handful of restaurants and takeout counters that occupy this large, airy brick building. The historic structure has stood in this corner spot since the 1920s, but it also boasts a modern feel, with large windows and exposed beams. The indoor market houses more eateries than actual market stalls, and the home stores and the fish market with exterior entrances are generally considered part of the complex. Grab oysters to grill on the barbecue from Taylor Shellfish Farms, a tenant of this indie version of Pike Place Market.

MAP 3: 1501-1535 Melrose Ave., 206/568-2666, www.melrosemarketseattle.com; hours vary by business

Sugarpill

This small Capitol Hill shop calls itself a mercantile, selling foodie gifts like flavored chocolates and jams and the kind of salts that make an impressive gift. It's also an apothecary where customers can find remedies in the form of herbs, spices, teas, and lotions. The herbalist behind the counter is the real resource, good at matching people to cures, or at least treatments that are gentle and natural.

MAP 3: 900 E. Pine St., 206/322-7455, www.sugarpillseattle.com; 11am-6pm Mon.-Sat., 11am-4pm Sun.

VINTAGE
Throwbacks Northwest

Vintage shopping doesn't always have to mean '60s dresses and yellow leisure suits. Throwbacks specializes in vintage sports gear, like Starter jackets and baseball hats. You can find a 1985 World Series crewneck (the year the two Missouri teams played) or various Air Jordan sneakers, vintage jerseys, or shirts from local sports teams that you won't see on every other fan at the sports bar. The store also sells its wares online, but it's worth the trip for the charm of the sports memorabilia and old-school decor.

MAP 3: 1205 E. Pike St., 206/402-4855, http://throwbacksnw.com; 11am-7pm daily

SHOPS

FREMONT

CLOTHING
Les Amis

Fremont's home for fashion with minimal sparkle but maximum elegance has been around for more than two decades. Expect to find classic pieces at high prices, the kind of sweaters or skirts you keep for a lifetime. Located in an old wooden building lined with flowering trees outside, it has the feeling of a charming forest cottage.
MAP 4: 3420 Evanston Ave. N, 206/632-2877, www.lesamis-inc.com; 11am-6pm Mon. and Wed.-Sat., 11am-5pm Sun.

Show Pony

To look the part in indie, expressive Fremont, look to this boutique full of print dresses and vintage-style T-shirts that announce "Ladies Love Outlaws" or "Born to Run." The style is meant for a semi-country, semi-retro woman who likes to combine prints and quirky jewelry. Keep an eye out for the shop dog.
MAP 4: 702 N. 35th St, 206/706-4188, www.showponyboutique.com, 11am-7pm Mon.-Sat., 11am-5pm Sun.

BOOKS
The Book Larder

The center of this cookbook shop is a demonstration kitchen, complete with white tile wall and large wooden counters for cooking demos. The surrounding white bookshelves are lined with cookbooks old and new, including some vintage titles that are more than a century old. It's as much a community event space as a shop, hosting free author talks, plus cooking classes helpfully scheduled around lunchtime.

It's a small space, but foodies will want to stay awhile.
MAP 4: 4252 Fremont Ave. N, 206/397-4271, www.booklarder.com; 11am-6pm Mon.-Fri., 11am-5pm Sat., noon-4pm Sun.

The Book Larder

Outsider Comics and Geek Boutique

The blossoming and mainstreaming of geek culture may be a national phenomenon, but Seattle and its techy population may've been ground zero for the celebration of all things geek. This store sells tabletop games and gifts ideal for those who self-identify as nerds. And of course there are comics. Outsider aims to serve female and LGBT populations often ignored by mainstream comic shops, so there's an inclusive, friendly vibe.
MAP 4: 223 N. 36th St., 206/535-8886, www.outsidercomics.com; noon-8pm Mon.-Thurs., noon-9pm Fri., 10am-9pm Sat., 10am-7pm Sun.

TOYS AND NOVELTIES
✪ Archie McPhee

If you've ever needed a rubber chicken, or just thought that rubber chickens represented the height of modern humor, then novelty shop Archie McPhee is a must-do. The shop began as a mail-order business, issuing colorful catalogs hawking whoopee cushions and fake fingers. With its red exterior and yellow trim, this Wallingford store, located just east of Fremont, is like a brick-and-mortar version of a circus tent. Inside are bins and shelves of every item imaginable, like wind-up chattering teeth, moustache bandages, and adult coloring books. Up front there's an entire bathtub of plastic octopus arms (labeled with strict instructions not to climb in). Here, two dollars of allowance money will go a long way. At Halloween time, Archie McPhee is a popular costume destination, but it also stocks horse masks year-round. A skeletal "Wallingford Beast" in a small diorama is a nod to the P. T. Barnum school of amusement. Archie McPhee brings out the goofball in everyone.

MAP 4: 1300 N. 45th St., 206/297-0240, http://archiemcpheeseattle.com; 10am-8pm Mon.-Sat., 11am-7pm Sun.

OUTDOOR EQUIPMENT
Brooks Trailhead

Though the Brooks brand is common in running stores nationwide, the running-shoe retailer has only one dedicated physical retail store. The Trailhead, as the shop on the ground floor of the Fremont headquarters is called, is a rainbow of sporty footwear, decorated with floor murals and a wall of shoelaces. The Skee-Ball in the corner is meant for customers only, but staff will tempt you into making a shoe purchase with treadmills available for running analysis. Joggers who stop by mid-run will find a water station near the entrance.

MAP 4: 3400 Stone Way N, 206/858-5700, www.brooksrunning.com; 10am-7pm Mon.-Sat., 10am-6pm Sun.

Evo

Though Seattle's outdoor retail industry is dominated by REI, Evo has quickly become an indie alternative to the downtown giant. Begun as a website in 2001 by an Oregon skier, it has become a small empire, with a flagship store in Fremont that has an art gallery space and an indoor skate park next door. Ski gear takes over most of the store in winter, but there are also skateboarding and biking areas, plus lots of the lifestyle wear that Seattle residents wear whether they're playing outdoors or not. Prices are cheaper on the company's online outlet, but the two-story space is much more pleasant for browsing.

MAP 4: 3500 Stone Way N, 206/973-4470, www.evo.com/seattle; 11am-7pm Sun.-Thurs., 10am-8pm Fri.-Sat.

MiiR

Though best known for water bottles beloved by cyclists, MiiR is actually a hybrid company whose Fremont flagship is one part store, one part coffee shop/gathering place. The brand's hard-sided tumblers, growlers, camp cups, and food canisters—ideal for bringing, say, hot soup on a bike ride—line the shelves, and a counter sells food, beer, and java. Located near Evo, it has the same hip, sleek outdoorsy style.

MAP 4: 3400 Stone Way N, 206/566-7207, www.miir.com; 7am-9pm Mon.-Fri., 8am-9pm Sat., 8am-8pm Sun.

CLOTHING AND ACCESSORIES

Monster Art and Clothing

While most of Ballard strives for sophistication, the wares at this small shop are a little kookier. Its racks are filled with graphic T-shirts and dresses printed with illustrated octopuses or dueling narwhals. There's a whole wall of colorful socks, and original artwork by local artists is for sale. During the neighborhood's regular art walks, held the second Saturday of every month, it's not unusual to see an aerialist performing here.

MAP 5: 5000 20th Ave. NW, 206/789-0037, www.monsterartandclothing.com; 11am-8pm Mon.-Wed., 10am-9pm Thurs.-Sat., 10am-6pm Sun.

Prism

If walking among the casually hip denizens of Ballard inspires you to fit in, this is the boutique for doing it. Statement necklaces made of carved wood and twisted brass hang from the wall, and the small clothing racks include graphic T-shirts and vintage-style sweaters. The store is part of a tiny collective that supports local makers, so many of the candles and gift-ready housewares sold here are crafted in the Northwest.

MAP 5: 5208 Ballard Ave. NW, 206/402-4706, http://prismseattle.com; 11am-9pm daily

SHOES

Re-soul

This small shoe shop carries a variety of lines, but the highlight is its in-house brand designed in Seattle and made in Italy. The owner, a former Nordstrom designer, specializes in simple flats and Oxfords for both men and women. This is a spot for fine leather and craftsmanship, not bargains; crisp two-tone saddle shoes can run in the hundreds of dollars.

MAP 5: 5319 Ballard Ave. NW, 206/789-7312, http://resoul.com; 11am-8pm Mon.-Sat., 11am-5pm Sun.

FARMERS MARKETS

✪ Ballard Farmers Market

Though Ballard Avenue is one of the busiest retail stretches of the city, it closes to car traffic every Sunday for one of the city's most beloved outdoor farmers markets, and one of the only to run year-round. A central aisle of stalls fills with produce vendors, meat sellers, and craftspeople, with a few prepared food stalls as well. On summer days the sidewalks are crammed with pedestrians carrying canvas totes or a leash—dogs are everywhere. This being Ballard, it's not unusual to see something whimsical, like a poet selling written-on-demand verses from his portable typewriter.

MAP 5: Ballard Ave. NW between Vernon Pl. NW and 22nd Ave. NW, www.sfmamarkets.com; 10am-3pm Sun.

OUTDOOR EQUIPMENT

Ascent Outdoors

This venue has long been an adventure store, but for a long time it was known as Second Ascent—a shop for secondhand gear. Renamed, the store now de-emphasizes the used equipment in favor of new stock, but it's still a welcome place to find a deal. Though there's lots of used hiking

Ballard Farmers Market

boots, ski gear, and some clothing, most of the shop is dedicated to samples that are new, if limited in the sizes available. The salespeople are helpful, almost to a fault, so don't expect to browse long before meeting a chatty climber or skier who wants to know what you're heading out to do, and not just so they can sell you the right gear. The shop also offers cross-country and alpine touring ski sales and rentals (but not downhill skis). The shop still buys used gear, useful for anyone who comes to the Pacific Northwest for an adventure and doesn't want to haul their stuff home.

MAP 5: 5209 Ballard Ave. NW, 206/545-8810, http://ascentoutdoors.com; 10am-7pm Mon.-Wed. and Sat., 10am-8pm Thurs.-Fri., 10am-6pm Sun.

MUSIC
✪ Bop Street Records

Bop Street has been in Ballard for more than 30 years. It holds more than half a million records and was named one of the five best music stores by the *Wall Street Journal*. Bop Street has proved itself a vinyl destination, all thanks to owner Dave Voorhees, who still likes to show customers around. Albums are stacked on shelves so high they can only be reached from the kind of ladder you see in fancy old libraries. Collections range from rock and soul to world music, and the store has more than 10,000 classical records. Even though the shop's had to down-size in recent years, it's still one of the most impressive music stores on the West Coast.

MAP 5: 2220 NW Market St., 206/297-2232, www.bopstreetrecords. com; noon-8pm Tues.-Wed., noon-10pm Thurs.-Sat., noon-5pm Sun.

RECORD STORES

Besides the rain, Seattle's music scene is perhaps its most famous attribute. This is the town that birthed Nirvana, Macklemore, and Jimi Hendrix. Though record stores are disappearing across the country as digital music takes over, there are still a few holding strong here, including Ballard's **Bop Street Records** (page 191) and **Sonic Boom Records** (2209 NW Market St., 206/297-2666, www.sonicboomrecords.com; 10am-10pm Mon.-Sat., 10am-7pm Sun.), across the street from each other. Capitol Hill also boasts **Everyday Music** (1520 10th Ave., 206/568-3321, www.everydaymusic.com; 10am-10pm daily)—helpfully located across from The Elliott Bay Book Company, another store that's bucking conventional wisdom by selling old-fashioned media—and **Wall of Sound** (1206 E. Pike St., #1C, 206/441-9880, www.wosound.com; 11am-7pm Mon.-Sat., noon-6pm Sun.), catering to more eccentric tastes. Most music shops sell both new and used vinyl, and Seattle's somewhat buried jazz reputation surfaces with a great selection at SoDo's **Silver Platters** (2390 1st Ave. S, 206/283-3472, www.silverplatters.com; 10am-10pm Mon.-Sat., 11am-7pm Sun.). Even the airport shows off the Seattle music tradition with a **Sub Pop Records shop** (Seattle-Tacoma International Airport, Concourse C, www.subpop.com/airport; 6am-10pm daily), offering vinyl and merchandise with the famous label's logo. Still, Seattle's music stores are not impervious to the changing tides of music consumption: **Easy Street Records** (4559 California Ave. SW, 206/938-3279; store 9am-9pm Mon.-Sat., 9am-7pm Sun., cafe 7am-3pm daily) closed its Queen Anne outpost in 2013, leaving only its West Seattle location—but this one has an in-store diner dishing up Jive Turkey and Culture Club sandwiches, plus—groan—the Salad of John and Yoko.

University District   Map 6

BOOKS
Amazon Books

Yes, the online retailer is known for being, well, online, but the web giant decided to try something different with a brick-and-mortar bookstore in University Village, a high-end outdoor mall near the University of Washington. The space is striking, partially due to how much it looks like a traditional bookstore. But there's a giant Kindle counter in the middle, and books are displayed with pull-quotes from online reviews underneath. Prices, notably, match Amazon's online amounts. The bookstore aims to not only highlight the highest-rated books online, but also serve as a hangout spot—though its small size makes it less successful in that domain. Indie fans might be cautious, but the store could represent a whole new future for bookstores.

MAP 6: 4601 26th Ave. NE, 206/524-0715, http://uvillage.com/amazon-books; 9:30am-9pm Mon.-Sat., 10:30am-7pm Sun.

Amazon Books

Third Place Books

The saying goes that the first place is home and the second place is work. Third Place Books is meant to be the third important component of a Seattle resident's life, a community center for reading and discussion. The bookstore, one of three locations in the city, sells new and used books and has a fiercely independent feel—staff make personal recommendations, kids are welcome to sprawl and explore, and the shelves are comfortably cluttered. The old brick building has free Wi-Fi throughout the space.

MAP 6: 6504 20th Ave. NE, 206/525-2347, www.thirdplacebooks.com; 8am-9pm Sun.-Thurs., 8am-10pm Fri.-Sat.

University Book Store

Not only does the University Book Store carry many of the Northwest authors that are taught at the University of Washington next door, but there's also every kind of Husky shirt, bag, sticker, and flag imaginable. The large store often holds events with visiting writers.

MAP 6: 4326 University Way NE, 206/634-3400, www.bookstore.washington.edu; 9am-7pm Mon.-Fri., 10am-6pm Sat., 10am-5pm Sun.

CLOTHING
Tommy Bahama

What in the world does a tropical clothing line have to do with rainy, temperate Seattle? The Tommy Bahama company, known for its flowered shirts and vacation caftans, is actually based in Seattle; perhaps no one understands the need for beachwear more than the residents of a gloomy Northwest city. The University Village store feels like a room inside a colonial Key West mansion, with the brand's scented candles giving off a crisp beachy smell. Since Seattle has more sunny days than its reputation would suggest, not all the lightweight polo shirts and linen tank tops sold here are worn on Hawaiian vacations.

MAP 6: 2600 NE 46th St., 206/826-8030, www.tommybahama.com; 9:30am-9pm Mon.-Sat., 11am-6pm Sun.

GIFTS AND HOME
✪ Glassybaby

It's a store known for one thing—a votive candleholder—but that one thing has earned quite the reputation. An artist who was attending a sick relative originally created the colored glass lights, and the company still supports cancer charities. Glassworkers make 500 of the product every day. Made in a dizzying array of colors, the solid-glass objects make ideal gifts, and the company even has a Glassybaby-of-the-month club to send a different color to recipients throughout the year. This store is located in the University Village outdoor mall, but there's a Glassybaby outpost in Sea-Tac Airport.

MAP 6: 2627 Northeast Village Ln., 206/274-4683, http://glassybaby.com; 9:30am-9pm Mon.-Sat., 11am-6pm Sun.

FARMERS MARKETS
University District
Farmers Market

Though it can't compare to the sheer size of Pike Place Market, the University District Farmers Market is a cheerful neighborhood gathering that goes year-round on the street known as "the Ave" (despite University Way not actually being an avenue). Two long blocks fill with a row of stands from which local farms and orchards sell fresh produce, cheeses, meats, and oysters, and there's a smattering of ready-to-eat food stands mixed in. Thanks to the neighborhood's student population that likes to sleep in, early hours aren't too crowded.

MAP 6: University Way NE between 50th and 52nd Sts., http://seattlefarmersmarkets.org; 9am-2pm Sat.

SHOPPING MALLS
✪ University Village

Most of Seattle's malls are located so far on the periphery of the city that they might as well be in the distant suburbs; only the University District's U Village is a truly urban mall. The outdoor complex has a grocery store, many restaurants, and shiny product display stores from Apple and Microsoft. Parking can be a bear, so the parking garages, while farther from stores than the few surface parking spots, are usually a good bet. The 120 stores include a number of high-end chains like Room & Board, Aritzia, and Jonathan Adler, plus local shops. It was the second place, after Pike Place Market, that Starbucks opened a coffee shop.

MAP 6: 2623 Northeast University Village, http://uvillage.com; 9:30am-9pm Mon.-Sat., 11am-6pm Sun.

International District and SoDo

Map 7

GOURMET GOODIES
✪ Uwajimaya

You could call this a grocery store, but it's so much more. Founded by a Japanese entrepreneur in the 1920s and enduring even after the owner was sent to an internment camp during World War II, the store is now recognized as the biggest Asian marketplace in the city. There are aisles of meats, prepared foods, spices, sakes, and imported treats, but also a gift section, an attached bookstore, food court, beauty salon, and more. The complex is still family run, and its flagship store takes up most of a city block. On Wednesday evenings there are free lessons in the game of Go in the food court.

MAP 7: 600 5th Ave. S, 206/624-6248; 8am-10pm Mon.-Sat., 9am-9pm Sun.

OUTDOOR EQUIPMENT
Filson

There's a distinct style to the high-end wares at Filson; they're what a gentleman hunter would wear, or perhaps a backwoods baron. The company's thick wool shirts, boxy jackets trimmed in white fur, and fishing vests have a timeless austerity. The new flagship store sits on the 2nd floor of the company headquarters, above the factory floor where Filson's famously rugged duffel bags and rucksacks are made—look for a window into the workspace. Inside the shop, there's a giant fireplace, a beautiful view to the industrial waterfront, and a repair shop. These wares are the kind of gear fathers bequeath to their sons (or mothers to their daughters, though the selection of women's wear is limited).

MAP 7: 1741 1st Ave. S, 206/622-3147, www.filson.com; 10am-6pm Mon.-Sat., noon-5pm Sun.

Outdoor Research

Seattle's many outdoorsy people know that OR gear stands up to harsh conditions. The company makes jackets, clothing, gloves, and hats, plus some non-wearable gear like dry bags and duffels. This store, located in the company's headquarters building, is a cozy space crowded with racks and staffed with knowledgeable salespeople (though on a busy weekend it can be hard to get someone's attention). It's known for blowout sales that take over the parking lot and adjacent buildings a few times a year, when lines form down the block despite the building being far from the bustle of SoDo. The company's gaiters (coverings that keep the rain from soaking your pants) are favorites among hikers in the wet Northwest.

MAP 7: 2203 1st Ave. S, 206/971-1496, www.outdoorresearch.com; 9am-6pm Mon. Sat., 11am 5pm Sun.

WHERE TO STAY

Being a well-appointed hotel in Seattle is not enough—you have to have a personality. Often that's expressed in art collections and modern decor, but it's

Hotel Max

also manifested in views, in-house dining, and programming for locals and visitors alike. Downtown Seattle is filled with hotels, many traditional and part of national chains. But there are also historic options like the Fairmont Olympic Hotel, which has hosted events and gatherings throughout its storied history.

In Belltown, accommodations are more eclectic, with Ace Hotel offering shared bathrooms and plenty of style, while the Edgewater sits on a pier jutting into Puget Sound. In Queen Anne and South Lake Union, cheaper hotels offer a place to stay that's still close to the center of action, especially for anyone visiting Seattle Center. Many of these spots have free bikes or a city shuttle to make transportation easier.

When visiting the University of Washington, the hotels of the University District are a natural choice, though they fill quickly during major events like graduation or home football games. In Ballard, a few very stylish hotels offer a quiet retreat away from downtown, but are still within walking distance of bars, restaurants, and sights.

Capitol Hill might be the city's hub for nightlife, dining, and youth culture, but there aren't many hotels in the area. The nearby Hotel Sorrento is a good option, a spot with old Italian charm and a monthly silent reading party in the lobby.

HIGHLIGHTS

✪ **MOST CLASSIC:** Downtown's elegant **Fairmont Olympic Hotel** is as much a landmark as a place to stay, and its spacious lobby is worth a visit even if you're not checking in (page 200).

✪ **MOST CHIC:** From the luxury amenities in the room to the views from the rooftop bar, everything at the **Thompson Hotel** is a cut above the properties that surround it (page 200)

✪ **BEST LOCATION:** The **Edgewater Hotel** isn't next to the water; it's on it. The Beatles once stayed here and fished right from their hotel room (page 203).

✪ **BEST BUDGET OPTION:** Seattle's **Ace Hotel** was the original in what's now a global chain dedicated to hip style and community (page 203).

✪ **BEST OLD-SCHOOL STAY:** The Italian-inspired **Hotel Sorrento** is updated but maintains a quirky style and hosts a monthly silent reading party in the fireplace lobby (page 204).

✪ **BEST INDOOR POOL: Hotel Ballard** offers complimentary 24-hour access to the Olympic Athletic Club and its chandelier-topped pool (page 205).

PRICE KEY

$	Less than $200 per night
$ $	$200-350 per night
$ $ $	More than $350 per night

Edgewater Hotel

CHOOSING WHERE TO STAY

Downtown

Most of Seattle's hotels are in the downtown core, and there are plenty to choose from. Most do not offer airport shuttles, but they are close to Link Light Rail (and thus access to the airport), and cabs have a set fare to reach these downtown blocks. It's the best place for first-timers and for those looking for an urban, pedestrian experience in Seattle.

Queen Anne and Belltown

The cheaper hotels just north of downtown appeal to budget travelers and those looking for a slightly quieter experience, while still staying within walking distance of major attractions. Expect a simpler setup, but with savings over the downtown towers.

South Lake Union

Adjacent to downtown but with easy access to Belltown, Queen Anne, and Lake Union, South Lake Union is an urban neighborhood with plenty of life—thank to the Amazon headquarters here. Expect hotels that capture the corporate-style whimsy of the tech companies and start-ups that call these blocks home, and note that the area's more about daytime activity than nighttime buzz.

Capitol Hill

This might be the most hopping neighborhood in the city, but there are few places to stay. The Hotel Sorrento in nearby First Hill appeals to visitors looking for a sedate sense of style, while the Silver Cloud Hotel in Capitol Hill has few frills but a central location.

Ballard

Staying in this northern neighborhood is like visiting a really great island—there's a lot to do, but getting there is a pain. Two hotels, next door to each other and sharing an owner, offer high- and low-end accommodations on a busy street.

University District

If you know a student or have business on campus, the high-quality hotels of the U District are invaluable. They're cheaper than downtown options and offer a few more perks. But since transportation options in the neighborhood are limited, they're not a good bet for anyone hoping to spend most of their time downtown.

International District and SoDo

There are few hotels south of downtown, save one notable exception right next to the football and baseball stadiums. This industrial zone is due for growth, and the increasing number of shops and eateries suggest that in a few years, it could be the new cool destination.

ALTERNATIVE LODGING OPTIONS

Hotels aren't the only option for visitors. **Short-term rentals** of privately owned properties are also gaining popularity, so much so that some civic leaders worry that these tourist rentals are crowding out affordable housing in the city. Companies like AirBnB and VRBO offer the opportunity to rent a room, apartment, or house directly from the owner, often for as little as one night. Sometimes, the owner will still be present, acting as host; for others, you'll have the place to yourself. The companies vet the owners and

WHERE TO STAY IF...

YOU ONLY HAVE A FEW DAYS...
...you'll want to be **downtown** in one of the hotels closest to Pike Place Market and other sights.

YOU WANT A WATERFRONT VIEW...
...ask specifically for a room on the upper floors of the **downtown** tower hotels or check into Seattle's only pier hotel, the Edgewater.

YOU WANT TO GET IN TOUCH WITH HISTORY...
...look to one of **downtown**'s older properties or one inside a funky old building in **Belltown.**

YOU'RE ON A BUDGET...
...save pennies in the slightly quieter neighborhood of **Queen Anne,** still close to many important sights but less frequented by business travelers.

YOU LIKE THE QUIET...
...roll up to **Capitol Hill.** The selection is small, but these places offer a quiet respite that's still next to one of the busiest neighborhoods in the city.

YOU WANT TO HANG WITH THE LOCALS...
...pack your bags for **Ballard,** where accommodations are close to the neighborhood's bars, restaurants, and shops, and there are fewer tourists.

YOU PLAN TO GET SERIOUS AT THE UNIVERSITY OF WASHINGTON...
...enjoy the high-quality and slightly less expensive **University District** hotels, which offer unparalleled access to the campus and student-filled blocks that surround it.

YOU'RE HERE TO ROOT ON THE HOME TEAM...
...unpack in **SoDo,** where reaching the football, soccer, and baseball games is a matter of minutes, and you can hear the roar of the crowd through every open window.

provide oversight and safety regulations, but be prepared to bring your own toiletries and food. Many rentals are found in Capitol Hill and Belltown, with few in the middle of downtown. Often these rentals are significantly cheaper than hotel options, especially if you're willing to branch out to the residential neighborhoods.

When lodging is scarce in Seattle—which can happen during large conferences or busy summer weekends—the hotels near **Sea-Tac Airport** are often still an option for travelers. Several border the airport, offering shuttles and easy access to the Link Light Rail to reach the city. The Hilton Seattle Airport, Seattle Airport Marriott, and Radisson Hotel Seattle Airport have some of the nicest rooms, while the Cedarbrook Lodge, just a few blocks away, is a true high-end retreat that hides its airport adjacency with wooded grounds.

There are few places to **camp** in Seattle, so anyone with a tent or RV will need to head to the outskirts of town. **Trailer Inns RV Park** (425/747-9181 or 800/659-4684, www.trailerinnsrv.com) is located in Bellevue, about a 30-minute drive from Seattle in normal traffic, with great access to the mountains that lie to the east of the city. Up north in Bothell, on the north side of Lake Washington, **Lake Pleasant RV Park** (425/487-1785) has spots overlooking a small pond but requires a membership fee. Tent camping near Seattle is even more difficult. State parks in the area are day-use only, though **Saltwater State Park** (253/661-4956, http://parks.state.wa.us), halfway between Seattle and Tacoma, does have nearly 50 sites and a stretch of waterfront on Puget Sound.

Downtown and Pioneer Square Map 1

DOWNTOWN

✪ Fairmont Olympic Hotel $$$

When presidents like John F. Kennedy visited Seattle, they stayed in the historic Fairmont Olympic Hotel. Not only was it the site of the original University of Washington, this longtime landmark was also the site of much planning for the 1962 World's Fair. Its more than 400 rooms are decked in pale luxury, with classic Victorian-inspired furniture and gray marble in the bathrooms. The large lobby is home to 2nd-floor interior balconies, red-carpeted stairs, and potted palms, while a tucked-away swimming pool sits inside a glass solarium, perfect for Seattle's not-so-warm days.

MAP 1: 411 University St., 206/621-1700, www.fairmont.com

✪ Thompson Hotel $$$

It felt like high time for a hotel like the Thompson to open in Seattle when it arrived in the mid-2010s; it had been a long time since an unapologetically fancy destination opened in the city. Just blocks from the waterfront and Pike Place Market, the Thompson, part of an international collection of high-end hotels, doesn't lean too far into hipster chic, though there are a few quirky touches throughout the hotel. Many rooms have stunning views of Elliott Bay, and all have top-notch beds, linens, and amenities. A rooftop bar with stunning views, The Nest, is a popular destination for guests and locals alike.

MAP 1: 110 Stewart St, 206/623-4600, www.thompsonhotels.com

Alexis Hotel

Alexis Hotel $$$

Though only a few blocks from the bustle of Pike Place Market and Pioneer Square, the Alexis Hotel is a quiet luxury property with about 120 rooms and very modern decor in deep blues and purples. The hotel has bikes available for guest use, and there's a free wine reception in the lobby every evening. Valet parking is $42 per night, but hybrid vehicles get it at half price. The cozy **Bookstore Bar & Café** (7am-midnight Mon.-Fri., 8am-midnight Sat., 8am-10pm Sun.), located on the 1st floor and with entrances from both the lobby and street, sells tomes ($5) along with whiskeys and salads.

MAP 1: 1007 1st Ave., 206/624-4844, www.alexishotel.com

Hotel Max $$

Every door in the boutique Hotel Max is covered in a local artwork, and each floor has a theme. Some of the hotel's 163 rooms can be tiny, but all are comfortable. Bold colors and mature art give the property an adult vibe, and meaty dishes from the wood-fired grill in the restaurant next door can be sent up as room service 24 hours a day.

MAP 1: 620 Stewart St., 206/728-6299, www.hotelmaxseattle.com

Hotel Monaco $$

The electric colors of the Hotel Monaco start in the lobby—where walls are blue and patterns are bright—and continue in guest rooms, where even the bathrobes are vivid in animal print. The downtown location is close to the Seattle Central Library and walkable to major attractions. Despite all the design pizzazz, the staff wants you to feel at home—so much so that you can get a complimentary loaner goldfish to act as your pet while

Hotel Monaco

you're there. The nearly 200 rooms are modern and equipped with high-end electronics, furniture, and linens.

MAP 1: 1101 4th Ave., 206/621-1770, www.monaco-seattle.com

Loews Hotel 1000 $$

The luxe Loews Hotel 1000 is a boutique property with just over 100 rooms. The staff puts special emphasis on service; there's usually more than one doorman out front to open the door for you. Bathrooms are large and include bathtubs whose faucets are on the ceiling. The rooms have creative but tasteful decor and fine linens. The basement spa (206/357-9490) is a special hidden gem, while the virtual Golf Club (8am-10pm daily) brings the links of the world to a small room. The hotel's All Water Seafood & Oyster Bar (206/357-9000, 6:30am-10pm Mon.-Fri., 7am-10pm Sat.-Sun.) is known for oysters and chowder fries.

MAP 1: 1000 1st Ave., 206/957-1000, www.hotel1000seattle.com

Mayflower Park Hotel $$

The traditional Mayflower Park Hotel is decked out in Queen Anne style, complete with chandeliers and brass knobs, a mark of its history—the hotel opened in 1927. With 160 rooms, it's a little bigger than a boutique property but not so large as to feel corporate or overwhelming. The central location is between downtown and Belltown, with the Mediterranean eatery Andaluca (6:30am-11am Mon., 6:30am-11am and 5pm-9pm Tues.-Fri., 7am-noon and 5pm-10pm Sat., 7am-noon and 5pm-9pm Sun.) just downstairs.

MAP 1: 405 Olive Way, 206/623-8700, www.mayflowerpark.com

Green Tortoise Hostel $

Few properties in the city can boast a location more convenient than that of the Green Tortoise Hostel, across the street from Pike Place Market and within walking distance of downtown, Pioneer Square, Belltown, and with a little trek, Seattle Center. The hostel has bunk beds with private lights, fans, and power outlets, plus curtains for a small amount of privacy. Some bunk beds are doubles. The beds are arranged in 30 different rooms, with combinations that range from dorms to private rooms. There's free wireless Internet and continental breakfast, and three times a week the hostel serves free dinner.

MAP 1: 105 Pike St., 206/340-1222, www.greentortoise.net

Pensione Nichols $

The homey Pensione Nichols is a bed-and-breakfast with killer views of Elliott Bay and an unbeatable location next to Pike Place Market. Of the dozen rooms, some have no windows (but do have skylights), and most share living space and bathrooms. Only the two apartments have private baths. The antique furnishings lean slightly toward the grandmother's-living-room aesthetic, but the house dogs are plenty welcoming.

MAP 1: 1923 1st Ave., 206/441-7125, www.pensionenichols.com

Queen Anne and Belltown

Map 2

QUEEN ANNE
Inn at Queen Anne $$

Billed as a historical property, the Inn at Queen Anne definitely has the dark corners of an older building. It's a relatively small property for Seattle, two three-story structures that look like an unassuming brick apartment building. Rooms are simple, but all have private bathrooms and some have stoves, and the Seattle Center is right across the street.

MAP 2: 505 1st Ave. N, 206/282-7357, www.innatqueenanne.com

MarQueen Hotel $$

The age of the MarQueen Hotel manages to convey luxury, with beveled glass doors and Alaskan marble in the floors. The midsized property has 59 rooms over three floors. Some rooms

MarQueen Hotel

have awkwardly placed but charming sitting parlors, and the Tin Lizzie bar on the 1st floor has vintage 1920s charm in the patterned ceiling and mod couches.

MAP 2: 600 Queen Anne Ave. N, 206/282-7407, www.marqueen.com

Maxwell Hotel $$

The Roy Street location of the Maxwell is good for visitors planning to spend a lot of time at Seattle Center; there are few hotels of this caliber quite so close. This boutique hotel specializes in loud pops of color—magenta patterned wallpaper and lime-green couches. The quirk doesn't outweigh comfort, however, with European duvets (two to a bed) and fluffy robes. Rooms don't vary much beyond size, though some suites have kitchenettes. With more than 100 rooms, it's one of the biggest hotels on this end of town. There are free bike rentals, and a shuttle branded with a giant yellow pineapple circles the city so guests can hit up the zoo or Pike Place Market. The Maxwell is also dog friendly.

MAP 2: 300 Roy St., 206/286-0629, www. themaxwellhotel.com

BELLTOWN
✪ Edgewater Hotel $$$

The Beatles stayed at the waterfront Edgewater Hotel when they came to town, famously posing with fishing poles out their window. You can try the trick yourself from about half of the hotel's 223 rooms; the rest face inland. The chic Pacific Northwest decor includes gas fireplaces and stuffed footstools shaped like brown bears. A waterfront restaurant, **Six Seven** (206/269-4575), is one of the chicest spots to mix fine dining and sunset views. Though city-side rooms are more affordable, it's worth the expense

to book a waterfront room and enjoy the dark expanse of Elliott Bay right out the window.

MAP 2: 2411 Alaskan Way, 206/728-7000, www.edgewaterhotel.com

✪ Ace Hotel $

Founded in Seattle, a collective of creative entrepreneurs turned an old boardinghouse into the Ace Hotel, putting turntables and reclaimed wood furniture in every room. Some rooms share hall bathrooms and some have original wood floors, and with less than 30 rooms it's basically a boutique property that's cheaper than almost everything in the downtown core. Original art in the rooms comes from the likes of Shepard Fairey. A large black table sits in the lobby, and a breakfast room serves waffles and coffee in the morning.

MAP 2: 2423 1st Ave., 206/448-4721, www.acehotel.com/seattle

City Hostel Seattle $

Don't be fooled by the beautiful building that looks more like an embassy than a cheap place to crash: City Hostel Seattle is indeed a hostel. The property has breakfast and free luggage storage, plus kitchens and an outdoor grill for guest use. Most rooms use shared hall bathrooms, and though there are only a handful of rooms, especially private ones, a nice community can fit in the shared four and six-room dorms. Each room is decorated with a different kind of mural or painting, many with glaringly bright colors, and the hostel also has a 20-seat movie theater.

MAP 2: 2327 2nd Ave., 206/706-3255, www.hostelseattle.com

South Lake Union
Map 2

Moxy Downtown Seattle $$

From the hot pink logo to the quirky lobby, the Moxy bursts with personality (for a subset of the Marriott hotel chain). There's no check-in desk—simply wave down the bartender and grab a few pieces of candy from the jar on one corner of the bar. The ground floor has board games, bright decorations and artsy antlers on the wall, plus a self-service food wall that reads "do it your damn self." Rooms are a little more standard, with gray, industrial decor, some with city views.

MAP 2: 1016 Republican St., 206/708-8200, http://moxyseattle.com

Capitol Hill
Map 3

✪ Hotel Sorrento $$

The Hotel Sorrento is like an Italian transplant next to the city's collection of world-class hospitals. It features the crooked, charming rooms of a historical building, and the cozy Fireside Room hosts a monthly silent reading party. With 76 rooms, it's bigger than a boutique property, but is classic and calm enough to never feel like a massive luxury hotel. It's the closest to old-world elegance that Seattle can pull off, and it has a distinctly more sedate vibe than the downtown properties.

MAP 3: 900 Madison St., 206/622-6400, www.hotelsorrento.com

Silver Cloud Hotel Seattle - Broadway $$

As one of the only hotels in Capitol Hill, the Silver Cloud Hotel earns cool points just for being so close to the city's best restaurant and bar scene. Otherwise the chain is standard but well appointed, with an indoor pool and in-room refrigerators and microwaves. The artsy vibe is meant to echo the apartments on trendy Capitol Hill. With five floors of rooms and an underground parking garage, it's one of the larger hotels outside the downtown core.

MAP 3: 1100 Broadway, 206/325-1400, www.silvercloud.com

Ballard

Map 5

WHERE TO STAY

✪ Hotel Ballard $$$

The Hotel Ballard is unusual in that it's an upscale boutique Seattle hotel, but isn't in downtown. It sits on Ballard's busiest street, right across from the buzziest bars, restaurants, and performance spaces, and above the high-end Olympic Athletic Club— sharing access to the club's giant salt-water pool. The top-floor open-air patio has a view of Ballard's industrial waterfront. Rooms are luxe and decorated in a modern European style,

Hotel Ballard

and the bathtubs are sizable. The lobby entrance can be hard to spot from the street because the 1st floor of the building is split between the athletic club and pizza restaurant Stoneburner.
MAP 5: 5214 Ballard Ave. NW, 206/789 5011, www.hotelballardseattle. com

Ballard Inn $

There's still a beautiful molded sign on the top of the Ballard Inn from when it was the American-Scandinavian Bank, as well as other bits of the property that also scream vintage, like the shared hall baths—though a few rooms do have en suite baths. The stark black-and-white aesthetic makes for clean lines and rooms that feel bigger than they are (which isn't very big). With just 16 rooms, the inn is dwarfed by its sister property, Hotel Ballard, across the street, but it also offers access to the Olympic Athletic Club. It doesn't skimp on amenities just because it's laid out in European style—beds are topped with goose-down comforters and all rooms have TVs and free Wi-Fi.
MAP 5: 5300 Ballard Ave. NW, 206/789-5011, www.ballardinnseattle.com

University District

Map 6

Watertown Hotel $$

The Watertown Hotel is owned by the Pineapple Hospitality Group, a fact only notable because the lobby is stocked with pineapple cupcakes; otherwise there's nothing tropical about the hotel. The modern building is a few blocks from the university, and the hotel offers free bike rentals. The 100 rooms are cheery, and some have city views. Rooms aren't cramped but not quite luxurious, though the service level is high. Free daily shuttles go to downtown Seattle, and there is a free laundry machine for guest use. A related property down the street has an outdoor pool that guests can use.

MAP 6: 4242 Roosevelt Way NE, 206/826-4242, www.watertownseattle.com

Graduate Hotel $

This property was once called the Hotel Deca, referring to the aesthetic that inspired the 16-story hotel—the property dates back to art deco's heyday in the 1930s, though there's little of the ornate decoration associated with that era in the building itself. Renamed in 2018, the decor has changed to include more local touches (like paintings of local star Bruce Lee) and scalloped bed headboards. Some of the 155 rooms have amazing mountain views. The street is a busy one, especially on weekend nights, but the building is tall enough that most disturbances are minimized. It's one of the few properties within walking distance of the main part of the University of Washington campus, so it books up quickly during (appropriately) spring graduation season, filling up six months or more ahead of time.

MAP 6: 4507 Brooklyn Ave. NE, 206/634-2000, www. graduatehotels.com/seattle

International District and SoDo

Map 7

Silver Cloud Hotel Seattle - Stadium $$

There aren't many places to stay in SoDo, but this hotel is practically inside the stadiums, sitting right between Safeco Field and CenturyLink Field. From the rooftop deck, you can see Elliott Bay and hear the roar of the crowds if a game is in progress. The lobby restaurant is standard, but there aren't many other options in the walkable vicinity. Wi-Fi is free and rooms are recently updated, some with Jacuzzi tubs positioned (somewhat oddly) in the bedrooms so they're next to the windows.

MAP 7: 1046 1st Ave. S, 206/204-9800, www.silvercloud.com/seattlestadium

DAY TRIPS

The Pacific Northwest encompasses mountains, trees, funky towns, and grand road trips. Every inch beyond Seattle reveals a little bit more nature, art, and culture.

Ferries head west from Seattle to Bainbridge Island once or twice an hour, and many who live across the water consider their island merely an extension of Seattle. But life is slower on Bainbridge, the art museum is free and welcoming, and the small shops that line its main downtown street are for rambling through, not rushing.

It doesn't take long heading east out of Seattle before you reach Bellevue, a kind of twin to Seattle. Located on the other side of Lake Washington, it's a suburb that has come into its own, offering restaurants, hotels, dining, and entertainment. Since its growth is largely thanks to big tech companies like Microsoft and Nintendo, it has a shiny, tech-forward vibe. The art museum is not to be missed, and the Kirkland waterfront is a welcome quiet space in a busy city. About 20 minutes past Bellevue, Snoqualmie Falls tumbles into the Cascadian foothills.

Mount Rainier

The city of Tacoma is so close that the Seattle airport is partly named for the city. It often gets overlooked, but the small metropolis is slowly becoming a favorite for arts aficionados and young people looking for an affordable place to live. The city's museums—notably the glass art museum and a car repository—and waterfront spaces rival those of Seattle.

You can't miss Mount Rainier on a Seattle visit. Even when it hides behind the clouds, you'll see it on every license plate and nearly every postcard. Even better is an actual trip to the mountain, which boasts visitors centers, trails, and a few classic park inns. Outside the national park proper are funky hotels and a ski resort with a sky-high restaurant; Rainier could be a whole trip unto itself.

HIGHLIGHTS

✪ **BEST EXCUSE FOR A FERRY RIDE:** The free **Bainbridge Island Museum of Art** celebrates local art in a beautiful building only a short walk from the ferry terminal (page 210).

✪ **BEST SHOW:** Watch glassblowers create new pieces at the **Museum of Glass** to gain an appreciation for the artistry of heat (page 220).

✪ **BEST WILDLIFE:** The charming **Point Defiance Zoo and Aquarium** is walkable and welcoming (page 221).

✪ **MOST ACCURATE NAME:** Whether covered in wildflowers in summer or under blankets of snow in winter, **Paradise** lives up to its name (page 232).

✪ **BEST RIDE:** The gondola ride at **Crystal Mountain** whisks visitors to a view of Mount Rainier in minutes (page 237).

PLANNING YOUR TIME

Got a day, or even just part of one? It's easy to escape Seattle to Bellevue or Bainbridge, reaching your destination in less than an hour and quickly getting to the sights and museums. Bainbridge is the best bet for a single excursion, since it combines a boat trip with a visit to a small town. Tacoma, to the south, requires a full day, mostly due to the traffic between the two cities but also because there's so much to do. With multiple days, head to Mount Rainier. The drive is longer but the views are greater, and there are old hotels and campgrounds that beckon for a longer stay.

Travel outside of Seattle usually requires a car, but Bainbridge Island is welcoming to pedestrians thanks to its ferry and small walkable blocks. Buses run from Seattle to Bellevue and Tacoma, but the commuter routes can be intimidating to visitors, and often take much longer than driving. A car rental is required for a trip to Mount Rainier, since public transportation doesn't reach the national park.

There are day-trip destinations on both the freeways that meet in Seattle, the north-south I-5 and the east-west I-90; head south on the former to reach Tacoma, or east on the latter to find Bellevue. No roads go west to Bainbridge, and it takes a combination of freeways and smaller highways to reach Mount Rainier. That means it's hard to combine trips in a single day, and you'll be returning through Seattle when going from one to the other. An exception—Tacoma is easily positioned as a stop on the way to Mount Rainier National Park from Seattle.

When heading to Bellevue or Tacoma, avoid weekday rush hours, since I-90 and I-5 both flood with cars. Bainbridge is a good choice at those times, since the walk-on ferry can handle scores of people. Mount

Day Trips

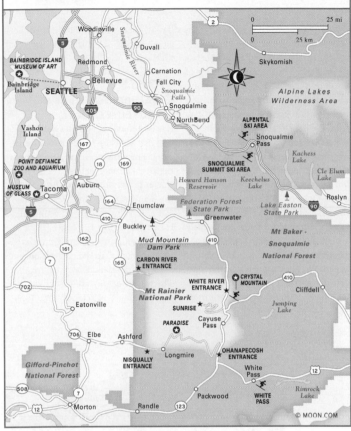

Rainier National Park can get very busy on summer weekends, with parking hard to find at main visitors centers. Aim for midweek, but avoid early spring or late fall because few amenities will be open.

Mount Rainier National Park, located in the Cascade Mountains, often has much different weather from Seattle and the surrounding area. It can be colder, rainy, and even snowy when things are mild down by Puget Sound. Only head to the area in winter if you're prepared for winter mountain driving and have an open destination, like the ski resort, in mind.

Bainbridge Island

Though just across Puget Sound from Seattle and home to many commuters, the small island of Bainbridge has its own personality. A tiny cluster of museums and eateries has grown up around the island's ferry terminal, making for a perfect no-car boat trip from the big city. Be sure to enjoy the trip, taking in postcard-perfect views of the city and scouring the waterways for Puget Sound sealife: harbor seals, waterfowl, sometimes even orcas. Once on the island itself, leave time to wander up and down Winslow Way and frequent the independently and locally owned stores, perhaps enjoying a cup of coffee on an outdoor bench. The ferry route is popular with commuters who leave their quiet island life for a job in the city, but most day-trippers will avoid the crowds because they're traveling the opposite direction.

SIGHTS
✪ BAINBRIDGE ISLAND MUSEUM OF ART

It wasn't that long ago that Bainbridge was just a sleepy residential suburb, albeit one with a unique commute to the city. The change to active destination is largely thanks to the birth of the Bainbridge Island Museum of Art (550 Winslow Way E, Bainbridge Island, 206/842-4451, www.biartmuseum.org; 10am-6pm daily; free), dedicated to the creative output of the Olympic and Kitsap Peninsulas. The building was constructed with environmentally friendly practices,

Bainbridge Island Museum of Art

Bainbridge Island

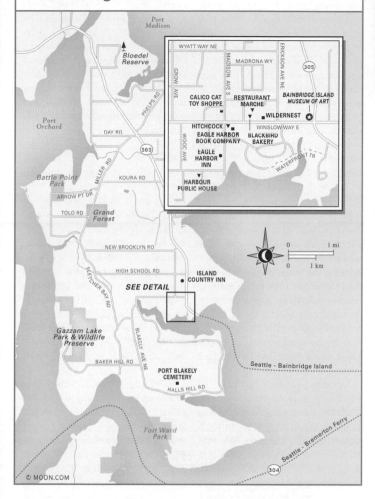

Port Madison

Bloedel Reserve

Port Orchard

Battle Point Park

Grand Forest

Gazzam Lake Park & Wildlife Preserve

Port Blakely Cemetery

Fort Ward Park

PHELPS RD
DAY RD
305
MILLER RD
KOURA RD
ARROW PT DR
TOLO RD
NEW BROOKLYN RD
HIGH SCHOOL RD
FLETCHER BAY RD
BLAKELY AVE NE
BAKER HILL RD
HALLS HILL RD

ISLAND COUNTRY INN

SEE DETAIL

Seattle - Bainbridge Island

Seattle - Bremerton Ferry

304

© MOON.COM

Detail inset:

WYATT WAY NE
GROW AVE
MADISON AVE S
MADRONA WY
ERICKSON AVE NE
305

CALICO CAT TOY SHOPPE
RESTAURANT MARCHE
BAINBRIDGE ISLAND MUSEUM OF ART
WILDERNEST
WINSLOW WAY E
HITCHCOCK
EAGLE HARBOR BOOK COMPANY
BLACKBIRD BAKERY
WOOD AVE
EAGLE HARBOR INN
HARBOUR PUBLIC HOUSE
WATERFRONT TR

0   1 mi
0   1 km

including insulation made of denim. The free museum is a good excuse to make the walk-on ferry trip across Puget Sound but doesn't take up much time for most art lovers. The 2nd floor has access to a small rooftop garden patio with handmade concrete boulders. Download the museum's free app for more artistic insight during your visit.

RESTAURANTS

The best day to hit the waterfront **Harbour Public House** (231 Parfitt Way SW, Bainbridge Island, 206/842-0969, http://harbourpub.com; 11am-midnight Mon.-Sat., 10am-10pm Sun.; $12-18) is probably Canada Day—the menu sports multiple versions of that country's favorite dish, poutine. Try it with black beans and yam fries, or get the classic version with gravy and cheese curds. The burger menu makes use of some local vendors, like Mount Townsend Creamery for the Trufflestack cheese or a veggie burger patty made in Port Townsend. Other options include local oysters and clams or baked russet potatoes. In winter there's a Friday oyster happy hour, and roast beef is featured on Sundays year-round.

Chef Greg Atkinson made his name at Seattle's Canlis, but at his own Restaurant Marche (150 Madrone Ln. N, Bainbridge Island, 206/842-1633, www.restaurantmarchebainbridge. com; 11:30am-2:30pm and 5pm-9pm Tues.-Sat.; $18-36) he created a bistro out of an old garage, albeit one that's now serving meals made with classic French techniques. It's much homier than the austere fine-dining destination he presided over across the water. At Marche, he specializes in elevating local produce to be the stars of the dish; try the moules-frites made with Puget Sound mussels and twice-fried potato fries.

Located in the middle of Bainbridge's main thoroughfare, Blackbird Bakery (210 Winslow Way E, Bainbridge Island, 206/780-1322, http://blackbirdbakery.com; 6am-6pm Mon.-Fri., 6:30am-6pm Sat., 7am-6pm Sun.) is the kind of hometown spot a bucolic village requires. The counters are crowded with European-style cakes, pastries, and other homemade treats, while the drink bar serves coffee from a Seattle roaster. Quiches and soups make a bid for full-meal status, but it's mostly dessert all the way with scones and fluffy cakes whose slices are as tall as they are wide.

The couple who created Hitchcock (133 Winslow Way E, Bainbridge Island, 206/201-3789, www.

hitchcockrestaurant.com; Tues.-Sun. 5pm-10pm; $25-35) traces family on the island back to the 1800s. The dishes on the restaurant's farm-to-table menu are just as local, with everything from the snap peas to the salmon Washington-sourced. The food is fancier than the exposed-wood dining room would indicate, and the chef's tasting menu ($65-90) is a worthy special occasion endeavor.

SHOPS

A bookstore of some ilk has anchored Winslow Way since the 1960s, and today Eagle Harbor Book Company (157 Winslow Way E, Bainbridge Island, 206/842-5332, www.eagleharborbooks.com; 10am-7pm Mon.-Fri., 10am-6pm Sat., 9am-6pm Sun.) is a warm community hub that hosts signings and celebrates local authors. The staff sometimes accepts used books for credit, filling the shelves of the downstairs used section of the store, but the front is dedicated to the crisp smell of new books.

Bainbridge Island isn't just a cute small town; it's a gateway to the wilds of the Olympic Peninsula. Outdoor store Wildernest (310 Winslow Way E, Bainbridge Island, 206/780-8527, www.wildernestoutdoorstore. com; 10am-7pm Mon.-Sat., 10am-6pm Sun.) is a logical stop for hiking boots, merino wool base layers, and, of course, rain jackets. The store also sells gear from first-aid kits to camping kitchen tools, plus rents snowshoes, climbing helmets, trekking poles, and bear canisters—the latter required for backpacking in much of the Olympics.

Sorry, cat lovers—the Calico Toy Shoppe (104 Winslow Way W, Bainbridge Island, 206/842-7720, www.calicocattoys.com; 10am-6pm Mon.-Sat., 11am-5pm Sun.) isn't actually full of catnip and feather toys for your feline. Rather it's a joyful toy store for kids, plus a puzzle and game store next door. Many of the playthings are simple, well-made items meant to inspire creativity, not suck batteries. Look for an in-store photo booth that posts pics right to social media accounts.

HOTELS

Nothing about Bainbridge Island is very big, but Eagle Harbor Inn (291 Madison Ave. S, Bainbridge Island, 206/842-1446, http://theeagleharborinn.com; $240-625) goes out of its way to show off its modest size, calling itself a "petit hotel." The brick exterior and outdoor umbrella-covered tables give off a Tuscan countryside feel, though the waterfront is close by. Accommodations range from simple rooms to bigger town homes with kitchens and offices, all decorated in warm, homey tones. With high-end linens and marble bathrooms, the space doesn't appeal much to kids; it's more a sedate retreat for a quiet couple or older family. Ask about getting an Eagle Harbor tour on an electric boat.

The Island Country Inn (4633 Woodson Ln NE, 206/842-7800, www.pleasantbeachvillage.com; $119-199) is a sweet little retreat on a quiet corner of Bainbridge Island. The 12-room hotel, whose exterior has light touches of Bavarian design, offers gas fireplaces and a pool with wading area, plus a hot tub. Suites are sizable. Note that the hotel is far enough from the ferry terminal and the Winslow Way shopping district to necessitate a car.

INFORMATION AND SERVICES

When on the Washington State Ferry to Bainbridge Island, look for free visitors guides and pamphlets in display cases on the passenger deck. Once on land, look for a tourism kiosk in the ferry terminal. The Bainbridge Chamber of Commerce (http://visitbainbridge.com) has visitor information and suggested itineraries.

GETTING THERE AND AROUND

Yes, Bainbridge is an island. But it's not completely isolated: It's linked to the Kitsap Peninsula by bridge on its northwest corner. It can be reached without a boat ride by heading south from Seattle on I-5 to Tacoma, then taking State Route 16 and the toll Tacoma Narrows Bridge northwest to Bremerton. From Bremerton it's 20 miles north to Poulsbo, then about 7 miles on State Route 305 to the Agate Pass Bridge onto Bainbridge Island.

Of course, that could take almost two hours, depending on Tacoma traffic, while a ferry from Seattle to Bainbridge is just a 35-minute ride. From the Washington State Ferry Terminal (http://www.wsdot.wa.gov/ferries/) downtown, be sure to pick a Bainbridge route, not a Bremerton-bound boat. Cars pay upon entering the waiting lot ($18.70 for car and driver, plus fees for additional passengers) and are directed to the correct waiting lane. Don't even try to skip a line; line control is a big deal on these commuter routes. Walk-on passengers ($8.35 adults, $4.15 children 6-18 and seniors, children under 6 free) enter the 2nd-floor terminal and can purchase tickets at a manned booth or a ticket machine. Cars pay in both directions, but walk-on passengers and vehicle passengers ride free on the eastbound (toward Seattle) trip.

Once on Bainbridge, most of the stores on Winslow Way and the Bainbridge Island Museum of Art are within a hearty walk from the ferry terminal; be prepared for a little ramble uphill. In summer, grab wheels at the nearby Bike Barn (260 Olympic Way SE, Bainbridge Island, www.bikebarnrentals.com; 10am-4pm Tues.-Sun. June-Sept.). Rides start at $25 and can be returned as late as 7pm. Bike routes hit the island's parks and the private Bloedel Reserve (7571 NE Dolphin Dr., Bainbridge Island, 206/842-7631, www.bloedelreserve. org; 10am-4pm Tues.-Wed., 10am-6pm Thurs.-Sun. summer, 10am-4pm Tues.-Sun. winter; $17 adults, $12 seniors, $10 children 13-18, $6 children 5-12, children under 5 free), an estate and garden about seven miles from the ferry terminal. The acres include a rhododendron garden and waterfalls, though pets and picnics are not allowed. Kitsap Transit buses (www. kitsaptransit.com/service/routed-buses/bi-ride) make limited trips to Bloedel Reserve for $2.

Eastside and Bellevue

Microsoft's headquarters isn't far from Bellevue, and the sleek, modern look of the city reflects that company's technological vision. Located just across Lake Washington from Seattle, Bellevue and its neighbors such as Kirkland and Woodinville have a more suburban feel and a slow, welcoming pace. Iconic Snoqualmie Falls is located just east of Bellevue off I-90. Those visiting Seattle on business trips could likely find themselves in this sister city, one slowly earning its own reputation separate from its neighbor across the pond.

SIGHTS
BELLEVUE ART MUSEUM
At various times the Bellevue Art Museum (510 Bellevue Way NE, Bellevue, 425/519-0770, www. bellevuearts.org; 11am-5pm Wed.-Sun.; $15 adults, $12 seniors and students, children under 6 free) has been located in places like an old funeral home and the top floor of downtown Bellevue's shopping mall; today it has a much-improved dedicated building not far from the shopping district. The 3rd floor has an outdoor sculpture garden with a wall that traces the direction of the 48th parallel, while indoor galleries display Northwest paintings, sculpture, and mixed-media pieces. There's a free tour daily at 1pm, and

downtown Bellevue

the museum hosts extended free hours (11am-8pm) on the first Thursday of the month.

BELLEVUE BOTANICAL GARDEN

Celebrating the very green, very lush Pacific Northwest, the Bellevue Botanical Garden (12001 Main St., Bellevue, 425/452-2750, www.bellevuebotanical.org; dawn to dusk daily, visitors center 9am-4pm daily; free) includes a water-wise garden that can grow without additional water resources and doesn't release chemicals into the environment; other sections are dedicated to fuchsias, rhododendrons, and dahlias. A volunteer staff keeps up the border of perennials, and a short nature trail, just a third of a mile in length, includes a suspension bridge over a ravine. The visitors center has a gift shop.

RESTAURANTS

The excitement was palpable when Din Tai Fung (700 Bellevue Way NE, No. 280, Bellevue, 425/698-1095, http://dintaifungusa.com; 11am-9:30pm Mon.-Thurs., 11am-10pm Fri., 10am-10pm Sat., 10am-9:30pm Sun.; $6-16) opened next to the Bellevue Square shopping area—the Taiwanese chain, best known for its soup dumplings, has a worldwide following. The sleek lines of the space highlight the workers constructing dumplings behind glass windows. Weekend brunches tend to have the longest waits, but the warm, soft dumplings, filled with meat and broth, became popular for a very good reason.

Many of Bellevue's eateries are second or third outposts of a local chain, concepts that worked well in Seattle before getting a more suburban copy over here. Monsoon East

(10245 Main St., Bellevue, 425/635-1112, www.monsoonrestaurants.com; 11:30am-3pm and 5pm-10pm Mon.-Thurs., 11:30am-3pm and 5pm-11pm Fri., 11am-3pm and 5pm-11pm Sat., 11am-3pm and 5pm-10pm Sun.; $18-25) is one of the most surprising of those second editions—the original is no downtown Seattle powerhouse, but rather a neighborhood joint in Capitol Hill beloved by locals. Here traditional Vietnamese dishes and techniques are mixed with Pacific Northwest ingredients and favorites, such as the Puget Sound oysters served with cilantro lime mignonette and duck confit buns with pickles and herbs. At the weekend dim sum brunch, the Bloody Marys are made with pho broth.

As yet another Bellevue version of a Seattle mainstay, El Gaucho (450 108th Ave. NE, Bellevue, 425/455-2715, http://elgaucho.com/dine/bellevue; 11:30am-2:30pm and 5pm-10pm Mon.-Fri., 5pm-10pm Sat.-Sun.; $37-75) manages to distance itself from the throwback original in a modern, glassy space. Though the menus include seafood and a Sunday prime rib dinner, the stars of the show are the 28-day dry-aged steaks and a chateaubriand for two carved tableside. A number of rich sauces can add flavor to the meats, and a baked potato with cheese sauce and scallions is fluffed by waiters at the table. Save room for a tableside bananas Foster or cherry jubilee flambé.

The white tablecloths at Bis On Main (10213 Main St., Bellevue, 425/455-2033, http://bisonmain.com; 11:30am-11pm Mon.-Thurs., 11:30am-midnight Fri., 5:30pm-midnight Sat., 5pm-9pm Sun.; $27-61) are classic, but nothing's too stuffy at this fine-dining bistro where pieces from Northwest artists hang on the wall. Late-night happy hour starts at 8:30pm and runs all night on Sundays. The menu features Italian and French classics, from a cipollini onion risotto to truffle pommes frites.

Café Juanita (9702 NE 120th Pl., Bellevue, 425/823-1505, www.cafejuanita.com; 5pm-9pm Tues.-Thurs., 5pm-10pm Fri.-Sat.; $16-55) isn't really near anything of note in a quiet neighborhood north of Lake Washington, and it's hard to find. But the Italian restaurant has a great reputation (it has racked up awards) and ardent fans. The northern Italian fare includes homemade pastas and rich dishes like braised rabbit. Though it's tucked away, the refined food and classy setting give it a sense of occasion.

Corporate Bellevue, home of power lunches and suburban diners, has a lot less funky charm than some of Seattle's older neighborhoods, but spots like Lot No. 3 (460 106th Ave. NE, Bellevue, 425/440-0025, www.lotno3.com; 11am-midnight Mon.-Thurs., 9am-2am Sat., 9am-midnight Sun.; $14-18) prove that there's plenty of character to be found in the city. In true Northwest style, the gastropub pairs craft brews with locally sourced comfort foods like crispy pork belly and chicken and waffles. There's no holding back on cravings here, where you can order a "plate o' bacon," goat cheese toast, or a Cubano made with slow-roasted pork. Rather than the sleek modernity that dominates tech-friendly Bellevue, the restaurant lives in a space designed with industrial boldness—dark, heavy wood tables and strings of vintage lights hanging from the ceiling.

No, you're not exactly on the water at The Lakehouse (10455 NE 5th Pl., Bellevue, 425/454-7076, http://thelakehousebellevue.com; 6am-10pm Mon.-Fri., 7am-10pm Sat.-Sun.; $38-82), but there are porch swings and Adirondack chairs outside anyway—a bit quirky since the restaurant's located inside the W Hotel. Inside, the dark floral wallpaper and black wood touches seem a bit more serious than most lake vacations, but much of the menu features seafood, from grilled prawns to Alaskan halibut, and all dishes are prepared with local produce. Reservations are recommended.

HOTELS

The Eastside's most welcome hotel district isn't even in Bellevue, but in next-door Kirkland, which has a small waterfront on Lake Washington and an even slower pace. The Heathman Hotel (220 Kirkland Ave., Kirkland, 425/284-5800, www.heathmankirkland.com; $309-409) sits a few blocks from the water in this quiet suburb. The sizable property has updated furnishings in rich tones of cream and gold, with a standard of service that far outdoes the neighborhood's calm and understated tone. There are soft robes in the closet and pillow-top or feather bed options for the bed. Downstairs at Trellis restaurant, afternoon tea is served daily, and Sundays and Mondays feature a three-course dinner special. The restaurant has a dedicated farm in nearby Woodinville that grows its produce. Hotel guests get complimentary tickets to Argosy boat cruises, SUV service to close-by attractions, and bike rentals.

Even farther from the center of action, the Woodmark Hotel (1200 Carillon Pt., Kirkland, 425/822-3700, www.thewoodmark.com; $319-541) is a calming spot next to a marina and flanked by two good dining spots, ideal for a city getaway that almost feels remote. Rooms have Lake Washington views, and some even have small balconies for catching the breeze off the water. Rooms feel comfortable and not too businesslike, appropriate for a hotel best suited to a quiet break that's still only a short drive to Bellevue's biggest companies. The Still Spa is one of the Eastside's best.

The best part of the **Bellevue Club Hotel** (11200 SE 6th St., Bellevue, 800/579-1110, www.thehotelbellevue. com; $190-299) isn't the rooms, though they do sport marble bathrooms and, for some, access to a private patio—it's the Bellevue Club, a private facility that guests are allowed to access. The club's two indoor pools, tennis courts, indoor track, and fitness classes are for getting the heart rate up, while the attached spa brings it right back down. Though the large fountains contribute to the retreat feel, the hotel is still close to Bellevue's commercial district.

Everything about the **Westin Bellevue** (600 Bellevue Way NE, Bellevue, 425/638-1000, www. westinbellevuehotel.com; $199-501) fits the modern, tech-built Bellevue downtown; it's an efficient chain hotel in a high-rise, close to the restaurants of Lincoln Square's shopping district. But it's also across the street from the Bellevue Museum of Art, and views reach to the sparkling waters of Lake Washington and far-off snow-topped mountains. The hotel has an indoor pool and Jacuzzi, plus an attached spa. To take a run even when you didn't bring workout gear, call the front desk to request a free running shoe and sports clothing rental, delivered right to your room.

INFORMATION AND SERVICES

Find ideas and itineraries for the Eastside at **Visit Bellevue** (www.visitbellevuewashington. com) or **Explore Kirkland** (www. explorekirkland.com).

GETTING THERE AND AROUND

There's little public transportation in and around Bellevue save the King Country Metro bus system (http:// metro.kingcounty.gov). The two main roads to Bellevue are bridges over the lake that separates the city from Seattle, and both get very crowded at rush hours. The I-90 bridge stops on Mercer Island before hitting the shore just south of Bellevue, while the Highway 520 floating bridge, which requires a toll, lands just north of Bellevue. Many restaurants in Bellevue offer free or reduced parking by request.

WOODINVILLE

Most of Washington's famed wine-making takes place east of Seattle, across the mountains. But go just a little east of the city for a town that's become a kind of emissary for the far-off vineyards. Woodinville is just 30 miles from the Space Needle but can feel like a different world, one with a slower pace and finer appreciation for sitting around and sipping spirits. Several of the larger wineries and tasting rooms cluster near where NE 145th Street meets Redmond-Woodinville Road, just east of Chateau Ste. Michelle, in the center of it all.

Chateau Ste. Michelle (14111 NE 145th St., 425/488-1133, www. ste-michelle.com; tastings and tours 10am-5pm daily; free) is a French-style behemoth that should look utterly out

Hiking is more than an occasional hobby to most Seattle locals; for many, it's a way of life. Trails short and long wind through the forests and mountains around the city. Many hikes are accessed from I-90, which travels east from Seattle toward the Cascades, but trails can be found around the entire region. Local outdoor group **The Mountaineers** (www. mountaineers.org) offers information on hikes as well as the "10 essentials," a list of hiking safety items including matches, water, and a headlamp. The **Washington Trails Association** (www.wta.org), a nonprofit organization, performs trail maintenance and offers a thorough online guide to the state's trails with the best and most up-to-date information. Given sometimes significant elevation gains on trails in the area, hiking times are highly variable; plan to give yourself some leeway in terms of daylight.

MOUNT SI

If you had to pick one trail as Seattle's favorite, it would be this mountain that towers over the town of North Bend. It's also famous, having appeared in the TV show *Twin Peaks*— the "twins" were this mountain and its neighbor. The trail is eight miles round-trip with significant elevation gain via switchbacks in the forest, but the reward is vast views from the rocky area near the summit. Budget 4-6 hours for this hike.

Getting There: The trailhead is about 35 miles, a 40-minute drive, east of Seattle. From exit 32 off I-90, turn left on 436th Avenue and left on North Bend Way, then right on SE Mt. Si Road. The trailhead, well signed about a half-mile later, gets crowded in summer, so King County Metro sometimes runs shuttles between Seattle and the trail's parking lot; schedules vary every year (check http://trailheaddirect.wordpress.com). A Discover Pass is required to park, and you can find one at North Bend gas stations.

RATTLESNAKE LEDGE

Don't worry, there aren't actual snakes about on this scenic rock balcony just south of North Bend (or if there are, they're harmless and not rattlers). This well-loved trail moves slowly uphill, through forest on a very well-maintained route, sometimes offering peeka-boo views of the lake below. After two miles you'll reach the flat ledge, a perfect, scenic lunch spot overlooking the watershed below. Stay far from the edge and keep an eye on children—falls off the precipice are deadly. It takes hikers about 2-4 hours to complete the four total miles.

Getting There: The trailhead is about 35 miles, a 40-minute drive, east of Seattle. From exit 32 off of I-90, head south on Cedar Falls Road SE for about 4 miles. The trailhead is at Rattlesnake Lake.

---

of place in grubby rural Washington. Instead the quaint shutters and giant wooden doors on the estate are welcoming, if a bit weird, and the winery gives tastings and hosts summer concerts on its well-trimmed lawns.

Located among wineries, **Sumerian Brewing** (15510 Redmond-Woodinville Rd. NE, 425/486-5330, www.sumerianbrewingco.com; 2pm-8pm Mon.-Wed., 2pm-9pm Thurs., noon-9pm Fri.-Sat., noon-8pm Sun.) isn't afraid of pouring something profoundly different. Known for crowd-pleasers like pilsners and IPAs, the brewery also stretches into stouts and a scotch ale. The tasting room (for adults only) is sizable, with outdoor seating available.

Drinks may be taken care of, but there's always dinner to consider, and the town has a clear favorite dining spot in **The Herbfarm** (14590 NE 145th St., 425/485-5300, http:// theherbfarm.com; seatings at 4:30pm and 7pm; $205-285). Originally home to an educational meal on the site of a small local farm, now it's relocated to a flowery spot among the wineries. Meals are a single-seating, nine-course affair preceded by a garden tour and introduction to swine named Basil and Borage—they're pets, not future pork dishes. As befits the wine-loving town,

POO POO POINT

The funny name of this part of West Tiger Mountain near Issaquah comes from the sound that steam whistles made when this was a logging center. There are two routes to the mountainside meadow you're aiming for, but the most direct is called the Chirico Trail. It offers quite a workout as it makes a few switchbacks up the mountain, but less than two miles up you'll reach a clear overlook where paragliders like to take off; on a nice day you'll see them unfurl their parachute-like contraptions and walk off the clearing into the sky. Thanks to the elevation gain, plan on around three hours for the 3.8-mile round trip—and more if you plan to hang out to watch the flyers.

Getting There: The trailhead is about 20 miles, a 30-minute drive, east of Seattle. From exit 17 on I-90, head south on Front Street/Issaquah-Hobert Road SE for about 3 miles. Look for the parking lot and field.

COAL CREEK FALLS

The Coal Creek Falls trail is located on Cougar Mountain, really more of a large hill, located in the foothills known as the Issaquah Alps. The wooded area is threaded with trails ideal for running, slow strolls, and small children. This out-and-back hike through the former coal mining area is a flat 2.5 miles total and there are mining holes and sometimes old equipment off the trail. The waterfall at the end is a 28-foot mossy cascade that runs most elegantly in winter. The well-signed network of trails on Cougar Mountain can get confusing, but if you end up on a wrong spur it's unlikely to take you too far. At a moderate pace, this hike takes about 1.5 hours.

Getting There: The trailhead is about 16 miles, a 25-minute drive, east of Seattle. From exit 13 on I-90, head south on Lakemont Boulevard about 3 miles, just after a sharp bend in the road. The parking lot will be to your left; the hike starts at Red Town Trailhead.

BILLY FRANK JR. NISQUALLY NATIONAL WILDLIFE REFUGE

The Nisqually National Wildlife Refuge protects the river delta where the waterway, filled by melting glaciers on Mount Rainier, empties into Puget Sound just outside the city of Olympia. The resulting wetlands drain and fill at various points of the year, but there are always a plethora of beavers, otters, owls, and ducks to see. There are five total miles of flat trail here, some on wooden boardwalks suspended over the delta, and much of it is wheelchair accessible.

Getting There: The trailhead is about 52 miles, about an hour's drive, south of Seattle. From exit 114 off I-5, turn right onto Brown Farm Road and follow signs to the refuge's parking lot. Parking is $3, and the visitors center offers maps.

the restaurant chooses pairings from a 26,000-bottle cellar.

GETTING THERE

Woodinville is just over 10 miles north of Bellevue on I-405, and about 20 miles—a 35-minute drive—northeast of Seattle via I-90 and I-405.

SNOQUALMIE FALLS

The roaring Snoqualmie Falls are farther east of Bellevue, just about 35 minutes from Seattle, and make a classic day-trip destination from the city, ideal for anyone looking for spectacular views without a hike. The falls are visible from a viewing platform (dawn-dusk daily; free). At 270 feet tall, they absolutely thunder over the edge at their fullest, usually in late spring. A short trail leaves from the observation platform down to the river, but the waterfall views are best right here on the platform next to the free parking.

Right next to the falls is the Salish Lodge and Spa (6501 Railroad Ave., 425/888-2556, www.salishlodge.com, $349-449), long a local favorite for a special occasion meal or easy getaway, and also an icon—it featured prominently in the TV show *Twin Peaks*, which was filmed here and in nearby North Bend. The Pacific

Northwest-inspired decor is woodsy, though rooms have a crisp modern feel, some with fireplaces and large soaking tubs. **The Dining Room** (800/272-5474; 7am-2pm and 5pm-9pm Mon.-Thurs., 7am-2pm and 5pm-10pm Fri., 7am-3pm and 5pm-10pm Sat., 7am-3pm and 5pm-9pm Sun.; $19-49) serves lunch and dinner as well as a famous, massive breakfast that includes its famous "honey from heaven," made from the hotel's own bees and poured from high above a plate of fresh pancakes. An on-site spa has a beautiful soaking pool and a riverside treatment tent.

GETTING THERE

Snoqualmie Falls is off I-90 about 25 miles east of Bellevue and 30 miles east of Seattle. Take exit 25 and follow Snoqualmie Parkway north about 4 miles, then turn left onto Railroad Avenue at a traffic circle; the way is well signed. Public buses run to the falls from downtown Seattle but involve a transfer in Issaquah—you'll take the 554 express and change to the 208 local bus—and the trip takes about 1.5 hours.

Tacoma

For a long time Tacoma was forgotten, the confusing half of Sea-Tac International Airport's name. At worst, it was the butt of jokes for its industrial smell, called "the Aroma of Tacoma." But recent years have seen an upswing for the waterfront city, including a spate of new museums and a rejuvenated downtown. A working industrial waterfront dwarfs the tourist areas, with most of the museums located along a finger of water that stretches into the city from Commencement Bay. Smaller than Seattle and embracing its workaday past, Tacoma is quietly becoming the unpretentious, artsy urban center of the region.

SIGHTS
✪ MUSEUM OF GLASS

Who knew that gritty Tacoma would eventually become known for a fragile, delicate art form? The **Museum of Glass** (1801 Dock St., 253/284-4750, www.museumofglass.org; 10am-5pm Mon.-Sat., noon-5pm Sun. spring-summer, 10am-5pm Wed.-Sat., noon-5pm Sun. fall-winter; $17 adults, $14 students and seniors, $5 children 6-12, children under 6 free) celebrates an entire artistic community made famous by Dale Chihuly, a glass sculptor born in Tacoma. The space was originally meant to focus on Chihuly—there's an outdoor bridge topped with his signature sculptures—but since then the artist has been part of a push to make the museum about the art form internationally. The body of the museum is shaped like a giant silver cone, inside of which is the Hot Shop Amphitheater where visitors can observe glass artists working in the studio. The museum café focuses on Argentinian-style sandwiches.

WASHINGTON STATE HISTORY MUSEUM

The Washington State History Museum (1911 Pacific Ave., 253/272-3500, www.washingtonhistory.org; 10am-5pm Tues.-Sun.; $14 adults, $1 seniors and students, children under 6 free) is quick to point out that the region's history didn't start with the arrival of the Europeans. The exhibits start with thousand year old evidence of Native American life in the area, eventually moving up to the eras of logging and women's suffrage fights to today's technology. A lab-themed exhibit turns history into a mystery game, and a permanent model railroad shows the region's rails in miniature.

LEMAY—AMERICA'S CAR MUSEUM

What looks like a giant silver slug from the interstate is actually LeMay—America's Car Museum (2702 E. D St., 253/779-8490, www.americascarmuseum.org; 10am-5pm daily; $18 adults, $16 seniors, $14 students, $10 children 6-12, children under 6 free), a relatively new addition to the Tacoma skyline and a welcome dash of modern architecture. More than 300 cars can be on display at a time, from Model Ts to Teslas. Take a free daily tour, get a free photograph in a 1923 Buick out front, or even take a turn at the wheel at the museum's race car simulators.

✪ POINT DEFIANCE ZOO AND AQUARIUM

The charmingly named Point Defiance is a thumb-shaped peninsula that juts north into Puget Sound a short drive from downtown. It's home to parkland and the Point Defiance Zoo and Aquarium (5400 N. Pearl St., 253/591-5337; hours vary by month; $18 adults, $17 seniors, $14

Fluent Steps by artist Martin Blank at Tacoma's Museum of Glass

Tacoma

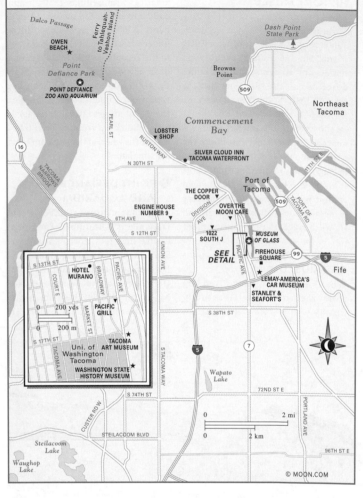

Dalco Passage

Ferry to Tahlequah-Vashon Island

OWEN BEACH ★

Point Defiance Park

★ POINT DEFIANCE ZOO AND AQUARIUM

Dash Point State Park

Browns Point

Commencement Bay

Northeast Tacoma

509

PEARL ST

16

TACOMA NARROWS BRIDGE

RUSTON WAY

LOBSTER SHOP ▼

N 30TH ST

SILVER CLOUD INN TACOMA WATERFRONT ●

Port of Tacoma

509

PORT OF TACOMA RD

11TH ST

Port of Tacoma

THE COPPER DOOR ▼

ENGINE HOUSE NUMBER 9 ▼

6TH AVE

DIVISION AVE

OVER THE MOON CAFÉ ▼

99

5

Fife

S 12TH ST

1022 SOUTH J

SEE DETAIL

MUSEUM OF GLASS ✦

PACIFIC AVE

FIREHOUSE SQUARE

★ LEMAY-AMERICA'S CAR MUSEUM

STANLEY & SEAFORT'S

UNION AVE

S 38TH ST

S 13TH ST

HOTEL MURANO ●

COURT E

BROADWAY

PACIFIC AVE

MARKET ST

PACIFIC GRILL

0   200 yds
0   200 m

S 17TH ST

TACOMA AVE

Uni. of Washington Tacoma

★ TACOMA ART MUSEUM

★ WASHINGTON STATE HISTORY MUSEUM

5

7

Wapato Lake

72ND ST E

PORTLAND AVE

S 74TH ST

CUSTER RD W

S TACOMA WAY

0   2 mi
0   2 km

96TH ST E

Steilacoom Lake

STEILACOOM BLVD

Waughop Lake

© MOON.COM

children 5-12, $10 children 3-4, children under 3 free). The zoo is smaller than Seattle's Woodland Park iteration but has a bonus: The Pacific Seas Aquarium opened in 2018 with more than 9,000 animals. Pacific Seas is, appropriately, home to Pacific walruses and harbor seals, plus five kinds of sharks, sea turtles, and many fish. Anyone over eight can do a dive into

the shark pool for a fee, and scuba-certified divers can venture beyond the cage. Back on dry land, the zoo has elephants, camels, and polar bears. Ask for a daily schedule of animal shows and keeper talks.

TACOMA ART MUSEUM

Though sometimes overshadowed by the striking glass museum,

Point Defiance Zoo and Aquarium

the **Tacoma Art Museum** (1701 Pacific Ave., 253/272-4258, www.tacomaartmuseum.org; 10am-5pm Tues.-Sun.; $15 adults, $13 students and seniors, children under 6 free) is a vital part of the increasingly popular downtown scene. The TAM has amassed thousands of works of Northwest and Pacific Rim art over 80 years, including Japanese woodblock prints and studio art jewelry. The Haub Family Collection of Western American Art is one of the country's most striking collections of frontier arts; it features pieces from Thomas Moran and Georgia O'Keeffe and includes works from contemporary Native American artists. In 2019, the striking, modern Benaroya Wing opened, adding exhibit space in an area designed by noted Seattle architects Olson Kundig.

RESTAURANTS

Located about a block from the Tacoma Art Museum, **Pacific Grill** (1502 Pacific Ave., 253/627-3535, www.pacificgrilltacoma.com; 11am-2pm and 4:30pm-9pm Mon.-Thurs., 11am-2pm and 4:30pm-10pm Fri., 10am-2pm and 4:30pm-10pm Sat., 10am-2pm and 4:30pm-9pm Sun.; $22-36) sits in a historic downtown building and features a varied menu that ranges from "the devil's eggs" to a rich, cheesy cauliflower melt sandwich. Though classics like filet mignon and grilled lamb have their place, the restaurant avoids a stuffy vibe by including a modern array of flatbreads, shared-plate starters, and vegetarian options. The decor is exposed brick with high windows and black wood tables; adults will feel at home but kids won't be charmed.

Something called the **Lobster Shop** (4015 Ruston Way, 253/759-2165, http://wp.lobstershop.com; 11:30am-3pm and 4:30pm-9pm Mon.-Thurs., 11:30am-3pm and 4:30pm-9:30pm Fri., 11:30am-3:30pm and 4:30pm-9:30pm Sat., 9:30am-1:30pm and 4:30pm-9pm Sun.; $20-52) seems as if it would be more at home in New England than on Tacoma's Commencement Bay, but the seafood selection here is the city's best—to say nothing of the waterfront views. Lots of the sea creatures really are local, from the Dabob Bay clams served with linguini to the Dungeness crab cakes. The wild king salmon is prepared with a maple glaze or on the traditional cedar plank. And yes, the lobster is indeed from Maine—it's served in a dip, by the tail, with pasta, or in a rich bisque.

Though the museums are located next to Tacoma's working industrial waterfront, the north end of downtown evolves into more charming streets packed with small businesses. Tucked into an alley behind bright red brick is **Over the Moon Café** (709 Opera Alley, 253/284-3722, http://overthemooncafe.net; 11:30am-2:30pm and 4:30pm-9pm Tues.-Thurs., 11:30am-2:30pm and 4:30pm-10pm Fri.-Sat.; $22-38). Characterized by exposed brick and wood beams, the restaurant has the eclectic clutter of an artistic collector, with little extra room. Dishes range from generous pasta bowls to duck breast served with a port reduction. Desserts are rich and sizable, deserving of some reserved space.

Stanley & Seafort's (115 E. 34th St., 253/473-7300, http://stanleyandseaforts.com; 3pm-9pm Mon.-Thurs., 3pm-10pm Fri., 10:30am-10pm Sat., 10:30am-9pm Sun.; $24-55) isn't a restaurant—it's an institution. The neon sign that sits on a hill above the city is as much a part of the landscape as the UFO-like Tacoma Dome below. Views, of course, are expansive from the window seats and the patio (and the parking lot, actually). The special-occasion joint has the classics on lock: prime rib roasted with rock salt, chilled crab cocktail, a seafood étouffée. It's the kind of place that gets so many eager celebrants that it advertises a special prom menu—and no, you can't have that option unless you're really sweating out the big dance, but the early-bird three-course special is for everyone.

NIGHTLIFE

One of Tacoma's best cocktail bars, **1022 South J** (1022 S. J St., 253/627-8588, www.1022southj.com; 11am-midnight Tues.-Thurs. and Sun., 11am-2am Fri.-Sat.) is dim and atmospheric, but still far from pretentious. Even though it's located many blocks from the downtown museums, it was discovered and praised by the *New York Times* and saw its reputation skyrocket. The tiny kitchen serves a number of sandwiches and small plates, but the real draws are cocktails built from local, small-batch ingredients and the conversation you can have with the bartender while they're made.

Every Washington town needs a craft beer bar, and **The Copper Door** (12 N. Tacoma Ave., 253/212-3708, www.thecopperdoor.net, 11am-11pm Mon.-Thurs. 11am-2am Fri.-Sat.) has 16 taps, more than 800 bottles, and a logo sporting hops, wheat, apples, and water. It's all behind, yes, a copper door in the neighborhood north of downtown, next to the castle-like Stadium High School. Every Sunday sees "Kill the Keg" specials to polish off the week's offerings before they change on Monday.

Finding **Engine House Number 9** (611 N. Pine St., 253/272-3435, www.ehouse9.com; 11am-midnight Mon.-Wed., 11am-1am Thurs., 11am-2am Fri., 8am-2am Sat., 8am-10pm Sun.) in Tacoma's 6th Avenue Business District isn't hard; as the name says, it's in an old firehouse. The 1907 brick building has touches of fire history inside, including a fire pole, and the exposed brick and big windows give it a warm burgers-and-beer feel. (It's also the city's first craft brewery.) Weekend breakfasts are hearty enough to fill the former firefighting inhabitants of the space.

SHOPS

Originally built as a train terminal, **Freighthouse Square** (2501 E. D St., 253/305-0678, www.freighthousesquare.com; hours vary) is now a shopping district with three blocks of indoor shops. Stores include Claudia's Attic for gifts, Noble Trove with its sports gear, and a knife sharpener called Vulcan Knife. There's also the world's only Lego demo studio, City Blocks, with impressive sculptures and do-it-yourself Lego stations. Among the several food options is a liege waffle joint called La Waffletz. In addition to its shopping options, Freighthouse will eventually be a train station again when the Amtrak terminal takes up residence.

Rough-and-tumble Tacoma may now be dotted with museums and craft cocktail bars, but its soul hasn't changed. Skateboarding fashion brand Bleach (1934 Pacific Ave., 253/292-1694, http://bleachlife.com; 11am-7pm Mon.-Thurs., 11am-8pm Fri.-Sat., noon-5pm Sun.) has the washed-out gray hoodies and T-shirts that skaters like, plus plenty of locally branded shirts that say things like "You'll Like Tacoma." They carry a line of Rainiers minor league baseball gear, and a T-shirt printing press sits in the front window.

The small Defiance Bicycles (411 S. Fawcett Ave., 253/777-5546, http://defiancebicycles.com; 10am-6pm Mon.-Sat.) is a friendly cycling destination for visitors who've come on two wheels. Though there's plenty of gear for sale, the staff's local knowledge of routes is more valuable. They'll even remind you that while their name is about defiance, they have to encourage you to obey the local helmet law.

Hotel Murano

HOTELS

If the Museum of Glass is Tacoma's signature attraction, Hotel Murano (1320 Broadway, 253/238-8000, www.hotelmuranotacoma.com; $200-280) is the accommodations equivalent. No other hotel in town can compare to this modern tower, which has a swooping glass sculpture out front and an ultramodern lobby. It's named for the Italian district near Venice known for its glass art, and it works the colors, aesthetic, and crisp appeal of the art form into the decor. The hotel offers so many accommodations that you can choose your pillows, religious tome, and Spotify channel. Rooms are pointedly non-corporate, and the downstairs lobby bar is buzzy. Kids are welcome—and will be entranced by the multicolor glass wonderland.

As part of a hotel chain known to be serviceable but never fancy, Silver Cloud Inn Tacoma Waterfront (2317 Ruston Way, 253/272-1300, www.silvercloud.com/tacoma; $259-370) is nicer than most. Its location on the Puget Sound waterfront—the only hotel in town on the water—means it's a bit removed from downtown but open to beautiful views; some rooms have fireplaces and Jacuzzi tubs that look right into Commencement Bay. There are a few restaurants within walking distance, but it's not particularly convenient for anyone without a car.

INFORMATION AND SERVICES

The Tacoma Visitor Information Center (1516 Commerce, 800/272-2662, www.traveltacoma.com; 10am-4pm Mon.-Fri., 10am-3pm Sat. summer, 10am-4pm Tues.-Fri., 10am-3pm Sat. fall-spring), with maps and downtown exploration suggestions, is located in the lobby of the Greater Tacoma Convention Center.

GETTING THERE AND AROUND

Though it's only a little more than 30 miles from Seattle to Tacoma via I-5, the drive can take an hour or more when traffic clogs the interstate. Look for carpool lanes if there are at least two people in the vehicle, but don't be tempted to cheat—state patrolmen will issue tickets to solo drivers in the lanes. Sound Transit's Route 590 Express bus (www.soundtransit.org) runs from downtown Seattle's 2nd Avenue to Freighthouse Station and the museum district in Tacoma. Even faster is the Sounder rail, a train that goes from Seattle's King Street Station to the Tacoma Dome Station. Within the city, the Tacoma Link Light Rail goes to six stops in the downtown area, starting at Tacoma Dome Station near Freighthouse Station, and is free.

Mount Rainier National Park

Look at any Washington State license plate and you'll see it: the towering hulk of mountain called Rainier. Though the 14,410-foot peak is imposing—it's so dangerous that climbers practice here before trying Mount Everest—the mountain welcomes everyone to its flanks, where wildflowers bloom in the summer and plentiful snow beckons skiers and sledders in the winter.

Although the mountain has been an icon for centuries, it didn't become a national park until 1899. Naturalist John Muir visited the area and sang its praises, wowed by the wildflower meadows that surround it like a floral skirt. Today hundreds of climbers use Camp Muir, halfway up the mountain, as a staging area for summit ascents.

VISITING THE PARK

Mount Rainier National Park (360/569-2211, www.nps.gov/mora; $30/vehicle) consists of five main regions: Longmire, Paradise, Ohanapecosh, Sunrise, and the remote Carbon and Mowich area. Even though the park is open year-round, summer is by far its most popular season. Snowdrifts can linger in Paradise well into the summer, and the Sunrise visitors center doesn't generally open until July. August weekends are the most crowded in the national park, when wildflowers are at their peak and sunny days are more common.

Snowflakes begin falling in September or October and lead to serious accumulation—for many years the mountain held a world record for the most snowfall in a year, a record only broken by nearby Mount Baker. When thick snow blankets the park in winter, the narrow (but plowed) roads make for slow going and cars need chains, and the only attractions open are the Jackson Visitor Center (on weekends) and the National Park Inn.

ENTRANCE STATIONS

The park has two major entrances. The southwest Nisqually Entrance goes to the largest visitor destination at Paradise but first passes through the Longmire encampment. The northeast White River/Sunrise entrance (May-Nov.) leads to the visitors center at Sunrise. Entrance stations charge $30 per car ($15 for walk-ins), which is good for up to seven days. Seniors age 62 and over can score a lifetime pass,

Mount Rainier

good for entrance to all National Park Service units, for $80.

The **Nisqually Entrance** is located in the southwest section of the park on State Route 706 approximately 6 miles from Ashford. The road from the entrance to Longmire stays open year-round (weather permitting) and provides the only winter access to the park. From November 1 through May 1 a gate closes the road from Longmire to Paradise (nightly at 5pm Mon.-Fri. and 7pm Sat.-Sun.), and it may stay closed longer if snow builds up. All cars, including those with four-wheel drive, are required to carry chains November-May.

Sunrise and **White River** form the northeast entrance to the park. This entrance is accessed via State Route 410, 13.5 miles south of Greenwater. The road into the park is only open May-November; through access from Ohanapecosh and Longmire is available seasonally. The road from the White River Entrance Station to Sunrise is open early July-October

(weather permitting) and closes nightly from its junction with the White River Campground (open seasonally) and reopens in the morning.

Other park entrances include the **Ohanapecosh Entrance,** the southeast entrance to the park. Packwood, 11 miles southwest, is the nearest gateway. State Route 123 from U.S. Highway 12 is open May-November; this entrance is inaccessible the rest of the year.

Carbon River is the northwest entrance to the park; vehicles are not permitted past the entrance station. The Mowich Lake hike-in campground lies south of the Carbon River entrance, at the end of an unpaved road (mid-July-mid-Oct.) that may be difficult for some cars to navigate. A machine near the park entrance collects the entry fee.

LONGMIRE

Most visitors enter the park on State Route 706. From there the road winds through forest and next to

Mount Rainier National Park

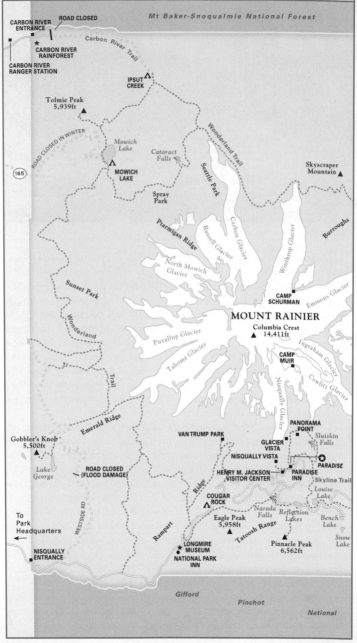

Mt Baker-Snoqualmie National Forest

CARBON RIVER ENTRANCE
ROAD CLOSED
Carbon River Trail
CARBON RIVER RAINFOREST
CARBON RIVER RANGER STATION

IPSUT CREEK

Tolmie Peak 5,939ft

Wonderland Trail

ROAD CLOSED IN WINTER

Mowich Lake

Cataract Falls

Seattle Park

Skyscraper Mountain

(165)

MOWICH LAKE

Spray Park

Ptarmigan Ridge

Russell Glacier

Carbon Glacier

Winthrop Glacier

Burroughs

North Mowich Glacier

Sunset Park

Wonderland

CAMP SCHURMAN

Emmons Glacier

Puyallup Glacier

MOUNT RAINIER
Columbia Crest
▲ 14,411ft

Ingraham Glacier

CAMP MUIR

Tahoma Glacier

Cowlitz Glacier

Trail

Emerald Ridge

Gobbler's Knob 5,500ft

Lake George

ROAD CLOSED (FLOOD DAMAGE)

WESTSIDE RD

VAN TRUMP PARK

GLACIER VISTA
NISQUALLY VISTA

HENRY M. JACKSON VISITOR CENTER

Nisqually Glacier

PANORAMA POINT
Sluiskin Falls

PARADISE

PARADISE INN

Skyline Trail

Louise Lake

COUGAR ROCK

Ridge

Eagle Peak 5,958ft

Narada Falls

Reflection Lakes

Bench Lake

Snow Lake

To Park Headquarters

Rampart

NISQUALLY ENTRANCE

LONGMIRE MUSEUM
NATIONAL PARK INN

Tatoosh Range

Pinnacle Peak 6,562ft

Gifford   Pinchot   National

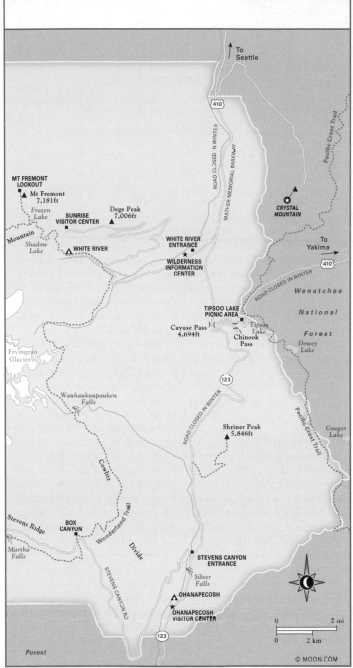

To Seattle

410

ROAD CLOSED IN WINTER

MATHER MEMORIAL PARKWAY

Pacific Crest Trail

MT FREMONT
LOOKOUT
▲ Mt Fremont
7,181ft
*Frozen
Lake*
SUNRISE
VISITOR CENTER ■   Dege Peak
7,006ft

CRYSTAL
MOUNTAIN

Mountain
*Shadow
Lake*   △ WHITE RIVER

WHITE RIVER
ENTRANCE ■
★
WILDERNESS
INFORMATION
CENTER

To
Yakima

410

ROAD CLOSED IN WINTER

Wenatchee

National

*Fryingpan
Glacier*

TIPSOO LAKE
PICNIC AREA ■
Cayuse Pass
4,694ft
Chinook
Pass

*Tipsoo
Lake*

Forest
*Dewey
Lake*

*Wauhaukaupauken
Falls*

ROAD CLOSED IN WINTER

123

Shriner Peak
5,846ft

Pacific Crest Trail

*Cougar
Lake*

Stevens Ridge

BOX
CANYON ■

Wonderland Trail

Divide

STEVENS CANYON RD

*Martha
Falls*

STEVENS CANYON
ENTRANCE ■
*Silver
Falls*
△ OHANAPECOSH

OHANAPECOSH
VISITOR CENTER

123

Forest

0   2 mi
0   2 km

© MOON.COM

229

VISITORS CENTERS

- **Longmire Information Center** (360/569-6575; 9am-5pm daily June-Sept., 9am-4:30pm daily Oct.-May) in Longmire, inside the Longmire Wilderness Information Center (7:30am-5pm daily May-Sept.)

- **Henry M. Jackson Memorial Visitor Center** (360/569-6571; 10am-7pm daily summer, 10am-5pm Sat.-Sun. fall-spring weather permitting) in Paradise

- **Ohanapecosh Visitor Center** (360/569-6581; 9am-5pm daily June-Aug., 9am-5pm Fri.-Sun. Sept.) in the southeast corner of the park on State Route 123

- **Sunrise Visitor Center** (360/663-2425; 10am-6pm daily July-Sept.) in Sunrise

- **Carbon River Ranger Station** (360/829-9639; 7:30am-5pm daily June-Sept.) in the Carbon and Mowich area

the Nisqually River, gaining elevation until it gets to the small gathering of buildings called Longmire (6.5 miles from the Nisqually Entrance on Longmire-Paradise Rd.). James Longmire settled the area in 1883 and found mineral springs nearby. Now it's one of the biggest recreation centers in the park. It holds the National Park Inn, a small general store full of gifts and snacks, a museum, a wilderness center, and historical displays in an old gas station. Most buildings are in the rustic national park style, made from large rocks and dark wood timbers.

LONGMIRE MUSEUM

Located in one of the historic stone-and-wood buildings that compose Longmire, the Longmire Museum (360/569-6575, www.nps.gov/mora; 9am-5pm daily June-Sept., 9am-4:30pm daily Oct.-Dec.; free) is home to exhibits and photographs that trace the history of the area, including the Longmire family and their use of the area as a resort. Books and maps are available; when the museum is closed, some exhibits move to the Wilderness Information Center next door.

HIKING

The Trail of the Shadows (under 1 mile) skirts past one of the Longmire family's old cabins and the mineral springs. For a longer hike, continue on the Rampart Ridge Trail. This trail tests the quads in a 4.6-mile loop, but the mountain views are worth it. The trailhead is located across from the National Park Inn.

Other short trails near Longmire include the Twin Firs Trail (under 1 mile), which starts about 2 miles west of Longmire and is marked by signs on the north side of the road. The loop travels through old-growth timber, including its namesake twin Douglas firs and cedar trees.

The Carter Falls Trail (2 miles) begins just west of the Cougar Rock Campground, about 8 miles from the Nisqually Entrance. Wander through old-growth trees and across a footbridge over the Nisqually River to gaze at Carter Falls, or continue another 150 feet to see Madcap Falls.

About 6 miles past Longmire, a one-way road provides a short detour to the Ricksecker Point parking area. Here you can take in views of the Tatoosh Range and the Paradise River before rejoining the road to Paradise.

on a trail at Mount Rainier

Dining Room (7am-11am, 11:30am-4pm, and 5pm-8pm daily year-round; $18-42) serves straightforward, hearty meals like pot roast, beef chili, and grilled cheese sandwiches, but the sweets—including blackberry cobbler and hot chocolate—are the best. Breakfasts include pancakes, biscuits and gravy, and eggs Benedict made with grilled portobello mushrooms.

CAMPING

Located just a couple of miles past Longmire, **Cougar Rock Campground** (2 miles past Longmire on the Longmire-Paradise Rd., www.recreation.gov; May-Oct.; $20) is one of the most popular places to camp in the state because of its proximity to Paradise. The 173 sites have access to flush toilets and an RV dump station, and 5 group sites ($60) can hold up to 40 people and five cars. There are no hookups, and RVs with generators must observe quiet hours. Across the road, a trail leads down to the Nisqually River, and a bridge crosses it to lead to a trail to Carter Falls. Ranger programs, sharing historical and natural information about the area, are held at a central amphitheater. Reservations are required in the busy summer months.

INFORMATION AND SERVICES

Longmire Information Center (360/569-6575), located in the Longmire Museum, is staffed by rangers who can offer suggestions on where to hike and explore within the park. During the winter months, the museum closes and information services move to the Wilderness Information Center next door.

In summer, the **Longmire Wilderness Information Center**

Located about 7.5 miles up the road from Longmire (and about 1 mile before Paradise), the 176-foot **Narada Falls** is reached by an easy 0.5-mile stroll from the road. Walk across the sturdy bridge and get a little damp from the spray. Picnic tables and restrooms are also available.

RESTAURANTS AND HOTELS

The **National Park Inn** (Paradise-Longmire Rd., 6 miles from the Nisqually Entrance, 360/569-2275, www.mtrainierguestservices.com; $128-158 shared bath, $172-257 private bath; open daily year-round) in Longmire is less grand than its Paradise cousin, but it has a cozier charm—plus it's open year-round. It has only 25 rooms in a building constructed in 1910 and has both a stone fireplace indoors and a long porch outside, lined with chairs for relaxing with ice cream or a hot chocolate (or a beer). Rooms are simple, small, and not particularly modern, but the rooms with a shared bath come with robes and slippers for trips through the hallway.

The casual **National Park Inn**

(360/569-6650, 9am-5pm daily June.-Sept., hours vary in winter) is headquarters for wilderness permits and backcountry information. In winter, it serves as an all-purpose information center for visitors. Rangers staff the center and can provide maps, outdoor suggestions, and updates on road closures and snow levels, which can affect travel into July.

GETTING THERE AND AROUND

Longmire is located inside the Nisqually Entrance to the national park, near the town of Ashford. To reach Ashford from Seattle, take I-5 south for 10 miles from Seattle, exiting onto I-405 north. Take exit 2 onto State Route 167 south. After a little more than 20 miles, take State Route 512 west for three miles. Take the State Route 161 exit toward Eatonville; you'll reach that small town in about 23 miles. Take a left onto Center Street, which becomes Alder Cutoff Road. Follow it for 6.5 miles to where it meets State Route 7. Turn left onto State Route 7, the National Park Highway. The small settlement of Elbe will be about 4.5 miles from the turn onto State Route 7. After that, the road turns into State Route 706 and heads 8 miles east to Ashford. Continue on State Route 706 and through the entrance booth. The road winds through the park; Longmire is 6 miles past the entrance.

✪ PARADISE

From Longmire, Paradise Road continues to climb and crosses the Nisqually River; pull over at the Christine Falls parking lot to see a dramatic two-tiered waterfall and charming stone bridge. After 11 miles, the road approaches the tree line and you'll see lush subalpine meadows—this is Paradise, home to a hotel, visitors center, and climbing center.

During the approach from Longmire, keep to the left and follow signs for access to Paradise (the road runs both directions until Paradise). After passing the parking lots, the road becomes Paradise Valley Road and continues one-way in a scenic five-minute loop. It runs under Mazama Ridge before meeting up again with the main Paradise-Longmire Road and Stevens Canyon Road, which continues east across the park.

Continue driving past Paradise and stop at Inspiration Point. The pullout and viewpoint is located on Stevens Canyon Road (just past where it meets the Paradise-Longmire Road and Paradise Valley Road outlet). The views here stretch up Paradise Valley and across the Tatoosh Range. Continue along Stevens Canyon Road to Reflection Lakes, three miles from Paradise. These subalpine lakes are accessible from the roadside and are an excellent place for photographers to capture Mount Rainier reflected in the icy-cold water.

JACKSON VISITOR CENTER

At the center of Paradise is the steep-peaked roof of the Henry M. Jackson Memorial Visitor Center (Paradise Rd. E, 360/569-6571, www.nps.gov/mora; 10am-7pm daily June-Sept., 10am-4:30pm Sat.-Sun. Oct.-May), shaped so it doesn't hold the snow during the winter. The center was built in 2008 to replace an old concrete structure. It has a theater showing a short history film and displays about the area's natural history, plus a café and gift shop. The Paradise Inn nearby has lodging, a restaurant, and a café of its own.

PARADISE INN

Regardless of whether you're staying the night, the lobby of the Paradise Inn (98368 Paradise-Longmire Rd., 360/569-2275, www.mtrainierguestservices.com; May-Sept.) is a must-see. The long room, anchored by massive stone fireplaces at each end, is marked by regular exposed log beams. It's decorated with a 14-foot-tall grandfather clock and a piano played by President Harry Truman during a visit (both pieces were built by the same German carpenter). Couches and long wooden tables dot the lobby and are often filled with as many recovering climbers as hotel guests.

HIKING

Paradise's real treasures are outside. The short Alta Vista Trail (1.2 miles round-trip) near the parking lot is paved to help preserve the fragile landscape of subalpine meadows, which burst in summer with purple lupine and orange-red Indian paintbrush. The Nisqually Vista Trail (1.25 miles round-trip) spur travels to an overlook with a view of the Nisqually Glacier, whose melt fills the river you followed on the way up.

As the trails get steeper, they become unpaved and the crowds thin out. For a longer hike, follow the Skyline Trail (5.5 miles round-trip) to Panorama Point, which in addition to great views has a bathroom that has been built into the rock. From Panorama Point the trail heads east before swinging back to Paradise, and hikers may encounter summit-bound climbers loaded with large packs and ice axes. The whole loop is well signed and has some of the very best views of the peak and the jagged Tatoosh Range to the south.

The Pinnacle Peak trail (2 miles

Christine Falls

one-way) gains more than 1,000 feet in elevation as it moves south of the road and into the Tatoosh Range. The trail ends at the rocky Pinnacle Saddle and offers a spectacular view of Mount Rainier; climbing any farther requires scrambling experience and is not advised. To reach the trailhead, take the Paradise-Longmire Road or the Paradise Valley Road to Stevens Canyon Road, and then go 3 miles to Reflection Lakes.

The **Bench and Snow Lakes Trail** (2.5 miles round-trip) includes boardwalks through wildflower meadows. The trail ends at Snow Lake, about 1.25 miles from the trailhead, where there's a small backcountry campground. The trail is snow covered at the start of summer and muddy until midsummer. The area is also popular with black bears. The trailhead is located 1.5 miles east of Paradise down Stevens Canyon Road.

RESTAURANTS AND HOTELS

The stately old **Paradise Inn** (98368 Paradise-Longmire Rd., 360/569-2275, www.mtrainierguestservices.com; May-Sept.; $134-209 shared bath, $209-309 private bath) is one of the country's most distinguished national park lodges. It was built in 1916 and decorated with rustic woodwork by a German carpenter who wanted to evoke alpine styles. Many of the cedar logs were from a grove nearby that had been decimated in a fire. The original structure had only a few dozen rooms, which today have shared hall bathrooms and cozy shapes under the steep roof. An annex built in 1920 added four floors of rooms, all of which have private bathrooms, and a major renovation in 2018 spruced up the whole place.

The attached **Paradise Inn Dining Room** (7am-9:30am, noon-2pm, and 5:30pm-8pm daily May-Sept.) is impressive in its elegant rustic style. While it serves a wide array of seafood, small plates, steak, and a bourbon-buffalo meatloaf, the decor is more impressive than the flavors. Reservations are not accepted.

The **Paradise Camp Deli** (10am-6:45pm daily June-Sept., 11am-4pm Sat.-Sun. Oct.-May), in the Jackson Visitor Center, is a fast-service restaurant serving salads, pizzas, and soft drinks. Enjoy soft-serve ice cream or coffee outside, or eat inside when the weather's bad.

INFORMATION AND SERVICES

The **Paradise Climbing Information Center** (360/569-6641; 6am-3pm Sun.-Thurs., 6am-5pm Fri.-Sat. May-Sept.), located in the historic Guide House, provides climbing permits for those attempting to summit Mount Rainier, as well as backcountry hiking and camping permits. For information on day hiking or less advanced outdoor activities, visit the Jackson Visitor Center.

GETTING THERE AND AROUND

Paradise is 13 miles east of Longmire on the Longmire-Paradise Road.

To reach the Sunrise area from Paradise and make a loop through the park, continue east from Paradise on Stevens Canyon Road for 11 miles to a T intersection with State Route 123. Turn left and follow State Route 123 north for 3.5 miles to the intersection with State Route 410. Stay to the left to take State Route 410 north 4.5 miles to the gate that marks the border of the national park. Stay north on State Route 410 to reach the towns of Greenwater and Enumclaw.

SUNRISE

The park's **Sunrise** area got its name the obvious way—by offering a spectacular view of the mountain when the sun first emerges from the east. Located on the northeast side of the park and situated at 6,400 feet elevation, Sunrise is covered in snow most of the year. This region is less developed than the west side of the mountain, with only a small visitors center, a nearby campground, picnic facilities, and limited food options. Sunrise Road stretches from the White River Entrance Station to the Sunrise Visitor Center, and the road is usually open by mid-July and closes by October. Overnight visitors may camp at White River Campground, but are not permitted at Sunrise. The road between the visitors center and the campground closes nightly.

Sunrise is accessible via State Route 410. The region is about 50 miles (1.5 hours) south of the town of Enumclaw and is a 2-hour drive from Paradise when the park road is open.

SUNRISE VISITOR CENTER

The **Sunrise Visitor Center** (Sunrise Rd., 360/663-2425, www.nps.gov/mora; 10am-6pm daily July-Sept.), in the northeast corner of the park, is even higher than the facility at Paradise. It offers views of the Emmons Glacier side of Mount Rainier, the White River Valley below, and Mount Baker and Glacier Peak to the north. It's particularly spectacular at—what else—sunrise, especially from the **Sunrise Point** overlook on the road that approaches the wood-sided visitors center. Inside are more

exhibits about the mountain and its history, and rangers lead programs and hikes. Services are less extensive than at Paradise, with only a snack bar and small bookstore.

TIPSOO LAKE

As State Route 410 enters the national park, it becomes Mather Memorial Parkway. In eight more miles, Mather Memorial Parkway meets State Route 123 at Cayuse Pass (elevation 4,694 feet). Head east to continue along Mather Memorial Parkway for three miles to **Tipsoo Lake.** The lake is surrounded by glorious mountain meadows, and picnic tables offer a spot to sit and soak in the views.

HIKING

Hikes around Sunrise lead through the Yakima Park meadows and rocky expanses inhabited by marmots and fuzzy white mountain goats. At the Emmons Vista Overlook near the visitors center, look on the south side of the parking lot for the trailhead for the **Silver Forest Trail** (2 miles), which offers great views with little elevation gain. Or head west from the same trailhead through meadows on the **Shadow Lake Trail** (3 miles), which includes Sunrise Camp, a backcountry campground.

Cross to the north side of the parking lot for the **Sourdough Ridge Trail** (1 mile), a quick loop up a ridge above Sunrise with views of the mountains north of Rainier, such as Glacier Peak and Mount Baker. More ambitious hikers can attempt the **Burroughs Mountain Trail** (7 miles), which travels through the rocky expanse of its namesake mountain.

The **Glacier Basin Trail** (6 miles round-trip) leaves the White River Campground and follows an old mining road. About 3 miles in, around the Glacier Basin camp, are the rusty remnants of a former mine.

Three miles south of the White River Entrance Station, follow State Route 410 east to Tipsoo Lake. The Naches Peak Loop Trail (3.4 miles round-trip) starts from the parking lot at the lake and circles Naches Peak for beautiful views of Mount Rainier.

RESTAURANTS

The Sunrise Day Lodge (www. mtrainierguestservices.com; 10am-7pm daily June-Sept.) includes a small snack bar that serves grilled burgers and hot dogs, sandwiches, and soft-serve ice cream. Although there's space to eat inside, the view from the picnic tables outside overlooks the subalpine meadows that skirt Mount Rainier. An attached gift shop sells books and small souvenirs. The snack bar provides the only food service in the area, and it can open as late as July in especially snowy years.

CAMPING

The 112-site White River Campground (360/569-2211, www. nps.gov/mora; June-Sept.; $20) lies three miles from Sunrise at 4,400 feet, a higher elevation than the other two major campgrounds in the park. A few of the 112 sites have prime locations next to the White River. A historic patrol cabin located between two of the campsite loops hosts ranger programs around its campfire circle. Amenities include water and flush toilets, but not an RV dump station (though RVs are allowed). Reservations are not accepted.

Though located outside the national park, the Silver Springs Campground (State Route 410, www.

recreation.gov; May-Sept.; $20-40) is just a mile west of the White River Entrance—useful when the White River Campground sites are all full. The forest here is full of old-growth cedar and western hemlock, and a small river flows through the 55 sites. Amenities include water, flush and vault toilets, and picnic tables; no electrical hookups are available.

INFORMATION AND SERVICES

The White River Wilderness Information Center (White River Entrance Station, 360/569-6670; 7:30am-5pm daily May-mid-Oct.) can provide permit information for backcountry hikers and campers on the mountain's north side. Climbers attempting to summit Mount Rainier from the north side must register here.

The Silver Creek Visitor Information Center (69211 SR 410 E, 360/663-2284, www.fs.usda.gov) is a classic log-cabin structure located about 1.5 miles north of the national park boundary. It's operated seasonally by the Snoqualmie Ranger District and staffed by U.S. Forest Service rangers who can offer advice on recreation and informational materials.

GETTING THERE AND AROUND

To reach Sunrise from Seattle, follow I-5 for 10 miles south and take I-405 north for 2 miles. Exit onto State Route 167 south and follow it a little less than 20 miles. Take the exit for State Route 410 east, and stay on State Route 410 for 15 miles to reach Enumclaw. Greenwater is 21 miles farther on State Route 410, and the national park gate is 13.5 miles farther south after that. A left turn right before the gate heads to Crystal Mountain.

The road into Mount Rainier National Park from the east is only open May-November. To reach Sunrise from the entrance gate, follow the road 4.5 miles through the park to a turnoff where a booth collects park entrance fees; Sunrise is 16 miles up a winding road that often isn't clear of snow until summer. Check road conditions and openings before attempting a trip; Sunrise Road is closed most of the year.

To reach Paradise from the Sunrise Road turnoff, continue south 3.5 miles on State Route 410 to its intersection with State Route 123. Bear right to follow State Route 123 south and go 11 miles to the intersection with Stevens Canyon Road. Take a right and follow Stevens Canyon Road 21 miles to Paradise. Many of the roads are only open during the summer, and all are winding mountain routes.

✪ CRYSTAL MOUNTAIN

Sprawling Crystal Mountain Resort (33914 Crystal Mountain Blvd., 360/663-2265, www.crystalmountainresort.com; $80 adults, $56 children 11-17, $24 seniors, children under 11 free) is the biggest ski resort in the state and has Washington's only gondola. It has bunny hills, new chairlifts, and backcountry skiing. The jib park is for trick skiers and snowboarders and has a giant airbag for aerial tricks ($5-25)—though anyone attempting to flip onto the cushion has to sign a waiver and wear a helmet. You can rent ski equipment at the base ($40-45 adults, $25-35 children), or visit a dedicated boot shop for fittings and adjustment.

Crystal Mountain Resort

Non-skiers can do more than just sip hot chocolate at the base lodge: **Snowshoe tours** ($85) include equipment rental and a cheese fondue dinner, plus a guide for the trek along a ridge near the summit. Scenic rides on the **Mount Rainier Gondola** (9am-3:30pm daily, closed fall and spring; $23 adults, $18 seniors, $15 children 4-15, children under 4 free) allow anyone to see the top, with the enclosed gondola car making a climb of 2,500 feet in less than 10 minutes—but be warned that in winter the wind at the top can be unforgiving.

Even though Crystal Mountain Resort is best known as a ski destination, the gondola runs during summer to carry hikers and sightseers up the hill. Guided hikes with a U.S. Forest Service ranger are free with a gondola ticket, as are wildflower hikes with naturalists. A disc golf course is free, at least if you're willing to hike uphill to hit all 27 baskets (otherwise buy a gondola ticket and work your way down). The **Mountain Shop** rents lawn games like bocce and croquet, and a taco truck is parked outside on weekends. From the summit, the **Crystal Mountain Trail** winds six miles to the base area, while the **Bullion Basin Trail** from the parking lot is a challenging three-mile hike to meet the Pacific Crest Trail, a good place to turn around. Find maps at the Mountain Shop.

If you're not looking to walk yourself, **Chinook Pass Outfitters** (800/726-3631, www.crystalmountainoutfitters.com; 8am-6pm daily in season; $35-200) leads horseback trips from parking lot C. Overnight and fishing trips are also available.

RESTAURANTS

The Austrian theme of the Alpine Inn at Crystal Mountain extends to the in-house restaurant, the **Snorting Elk Cellar** (33818 Crystal Mountain Blvd., 888/754-6400, www.crystalhotels.com; 3pm-10pm Mon.-Fri., 2pm-10pm Sat.-Sun. summer, 11am-10pm Sun.-Thurs., 11am-midnight Fri.-Sat. winter; $10-26). Low arched ceilings cover a fireplace and walls painted in floral designs that wouldn't be out of place at any Oktoberfest. Seattle brewery Elysian creates the bar's namesake beer, but there are plenty of other taps for après-ski or après-hike visits. The menu leans toward hearty fare like stone-fired pizzas and thick sandwiches. The hot-drinks menu includes a hot toddy, hot buttered rum, hot spiced wine, and a drink called the Face Plant—imagine a rummy hot chocolate with peppermint schnapps and whipped cream.

You can't get much higher than the **Summit House** (33914 Crystal Mountain Blvd., 360/663-3085, http://crystalmountainresort.com; 10:30am-2:45pm daily weather permitting, open some evenings, $12-25) and still get waiter service; located at 6,872 feet at the top of Crystal Mountain, Summit House claims to be Washington's highest restaurant (and no one's arguing). Sitting at the top of the Mount Rainier Gondola, it's a meal that requires serious planning. Skiers swarm the area during the winter months, and the wind can be significant. Even in summer, clouds can obscure the spectacular Mount Rainier view, and sunset dinners mean a flashlight-led walk back to the gondola. Still, the wood-trimmed dining room with stone fireplace and antler chandeliers is worth the trip, and the menu includes gourmet fondue, fish specials, and filet mignon. Reservations and gondola tickets are required.

HOTELS

Of the three hotels at the base of the Crystal Mountain ski area, the Alpine Inn (33818 Crystal Mountain Blvd., 360/663-2262, www.crystalhotels. com; $200-365) has the most charm. The exterior is all Bavarian, complete with bright-green shutters and a large porch, and the hotel itself is located across the creek from the parking lot. A small fireplace anchors the lobby, and the hallways are lined with vintage black-and-white photos of skiers with wooden equipment and jaunty old ski outfits. Rooms are small but come in combinations with a sleeper sofa or bunk beds to accommodate families. Most don't have a TV or phone—the mountain is your entertainment.

The simpler Village Inn (33818 Crystal Mountain Blvd., 360/663-2262, www.crystalhotels.com; $260-295), just across the parking lot, has rooms only with a queen bed or two twins. Headboards are made of thick wooden logs, and rooms have balconies facing the ski mountain. Rooms come with refrigerators and, unlike the Alpine Inn across the way, a TV. But like the Alpine Inn, it's only a short walk to the Mount Rainier Gondola.

The Alta Crystal Resort (68317 SR 410, 360/663-2500, www. altacrystalresort.com; $299-369) is a small complex of suites, some two stories with two bedrooms. All have wood-burning fireplaces and either a kitchenette or full kitchen, and rooms aren't cramped. A large honeymoon cabin is on a creek and located away from the rest of the buildings. Steam rises from the hot tub and heated pool (set to 90 degrees in the winter), and a recreation lodge holds board games and a foosball table. Unlike some cabins in the area, the hotel has indoor distractions like wireless Internet and cable television, plus movie rentals and facilities to cook meals in the room. It also hosts campfires, s'more making, and other evening activities during weekends, holidays, and summer months.

GETTING THERE AND AROUND

To reach Crystal Mountain from Seattle, follow I-5 for 10 miles south and take I-405 north for 2 miles. Exit onto State Route 167 south and follow it for a little less than 20 miles. Take the exit for State Route 410 east, and stay on State Route 410 for 15 miles to reach Enumclaw. Greenwater is 21 miles farther on State Route 410, and the national park gate is 13.5 miles beyond that. Right before the gate, a left turn goes to Crystal Mountain Boulevard. The ski area is 6 miles up the winding road.

BACKGROUND

The Landscape

GEOGRAPHY

Elliott Bay and Mount Rainier

Seattle is a city trapped between the mountains and the sea. Or, to be more accurate, between the foothills of the Cascade Mountain Range and Puget Sound, a giant saltwater cut that forms a deep V in the state; the sound is linked to the Pacific Ocean by the Strait of Juan de Fuca, which forms the northwestern border with Canada. Dug by glaciers to be 800 feet deep in some spots, Puget Sound is home to salmon, seals, and pods of killer whales, some of whom can be spotted from shore in Seattle's Elliott Bay.

Some of Seattle's hills have been reshaped by city planners, shaved down to produce the landfill used to create more flat land around the water—take the city's famous Underground Tour to peek at the buried city blocks lost to the remodeling. But plenty of the mounds are still there, including First Hill, Queen Anne Hill, and Capitol Hill. From these vantage points one can see the jagged Olympic Mountains to the west and the distant, longer line of the Cascades to the east, including spectacular Mount Rainier.

True to Seattle's nickname, the Emerald City stays verdant year-round with plenty of evergreen trees throughout the city, and the streets are awash in color in the spring when flowering cherry trees erupt into bloom.

CLIMATE

Though it has a reputation for being a place of rain, Seattle isn't actually the wettest city in America. It receives about 36 inches of precipitation annually, less than Miami or Mobile, Alabama. However, rain here doesn't come in sheets and torrents, but rather tends toward light drizzles on gray days—about 155 days per year.

Thanks to the marine climate of Puget Sound, temperatures don't reach extremes. Summer highs top out around the low 80s, and the winter, which brings little to no snow, has lows in the upper 30s. Older private homes may not have air-conditioning for the city's few hot August days, but most newer construction can adapt to the worst "heat waves." The breezes off Elliott Bay mean many outdoor outings in Seattle call for a backup light cover or jacket. When the forecast predicts rain, most locals turn to a sturdy raincoat with a hood rather than an umbrella—though it's a myth that no Pacific Northwesterners will be seen with an umbrella.

ENVIRONMENTAL ISSUES

Seattle doesn't only get its green reputation from the evergreens and rain-watered lawns. The city prides itself on being environmentally friendly, instituting sustainable practices as law. Stores are banned from providing plastic bags to customers, and paper bags come with a small fee (usually $0.05). Not only is plastic, paper, and metal recycling compulsory—look for marked bins in public places—but so is composting in private homes and businesses. Most locals do this with a small container for food scraps, and the systems mean that more than half the city's waste is recycled or composted.

Capitol Hill's Bullitt Center, an office building and event center near downtown, bills itself as the greenest commercial building in the world, meant to be a model for how construction can use innovation to be more environmentally stable—there are solar panels, composting toilets, rainwater harvesters, and even a constructed wetland to treat graywater. It's an extreme version of what's popping up around the city—tech solutions to the challenge of minimizing human impact in the Pacific Northwest.

Despite pushes for public transit and sustainable building to keep the air and region clean, the city of more than 650,000 does create some environmental issues. Pollution and invasive species in Puget Sound may have contributed to reduced populations of certain kinds of sealife, including the fish that feed the region's famous orcas. Some beaches occasionally have pollution notices, advising people against entering the water, though they are rare. Air quality, however, is rarely a problem, though statewide wildfires in the late summer can lead to hazy days with a light layer of smoke in the air.

History

NATIVE AMERICAN CULTURE

For thousands of years, what would become the Seattle area was home to Coast Salish tribes, descended from people that crossed over from Siberia during the ice age. Many place-names in the area come from the Lushootseed or Chinook trading languages; the Duwamish River, Snoqualmie Pass, and the town of Puyallup are examples. The region's Native Americans lived in large cedar-log houses and carved totem poles with important animals and spirit figures. Authentic versions of these totem poles are found throughout the region, and new ones are carved to this day.

The tribes that lived around Puget Sound looked to the water for their livelihood, and salmon was more than a food—it was a way of life. The fish were caught from shore or from carved cedar canoes, and hunting parties also went after elk, seals, and smaller animals. Culturally, the tribes were known for their songs, dances, and storytelling.

TRADERS AND EXPLORERS

When George Vancouver entered Puget Sound in 1792 at the head of a British exploration of the uncharted-by-whites Pacific Northwest, he made a lasting mark on the land—and not just through his names. (Many of the monikers he gave to mountains, bays, and peninsulas have stuck, including Mount Rainier and Whidbey Island.) He brought back reports of calm bays ideal for accessing the natural bounty of the area, and a few years later the

Lewis and Clark expedition surveyed the Columbia River area by land. Soon after, the Hudson's Bay Company established an outpost near present-day Vancouver, Washington, bringing more European trappers and traders to the area. The area north of the Columbia River became the Washington Territory of the United States in 1853; it was originally to be named Columbia, but was instead given the name of the first president in order to avoid confusion with the District of Columbia. Of course, it would eventually be confused with Washington, D.C. anyway.

In the mid-19th century, a group of settlers led by Arthur Denny took the Oregon Trail across the country but found present-day Oregon to be too crowded. They traveled by boat up the Pacific coast to the mouth of the Duwamish River, landing at what is now called Alki Point in 1851. A local chief named Seattle met them at the beach. The chief later invited an important trader to relocate from Olympia to the village that was being called Duwamps. When the village was incorporated in 1853, the trader convinced the founders to rename it Seattle.

THE GOLD RUSH

It may have been called the Klondike gold rush, but the discovery of precious ore in the far north had an even bigger effect in a city hundreds of miles to the south. Headlines screamed the discovery of gold in northwest Canada in 1897, claiming that the steamer *Portland* was arriving from the Klondike loaded with more than a ton of gold aboard (it was actually double that). Prospectors soon started making their way to the remote goldfields. The fledgling city of Seattle quickly became the gateway to the north, the place where miners loaded up on supplies and frequented brothels before heading up the Inside Passage to Alaska and over rough terrain to the Klondike. The economic boom to the city was huge, with some 15,000 miners moving through town in one three-month period.

While Seattle was well positioned to serve as a launching point, it was no accident that it became known as the first stop to golden riches. The Seattle Chamber of Commerce made a concerted effort to link the city to the gold rush, taking out advertisements and writing letters to newspapers to show off the possibilities. An official gold assay office opened in Seattle.

As the Klondike Gold Rush National Historical Park shows in its hands-on exhibits, the gold rush didn't deliver for most of the rushers. It was the merchants that did best, like the Seattle hardware stores that made money from selling supplies to the miners. The city population boomed, and the increased infrastructure led to Seattle becoming an international trade crossroads. Even though the gold rush soon died, the city strengthened its connection to the north when it hosted the 1909 World's Fair, calling it the Alaska-Yukon-Pacific Exposition.

THE 20TH CENTURY

Seattle continued to grow as a timber hub and business center, and when World War II hit it was one of the leading producers of war materials, including Boeing airplanes (the company was founded in a Seattle shipyard in 1916). Seattle citizens with Japanese roots suffered after the bombing of Pearl Harbor, Hawaii, in 1941, when the city's large Japanese American population was rounded up and sent to internment camps along the West Coast, decimating the economic and civic positions they had achieved.

After the country recovered from World War II, Seattle looked to the future. Again hosting the world's fair in 1962, the city's theme became futuristic technology. The Space Needle and the Monorail were built for the exposition, and everyone from astronauts to royalty visited the science exhibits. The fair is generally credited with giving Seattle a reputation as a modern, global city.

THE TECH BOOM

Though one of Seattle's most famous hometown companies, Boeing, dates back a hundred years—and has since moved its headquarters out of town—two of its flagship names were born toward the end of the 20th century. First came a company that introduced much of the world to computing: Microsoft. Bill Gates first tinkered with electronics in his Seattle prep school, and the software company he cofounded with Paul Allen eventually settled in a Seattle suburb. Today Microsoft's newest operating system runs more than 200 million devices, and Gates has moved on to running a charitable foundation, one that also has a significant Seattle footprint. Seattle's other tech titan, Amazon, started as an e-commerce company in 1996 and is now a vendor, hardware and software producer, and tech innovator worth $175 billion.

Between the births of these two businesses, Seattle became famous for its grunge music, popularized nationwide by the band Nirvana.

During the 1990s, the city dictated national style—turning the casual flannel plaid into a fashion statement.

CONTEMPORARY TIMES

Often hailed as the next San Francisco or Silicon Valley—or, in other words, the next city to experience an overwhelming boom thanks to tech companies—Seattle has maintained its status as an outdoor haven and cultural hub. The 21st century has meant expansions in public transit and worldwide recognition for the arts. Laws legalizing marijuana and raising the minimum wage are being closely monitored nationwide for signs of success. The city has grown to more than 650,000 people, with a greater metropolitan sprawl of almost 4 million. Since the population started to grow in the 19th century, Seattle has never stopped growing, and that shows few signs of changing now.

Local Culture

DIVERSITY

The majority of Seattle residents are white, almost 70 percent. The city is known specifically for its Scandinavian roots, thanks to the Nordic fishermen who flocked to present-day Ballard soon after Seattle was founded. People with Asian roots make up another 14 percent of the population, including Chinese, Japanese, Korean, and Vietnamese communities. About 8 percent are black, and less than 1 percent are Native American. About 17 percent of the population was born outside the United States, with the city now home to growing Ukrainian and Somali communities.

INDIGENOUS CULTURES

Though Native American tribes once occupied all the lands around Puget Sound, 19th-century treaties led to the creation of reservations in exchange for fishing rights, education, and medical care. In recent years members of the Duwamish, whose tribe claims city namesake Chief Seattle as a member, have had to fight for enforcement of those treaties. Some Puget Sound tribes have opened casinos to boost revenue and jobs in their territories, including the sizable Tulalip Resort Casino just north of Seattle. Many have tribal cultural centers and museums, including those at Tulalip and the Suquamish Museum on the Kitsap Peninsula.

SUBCULTURES

Back in the 1990s, when grunge music ruled the airwaves, there was a growing segment of people living a grunge lifestyle, mostly young white adults committed to eschewing corporate ties and their formal trappings. Ballard was still noticeably a Scandinavian fishing enclave. The LGBT community was flourishing on Capitol Hill, the center for artists and musicians, while in Fremont a throwback group of hippies ran the semi-pagan, often nude Solstice Parade every summer. Today many of these subcultures survive, though LGBT representation has spread throughout the city and grunge has morphed into the hipster lifestyle focused on artisanal foods and local art. Fremont still holds the annual Solstice Parade and has unusual public art pieces, and fishing boats are still moored along Ballard's industrial waterfront, but rising real estate costs have turned both into more expensive residential neighborhoods with high-end restaurants and stores.

RELIGION

Though the city has the reputation for being unchurched, about 38 percent of King County residents reported affiliations with organized religion in 2010. Nearly all religions saw growth in the first decade of the 21st century, as did the total population. The most popular religions are Catholic, with more than 14 percent of locals, and evangelical Protestant, with more than 10 percent. There are also Mormon and Buddhist communities, along with smaller numbers of Muslim, Jewish, and Hindu adherents. The megachurch Mars Hill, which once boasted tens of thousands of members, grew in Seattle in the early 2010s but disbanded in 2015 after scandal surrounding its leadership.

LITERATURE

The city's literary history is kind of like the Blue Moon Tavern, the University District pub long known for its open mics and writer gatherings—not everyone knows about it, but it's bustling and well loved. Pulitzer Prize-winning poet Theodore Roethke, a midcentury writer known for his brutal honesty and introspection, moved to the city to teach at the University of Washington and later died on Bainbridge Island. He taught poet Richard Hugo, whose legacy includes a creative writing center on Capitol Hill that hosts classes and readings. The modern Pacific Northwest literary canon includes David Guterson's *Snow Falling on Cedars*, a fictional novel about the impact of the Japanese internment set around Puget Sound, and Maria Semple's *Where'd You Go, Bernadette*, a novel gently mocking the city's neuroses. Seattle's downtown library, in a glassy, cubist Rem Koolhaas-designed building, is a modern temple to the book, and the city is dotted with well-loved bookstores. The Elliott Bay Book Company on Capitol Hill is perhaps the most well regarded, but there are also beautiful technical bookstores, hidden mystery bookstores, and mouthwatering cookbook stores. There's a reason Seattle has been called the most literate city in America.

VISUAL ARTS

The city's most famous visual artist is probably Dale Chihuly, and his glass sculptures can be found in public spaces around town—look up for giant tangles of color that serve as chandeliers—and in his own Chihuly Garden and Glass in Seattle Center. Striking sculptures blanket the city, from the expected places like the Olympic Sculpture Park to unexpected locales like under a bridge (the Fremont Troll) and a tiny Fremont corner (the statue of Lenin). Downtown, the Seattle Art Museum has a large repository of Western art, and the small gallery in its gift shop highlights young working artists from around the region. On the first Thursday of every month, Pioneer Square galleries stay open late and launch new shows, and the streets fill with arts fans.

MUSIC AND DANCE

Seattle has come a long way since its music scene became nationally famous in the 1990s with Nirvana, Pearl Jam, and Mudhoney (though before that it claimed Jimi Hendrix). Back then grunge, a type of rock and roll with a rough, garage-band feel, was popular; today the city has a much more eclectic musical landscape. Rapper Macklemore was well known around the city before his independently produced album became a national hit; though he's famous for his salute to thrift shopping, he also wrote a popular ode to the city and its beloved baseball announcer Dave Niehaus called "My Oh My."

Indie is the Seattle buzzword; Sub Pop Records, a local label, rose to prominence with Nirvana but has since launched the careers of Death Cab for Cutie, Modest Mouse, and the Postal Service. The city's most influential radio station is KEXP, now grown into a national brand known for its independent rock tastes and live studio performances.

FOOD

Back in 1962, when the world's fair hit Seattle, the populace was delighted by Belgian waffles, a treat new to the United States. Since then the city's food scene has been less about importing novelty and more about an emphasis on the fresh and local. Salmon, the same food that sustained the Native American tribes that lived here for centuries, is one of the most popular dishes in downtown restaurants, often served grilled on a cedar plank. Oysters are another signature delicacy, grown in the waters of Puget Sound or south of the city in Willapa Bay. The region's mild climate makes for fresh produce, and some chefs delight in foraging for ingredients like mushrooms, berries, and fennel blossoms. Belltown restaurant Local 360 prides itself on gathering all its food from no more than a 360-mile radius around the kitchen.

Food isn't the only arena with an emphasis on the local; the city is famous for its coffee traditions, and not just the one called Starbucks. City-based roasters feed beans to smaller independent chains, where complex orders and pour-over coffee is the rule rather than the exception. Espresso, note many locals, gets us through the gray winters.

From its spot on the Pacific Rim, Seattle also has a strong Asian food community, centered on the International District downtown but radiating throughout the city. Vietnamese soup called pho (pronounced fuh) has practically supplanted salmon as the city's signature dish; restaurants around town serve the hot noodle bowls filled with seasoned broth and vegetables.

MARIJUANA

In 2012, Washington state voters made a revolutionary move, legalizing the use of recreational marijuana products in the state. It happened at the same time that Colorado did likewise, making the West the experimental grounds for legalized drug use. Though pot is legal, there are still strict guidelines on its use; smoking in public carries a fine, as does buying from an unauthorized dealer. Official shops, which must obtain licenses and be located a prescribed distance from schools, will only sell to those over 21 (though you do not need to be a Washington resident). On a single trip you can buy an ounce of marijuana or 16 ounces of edible products like brownies and candies—with cash.

ESSENTIALS

Getting There

cars on I-5 in Seattle

AIR

There is no "Seattle Airport." When approaching the Emerald City, flights land at the **Sea-Tac International Airport** (SEA, 17801 International Blvd., 800/544-1965, www.portseattle.org/sea-tac), so named because it sits between the cities of Seattle and Tacoma. Although its name is half and half, it's undeniably the Seattle airport, and it lies about 14 miles south of the city.

The vast majority of visitors that fly to the Seattle area come to Sea-Tac. A few flights from Boeing Field (a mostly private airport near downtown) go to San Juan Island, Orcas Island, and Port Angeles on the Olympic Peninsula through **Kenmore Air** (866/435-9524, www.kenmoreair.com). Kenmore also runs floatplane trips that leave from Lake Union to Victoria, British Columbia; Port Angeles; and spots all around the San Juan Islands. It is rumored that commercial flights will soon leave from Paine Field north of the city in Everett, but currently the large airfield is used only by private planes and one of Boeing's giant factories.

AIRPORT TRANSPORTATION

To reach downtown Seattle from the airport via public transportation, take the **Link Light Rail** (888/889-6368, www.soundtransit.org). The train starts in the University District and runs to Capitol Hill and Westlake Center in downtown Seattle, and then continues south with stops in neighborhoods like Columbia

City, Rainier Beach, the International District, and the stadium area. The trip between downtown and Sea-Tac is about 40 minutes, and passengers can buy tickets ($2.25-3 each way) at the station before boarding. (Don't try to board without a ticket because fare-enforcement staff regularly board the train to make sure everyone has a valid ticket.) Trains arrive every 7-15 minutes and operate 5am-1am Monday-Saturday and 6am-midnight on Sunday. The station is located across from the main airport terminal; exit on the mezzanine level to the parking garage and follow signs for the Link Light Rail.

Taxis depart Sea-Tac airport from the third level of the parking garage; look for a row of yellow cabs. A dispatcher is usually managing the line. A set fare of $40 covers trips from the downtown Seattle district to the airport; the trip from the airport to downtown is not set, but will cost about the same. Cabs are subject to the same traffic considerations as private cars, and congestion on I-5 can be intense. Trips from the airport to downtown Seattle can take as little as 20 minutes or over an hour during rush hour. Rideshares Lyft (www.lyft.com) and Uber (www.uber.com) depart from the marked section of the third level of the parking garage near the cabs.

Shuttle vans can also take travelers to downtown Seattle or throughout the city. Shuttle Express (425/981-7000, http://shuttleexpress.hudsonltd.net; $18 to downtown) organizes shared van rides to hotels or the convention center in downtown Seattle. Advance reservations are not required but are recommended, especially during peak travel times.

Car Rentals

The car rental center (3150 S. 160th St., www.portseattle.org/sea-tac) is separate from the main airport, accessible via regular shuttles that leave outside the baggage claim area. The energy-efficient facility holds 13 different car rental companies, and shuttles run 24 hours a day.

CAR

Two freeways lead to Seattle: I-5 and I-90. I-5 runs north-south, running from the Canadian border south all the way to Oregon, California, and the Mexico border. It slices through the city and has express lanes to relieve traffic at rush hour, but delays and stoppages are still common. When a rare traffic-free day occurs, it takes about 1.5 hours to reach Seattle from Portland, Oregon, and about 2 hours to reach Seattle from the Canadian border.

I-90, one of America's major east-west routes, ends in Seattle after a cross-country trip from Buffalo, Chicago, and Spokane. It crosses Lake Washington before ending at I-5 near the stadiums, just south of downtown Seattle.

Seattle is famous for its gridlock, and it's hard to avoid at least one or two delays thanks to clogged roads. Freeways, highways, and surface streets are especially crowded at rush hour—7am-9am and 4pm-6pm—but backups can happen any time. Visitors who expect to stay in downtown can do without a car, utilizing the light-rail or taxis to go to and from the airport. Even a brief trip to Capitol Hill or Ballard may not be worth the hassle and parking prices of a car, thanks to bus and taxi service. For day trips outside the city and movement around

Seattle's outer neighborhoods, a car may be needed.

TRAIN

Several major **Amtrak** (800/872-7245, www.amtrak.com) lines run through the Pacific Northwest to Seattle, stopping at Seattle's King Street Station. Most trains offer wireless Internet access and bistro cars that serve a limited menu and drinks.

- *Cascades:* Travels from Vancouver, British Columbia, to Seattle, then south to Eugene in central Oregon, including a stop in Portland. (Business-class seats on the *Cascades* trains offer more room.)
- *Coast Starlight:* Travels from Los Angeles to Portland and eventually Seattle. For longer trips, sleeper cars offer "roomettes" with simple bunk beds and larger rooms with private bathrooms.
- *Empire Builder:* This east-west line connects Seattle to Chicago and Milwaukee; it has sleeper accommodations, but no wireless Internet.

BUS

Greyhound (800/231-2222, www. greyhound.com) operates routes between Seattle and Vancouver and Portland, as well as the Olympic Peninsula and Oregon coast. However, service outside of major cities may not be common, and public transportation within those regions is limited. Travelers without cars in those areas may find it difficult to reach sights and services.

Although owned by Greyhound, **Boltbus** (877/265-8287, www.boltbus. com) is more popular with younger travelers. Buses travel from a stop near Seattle's King Street Station to Vancouver, BC, and Portland. Fares start low, as little as $1 for a trip, but those deals sell out quickly. Buses offer plug-ins and wireless Internet, as well as reserved seating.

Getting Around

PUBLIC TRANSPORTATION

The most expansive public transportation option in Seattle is the bus system, run by **King County Metro Transit** (206/553-3000, http://metro. kingcounty.gov), though the labyrinthine routes can be hard for newcomers to decipher. Route maps and trip planners can be found online, but most stops do not have detailed maps. Passengers board at the front of the bus, either using a prepaid ORCA fare card purchased at a light-rail station or paying cash ($2.75 adults, $1.50 children 6-18, $1 seniors, children under 6 free). Have exact amounts of cash ready; drivers cannot make change. Specially marked express buses make few stops, but the majority of routes stop regularly.

There are several other more limited forms of public transportation in the city, including the slowly growing **Link Light Rail.** So far a single line runs from the University of Washington to Capitol Hill and then Westlake downtown, continuing south with stops in Pioneer Square, the International District, and SoDo near the stadiums before veering to Columbia City and continuing to

Sea-Tac airport. The downtown stops are in underground stations that also serve as bus tunnels. Purchase an ORCA card or single-ride ticket at automated machines; rides cost $2.25-3.25 depending on distance. If using an ORCA card that can be loaded with a deducting balance, be sure to tap it on the yellow card readers before boarding; tap again when leaving to deduct the correct fare. When fare-enforcement officials board a car, their handheld devices can determine whether an ORCA card has been properly tapped before boarding. ORCA cards can also be loaded with an all-day pass ($8 adults, $6 seniors).

Two streetcars operate in Seattle (206/553-3000, http://seattlestreetcar.org; $2.25 adults, $1.50 children 6-18, $1 seniors, children under 6 free). The South Lake Union Streetcar runs from Westlake at 5th Avenue and Olive Way through South Lake Union to MOHAI and to the Eastlake neighborhood at Fairview Avenue North and Ward Street. The First Hill Streetcar goes from Pioneer Square at South Jackson Street and Occidental Avenue South up to First Hill before continuing north on Broadway to Capitol Hill, ending at Broadway and Denny Way near the Capitol Hill light-rail station.

Finally, a water taxi operates between West Seattle and downtown Seattle, though its West Seattle terminus is a good mile from the neighborhood's most popular attraction, Alki Beach. The King County Water Taxi (Pier 50, 801 Alaskan Way, www.kingcounty.gov; $5.75 adults and children 6-18, $2.50 seniors, children under 6 free) offers many of the same breathtaking downtown views as the larger ferries and is much faster.

TAXIS AND RIDE-SHARING APPS

To hail a taxi in Seattle, try Yellow Cab (253/872-5600, www.yellowtaxi.net) or hail one on the street in the downtown core. Taxi rates in Seattle are $2.70 per mile with an initial charge of $2.60. The city also has private car companies like Uber (www.uber.com) and Lyft (www.lyft.com), which use phone apps to assign cars to customers. Both Uber and Lyft operate from Sea-Tac airport; after ordering a car online, look for the pickup point on level 3 of the parking garage near the taxi stand.

DRIVING

Seattle is covered in SmartCar rentals from car2go (877/488-4224, http://seattle.car2go.com), where very small cars are rented by the minute—gas and insurance included—and can be picked up on the street around the city or at the airport. Advance registration is required, since users are sent a card that opens and activates their rental car.

Most roads in the greater Seattle area do not have tolls, with the exception of State Route 520 over Lake Washington to Bellevue; tolls are collected both ways but cars do not stop at a tollbooth. Automated cameras capture license plates and send bills to the corresponding address, and rental car companies will charge for tolls accrued. Tolls can be paid online (www.wsdot.wa.gov/goodtogo) after a bill is logged and sent. Reduced fares are available with a Good2Go pass, which can be ordered at the same website. The same system applies to express toll lanes on I-405, which runs north-south through Bellevue; cars with two or more passengers can use the lanes for free, but single-passenger cars are charged the corresponding toll. For both, tolls fluctuate based on time of day and road usage.

FERRIES

The Washington State Ferry boats (Pier 52, 801 Alaskan Way, 888/808-7977, www.wsdot.wa.gov/ferries; passenger fares: $8.35 adults, $4.15 seniors and children one way to Bainbridge Island or Bremerton), white with green trim and constantly crossing Puget Sound in front of downtown, are state icons. They allow commuters to travel to islands around Puget Sound and from the Olympic Peninsula on a daily basis, but can also be a fun, cheap ride for tourists. Tickets can be purchased from machines in the terminal lobby. Walk-on passengers are not charged on Seattle-bound boats from Bainbridge Island or Bremerton, though vehicles are charged both ways.

Travel Tips

The drinking age in the United States is 21 years old, and most bars and restaurants will ask for identification. Almost all grocery stores and liquor stores will require identification as well.

Bars in Seattle stay open until about 2am and often close earlier on weeknights. Laws regarding when alcohol can last be served are very strict, but some dance clubs will stay open later after their bars have stopped serving alcohol.

Smoking in bars, restaurants, and indoor places is prohibited. Seattle parks, as well as state parks, prohibit smoking in outdoor public places. Cigarettes are not sold to anyone under the age of 18, and identification is required.

In 2012, possession of marijuana for recreational use became legal in Washington State. That doesn't mean it's a free-for-all, however. Adults age 21 or older can possess up to one ounce of marijuana, but cannot smoke in a public place or drive under the influence. Stores selling marijuana are slowly becoming a reality as the state works out regulations and taxation. However, marijuana is still illegal on federal lands; it is also against the law to cross any borders while in possession of the substance.

ACCESS FOR TRAVELERS WITH DISABILITIES

Seattle is a hilly city, one with historic roots reaching back a century or more, so travelers with disabilities may find getting around some areas challenging. Wheelchair users will appreciate the number-one ranking the city received from WheelchairTravel.org; the sidewalk quality around Seattle can be uneven, but the area is largely welcome to visitors on wheels.

There is widespread adherence to federally mandated regulations regarding access, plus a general acceptance of accommodating those with disabilities. Museums, hotels, and major sites all have accommodations for visitors with disabilities, and most restaurants can find ways to work with diners that need special attention; it's advisable to call ahead if you foresee difficulties.

Disabled parking is labeled around the city, but cannot be used without an official parking pass; parking attendants will ticket without one.

TRAVELING WITH CHILDREN

Seattle is a wonderful destination for families because of its affordability, relaxed pace, and large number of activities for children. The city has parks, zoos, museums, and aquariums that cater especially to kids, as well as educational destinations such as the Pacific Science Center. Look for family rates at museums and at gardens that require admission.

When traveling with children in the Seattle area, be sure to make plans that include indoor stops. Kids can get stir-crazy in the event of a rainy day, which is common in the area. But there is also a prevalence of creative transportation options in the region: Rides on ferries, trams, and light-rail trains can be exciting for travelers of any age. Most hotels will happily accept children and can offer rooms away from noisy bars or events. Be sure to check before booking a bed-and-breakfast room, as some establishments may limit guests to adults only.

SENIOR TRAVELERS

Many older travelers will find discounts at bars, restaurants, museums, and transportation options. Age requirements vary. At hotels, ask for senior rates when booking. American travelers can also get discounts with membership in the AARP.

GAY AND LESBIAN TRAVELERS

Seattle is generally very friendly to gay and lesbian travelers. The city holds an annual pride parade and runs **Travel Gay Seattle** (614 Broadway E., 206/363-9188, www.travelgayseattle. com; 9am-5pm Mon.-Thurs., 9am-6pm Fri., 10am-2pm Sat.), a visitor information booth located in a 1st Security Bank branch in Capitol Hill, traditionally the city's most LGBT-friendly area. It has maps that show businesses that specifically support the city's growing gay and lesbian travel industry.

Gay marriage was legal in Washington State before it was legalized nationally, and the state has been a destination wedding spot for gay and lesbian couples looking to tie the knot. Check local city hall websites for more about the process of obtaining a wedding license.

INTERNATIONAL TRAVELERS
PASSPORTS AND VISAS

When visiting the United States from another country a valid passport is required. Depending upon your country of origin, a visa may also be required. For a complete list of countries exempt from U.S. visa requirements, visit http://travel.state.gov/visa.

Canadian citizens can visit the United States without a visa, but must show a passport or enhanced driver's license at the border. All car, train, and bus crossings may entail questioning from border-control agents about the purpose of the visit, destination (including hotel address), and purchases made while in the country.

To protect the agricultural industries of each country from the spread of pests and disease, the transportation of fresh fruit and plants may be prohibited. More information on crossing into the United States can be found at www.cbp.gov.

CUSTOMS

When entering the United States by plane, you will have to fill out a customs form. Be sure to have handy the information on your destination— name, address, and phone number.

There are monetary limits on the gifts you can bring into the country as well as on the amount of tobacco and alcohol you can bring.

If you take prescription medications, bring documentation for your medicines. Those that require the use of syringes should be packed in checked luggage along with proper documentation. You can find exact regulations on customs and duties for the United States online at www.cbp. gov.

Health and Safety

HOSPITALS AND EMERGENCY SERVICES

For urgent but not emergency cases of medical need, try one of the city's many urgent-care clinics, such as ZoomCare (531 Broadway, 206/971-3728, www.zoomcare.com; 8am-midnight Mon.-Fri., 9am-6pm Sat.-Sun.). Appointments can be booked online or over the phone, and doctors can treat minor injuries and illnesses.

The city's major emergency room is at Harborview Medical Center (325 9th Ave., 206/744-3300, www.uwmedicine.org), where helicopters often land carrying trauma patients from around the Northwest.

Emergency services can be reached by dialing 911 from any phone.

PHARMACIES

Most grocery stores have pharmacies, and downtown is home to several outposts of hometown chain Bartell Drugs (910 4th Ave., 206/624-2211, www.bartelldrugs.com; 6am-8pm Mon.-Fri., 8am-7pm Sat., 10am-6pm Sun.), a quick-service market with a sizable pharmacy section for over-the-counter and prescription medical supplies.

CRIME

Seattle is known as a fairly safe city by American standards, but it does have occasional street crime. The downtown core and outlying neighborhoods are usually safe for pedestrians during daylight hours, though it's important to keep valuables close when maneuvering in crowds. In evening hours, downtown, Capitol Hill, Ballard, Fremont, and other highly trafficked neighborhoods remain safe and are generally populated with pedestrians. Late at night some streets may be dark, and solo travelers should stick to better-lit main routes when walking. Panhandlers request change throughout the city, including at major vehicle intersections, but are not known to bother those who do not donate. To make a substantive donation to the city's homeless population, look for those hawking a newspaper called *Real Change* (http://main.realchangenews.org/about); produced by a nonprofit, it directly benefits Seattle's most vulnerable.

Information and Services

VISITORS CENTERS

If you wish to pick up maps, book tours, and get information, head to one of downtown's two visitors centers operated by the city. **Seattle Visitor Center and Concierge Services** (Washington State Convention Center, 7th Ave. and Pike St., 866/732-2695, www.visitseattle.org; 9am-5pm daily summer, 9am-5pm Mon.-Fri. fall-spring) is on the uphill end of downtown, while the **Market Information Center** (Pike Place Market southwest corner, 1st Ave. and Pike St., 866/732-2695, www. visitseattle.org; 10am-6pm daily) is closer to the waterfront.

POST OFFICE

The central **Seattle Post Office** (301 Union St., 206/748-5417, www. usps.com; 8:30am-5:30pm Mon.-Fri.) branch is in the middle of downtown; a small stand in the lobby sells packing materials while the official desk has national and international shipping options. Look for the automated postage machine in the lobby for faster service.

RESOURCES

Suggested Reading

HISTORY

Becker, Paula, Alan J. Stein, and the HistoryLink staff. *The Future Remembered: The 1962 Seattle World's Fair and Its Legacy*. Seattle: Seattle Center Foundation, 2011. With the staunch historic basis of local site HistoryLink.org, this beautiful coffee-table book explores the world's fair that changed Seattle's place in the world.

Morgan, Murray. *Skid Road: An Informal Portrait of Seattle*. Seattle: University of Washington Press, 1982. As it says right in the title, author Murray Morgan tells the city's story with all the bawdy, weird, and rambling bits left in; it's appropriate for a city that got big during the freewheeling days of a gold rush.

Thrush, Coll. *Native Seattle: Histories from the Crossing-Over Place*. Seattle: University of Washington Press, 2007. Coll Thrush's account of the region's Native American history challenges the easy narrative and explores how the modern West emerged.

LITERATURE

Alexie, Sherman. *The Lone Ranger and Tonto Fistfight in Heaven*. New York: Atlantic Monthly Press, 1993. Another local short story craftsman, Sherman Alexie tells stories about the hard life and complicated relationships on an eastern Washington Indian reservation.

Carver, Raymond. *What We Talk About When We Talk About Love: Stories*. New York: Vintage Books, 1989. Though he grew up in nearby Yakima, short story expert Raymond Carver eventually left Washington; still, he's probably the most famous writer the state can claim as a hometown hero.

Ford, Jamie. *Hotel on the Corner of Bitter and Sweet*. New York: Ballantine Books, 2009. Jamie's Ford's 2009 novel addresses the trauma and cultural impact of the Japanese internment of World War II among Seattle's Asian population.

Guterson, David. *Snow Falling on Cedars*. San Diego: Harcourt, 1994. A bestseller in the 1990s, David Guterson's novel about a death on a fictional Puget Sound island wove tales of romance, mystery, and trials faced by Northwest Asian Americans in the mid-20th century.

Roethke, Theodore. *The Collected Poems of Theodore Roethke*. New York: Anchor Books, 1975. Well known at the University District's Blue Moon Tavern before he died on Bainbridge Island, Theodore Roethke was the city's most famous poet.

Semple, Maria. *Where'd You Go, Bernadette?* New York: Little, Brown and Company, 2012. The comic novel about a loopy Seattle mother shot author Maria Semple into fame and exposed some of the city's funniest peccadillos (like the disaster of the five-way intersection).

Wolff, Tobias. *This Boy's Life: A Memoir.* New York: Grove Press, 1989. Tobias Wolff's memoir about a troubled childhood in Seattle and a small town in the North Cascades later became a movie starring Robert De Niro and Leonardo DiCaprio.

Internet Resources

GENERAL INFORMATION
Visit Seattle
www.visitseattle.org

Seattle Premier Attractions
www.seattleattractions.com

HISTORY
HistoryLink
www.historylink.org

NEWSPAPERS
Seattlepi.com
www.seattlepi.com

Seattle Weekly
www.seattleweekly.com

The Seattle Times
www.seattletimes.com

The Stranger
www.thestranger.com

PARKS AND RECREATION
Seattle Parks and Recreation
www.seattle.gov/parks

Washington Trails Association
www.wta.org

TRANSPORTATION
Metro Online
http://metro.kingcounty.gov

Seattle Department of Transportation
www.seattle.gov/transportation

Index

Restaurants

Nightlife

Shops

Hotels

Photo Credits

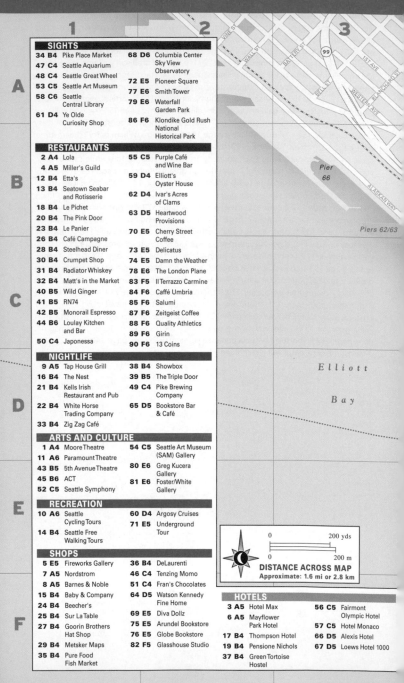

1   **2**   **3**

SIGHTS

34 B4 Pike Place Market	**68 D6** Columbia Center Sky View Observatory
47 C4 Seattle Aquarium	
48 C4 Seattle Great Wheel	**72 E5** Pioneer Square
53 C5 Seattle Art Museum	**77 E6** Smith Tower
58 C6 Seattle Central Library	**79 E6** Waterfall Garden Park
61 D4 Ye Olde Curiosity Shop	**86 F6** Klondike Gold Rush National Historical Park

RESTAURANTS

2 A4 Lola	**55 C5** Purple Café and Wine Bar
4 A5 Miller's Guild	
12 B4 Etta's	**59 D4** Elliott's Oyster House
13 B4 Seatown Seabar and Rotisserie	**62 D4** Ivar's Acres of Clams
18 B4 Le Pichet	**63 D5** Heartwood Provisions
20 B4 The Pink Door	
23 B4 Le Panier	**70 E5** Cherry Street Coffee
26 B4 Café Campagne	
28 B4 Steelhead Diner	**73 E5** Delicatus
30 B4 Crumpet Shop	**74 E5** Damn the Weather
31 B4 Radiator Whiskey	**78 E6** The London Plane
32 B4 Matt's in the Market	**83 F5** Il Terrazzo Carmine
40 B5 Wild Ginger	**84 F6** Caffè Umbria
41 B5 RN74	**85 F6** Salumi
42 B5 Monorail Espresso	**87 F6** Zeitgeist Coffee
44 B6 Loulay Kitchen and Bar	**88 F6** Quality Athletics
50 C4 Japonessa	**89 F6** Girin
	90 F6 13 Coins

NIGHTLIFE

9 A5 Tap House Grill	**38 B4** Showbox
16 B4 The Nest	**39 B5** The Triple Door
21 B4 Kells Irish Restaurant and Pub	**49 C4** Pike Brewing Company
22 B4 White Horse Trading Company	**65 D5** Bookstore Bar & Café
33 B4 Zig Zag Café	

ARTS AND CULTURE

1 A4 Moore Theatre	**54 C5** Seattle Art Museum (SAM) Gallery
11 A6 Paramount Theatre	
43 B5 5th Avenue Theatre	**80 E6** Greg Kucera Gallery
45 B6 ACT	**81 E6** Foster/White Gallery
52 C5 Seattle Symphony	

RECREATION

10 A6 Seattle Cycling Tours	**60 D4** Argosy Cruises
14 B4 Seattle Free Walking Tours	**71 E5** Underground Tour

SHOPS

5 E5 Fireworks Gallery	**36 B4** DeLaurenti
7 A5 Nordstrom	**46 C4** Tenzing Momo
8 A5 Barnes & Noble	**51 C4** Fran's Chocolates
15 B4 Baby & Company	**64 D5** Watson Kennedy Fine Home
24 B4 Beecher's	
25 B4 Sur La Table	**69 E5** Diva Dollz
27 B4 Goorin Brothers Hat Shop	**75 E5** Arundel Bookstore
29 B4 Metsker Maps	**76 E5** Globe Bookstore
35 B4 Pure Food Fish Market	**82 F5** Glasshouse Studio

HOTELS

3 A5 Hotel Max	**56 C5** Fairmont Olympic Hotel
6 A5 Mayflower Park Hotel	**57 C5** Hotel Monaco
17 B4 Thompson Hotel	**66 D5** Alexis Hotel
19 B4 Pensione Nichols	**67 D5** Loews Hotel 1000
37 B4 Green Tortoise Hostel	

Pier 66

Piers 62/63

Elliott

Bay

0   200 yds
0   200 m

DISTANCE ACROSS MAP
Approximate: 1.6 mi or 2.8 km

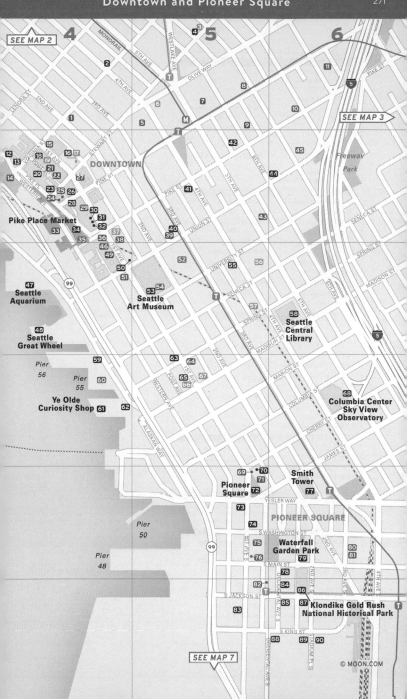

SEE MAP 2

4

MONORAIL

WESTLAKE AVE

5TH AVE

4

3

5

6

SEE MAP 3

2

OLIVE WAY

11

5

PIKE ST

4TH AVE

6

8

7

10

2ND AVE

LENORA ST

3RD AVE

5

9

Freeway Park

1

42

45

15

16

17

12

13

18

19

VIRGINIA ST

44

DOWNTOWN

6TH AVE

20

21

22

27

41

43

5TH AVE

14

WESTERN AVE

23

25

26

UNION ST

4TH AVE

24

28

29

30

31

3RD AVE

Pike Place Market

33

34

35

36

37

38

40

39

2ND AVE

PIKE ST

UNIVERSITY ST

46

49

50

51

52

55

56

SEATTLE AQUARIUM

47

53

54

Seattle Art Museum

SENECA ST

57

58

Seattle Central Library

99

SPRING ST

Seattle Great Wheel

48

Pier 56

59

63

64

67

66

65

1ST AVE

MARION ST

68

Columbia Center Sky View Observatory

Ye Olde Curiosity Shop

61

62

60

Pier 55

WESTERN AVE

POST AVE

COLUMBIA ST

CHERRY ST

JAMES ST

ALASKAN WAY

69

70

71

Smith Tower

77

72

Pioneer Square

73

YESLER WAY

PIONEER SQUARE

74

Pier 50

99

75

76

S WASHINGTON ST

Waterfall Garden Park

79

80

81

2ND AVE S

Pier 48

S MAIN ST

82

84

86

85

87

Klondike Gold Rush National Historical Park

83

S JACKSON ST

88

89

90

S KING ST

STADIUM PL S

SEE MAP 7

© MOON.COM

SEE MAP 4

SIGHTS

6 C5	Museum of History and Industry	
24 D4	Seattle Center	
25 D4	Bill & Melinda Gates Foundation Visitor Center	
27 D5	Center for Wooden Boats	
34 E3	Olympic Sculpture Park	
35 E4	Seattle Children's Museum	
36 E4	Seattle Center Monorail	
37 E4	Museum of Pop Culture	
39 E4	Chihuly Garden and Glass	
40 E4	Space Needle	
41 E4	Pacific Science Center	
70 F5	South Lake Union Streetcar	

RESTAURANTS

2 A3	How to Cook a Wolf
3 A4	Canlis
4 B3	The 5 Spot
9 D3	Toulouse Petit
13 D3	Uptown Espresso
15 D3	Pung Kang Noodle Place
20 D4	Caffe Vita
28 D5	Revel
30 D6	Re:public
31 D5	Serious Biscuit
42 E5	Cactus
44 E5	Flying Fish
45 E6	Lunchbox Laboratory
48 F3	AQUA by El Gaucho
49 F3	Six Seven
51 F4	Black Bottle
53 F4	El Gaucho
60 F4	Local 360
69 F5	Serious Pie

NIGHTLIFE

1 A3	Hilltop Ale House
7 D2	Holy Mountain Brewing
8 D3	The Sitting Room
10 D3	Tin Lizzie Lounge
14 D3	Mecca Café and Bar
18 D3	Triumph Bar
32 D6	Feierabend
33 D6	Lo-Fi Performance Gallery
43 E5	Brave Horse Tavern
52 F4	Some Random Bar
56 F4	Rob Roy
57 F4	Buckley's
61 F4	Shorty's
62 F4	The Crocodile
64 F4	Bathtub Gin and Co.
66 F4	The Whisky Bar
68 F5	Dimitriou's Jazz Alley
71 F5	Pennyroyal

ARTS AND CULTURE

16 D3	SIFF Uptown
19 D3	Seattle Repertory Theatre
22 D4	Pacific Northwest Ballet
23 D4	Seattle Opera
54 F4	Big Picture
67 F5	Cinerama

RECREATION

5 C3	Kerry Park
26 D5	Lake Union Park
38 E4	Ride the Ducks

SHOPS

12 D3	Mercer Street Books
46 E6	Feathered Friends
47 E6	REI
59 F4	Endless Knot
63 F4	Singles Going Steady
65 F4	Alhambra

HOTELS

11 D3	MarQueen Hotel
17 D3	Inn at Queen Anne
21 D4	Maxwell Hotel
29 D4	Moxy Seattle Downtown
50 F4	Edgewater Hotel
55 F4	Ace Hotel
58 F4	City Hostel Seattle

W SMITH ST

W MCGRAW ST

W BOSTON ST

W CROCKETT ST

West Queen Anne Park

W BLAINE ST

QUEEN ANNE

W GARFIELD ST

GALER ST

W HIGHLAND DR

Kerry Park

W PROSPECT ST

W KINNEAR PL

W OLYMPIC PL

W ROY ST

To Holy Mountain Brewing

W MERCER ST

ELLIOTT AVE W

W REPUBLICAN ST

W HARRISON ST

W THOMAS ST

Chihuly Garden and Glass

W JOHN ST

DENNY WAY

Olympic Sculpture Park 34

Elliott

Bay

© MOON.COM

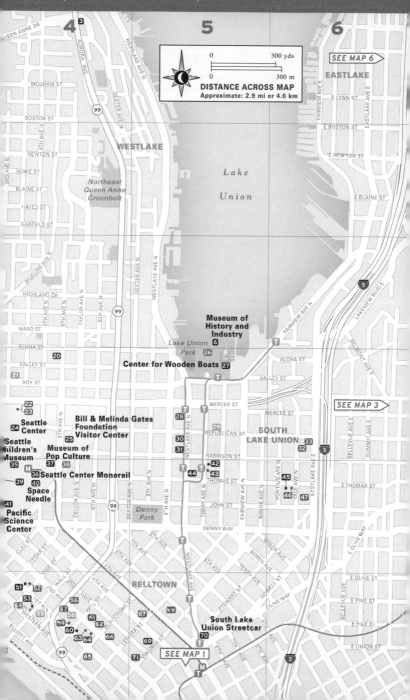

SEE MAP 6

0   300 yds
0   300 m

DISTANCE ACROSS MAP
Approximate: 2.9 mi or 4.6 km

4
5
6

QUEEN ANNE DR
3
AURORA AVE N
WESTLAKE AVE N

FAIRVIEW AVE E
EASTLAKE AVE E

EASTLAKE

MCGRAW ST
E LYNN ST

99
E BOSTON ST

BOSTON ST
DEXTER AVE N
E NEWTON ST

4TH AVE N
NEWTON ST

HOWE ST
WESTLAKE

BLAINE ST
Lake
E BLAINE ST

3RD AVE N
Northeast
Queen Anne
Greenbelt
Union

HAYES ST

GARFIELD ST

BIGELOW AVE N
HIGHLAND DR
TAYLOR AVE N
DEXTER AVE N
WESTLAKE AVE N

4TH AVE N
5TH AVE N
6TH AVE N
99
FAIRVIEW AVE N

LAKEVIEW BLVD E
5

WARD ST

ALOHA ST
Museum of
History and
Industry
6

BELMONT AVE E

20
Lake Union
Park **26**
ALOHA ST

VALLEY ST
Center for Wooden Boats **27**
VALLEY ST

21
ROY ST

MERCER ST
MERCER ST

22
23
28
WESTLAKE AVE N

SEE MAP 3

24 Seattle
Center
Bill & Melinda Gates
Foundation
25 Visitor Center
29
REPUBLICAN ST
SOUTH
LAKE UNION
33
32

BELLEVUE AVE E
SUMMIT AVE E

5TH AVE N
30
31

Seattle
Children's
Museum
35
Museum of
Pop Culture
37 **38**
HARRISON ST
5

36 **Seattle Center Monorail**
42
44
43
THOMAS ST
PONTIUS AVE N
45
YALE AVE N
46 **47**
E THOMAS ST

TAYLOR AVE N
6TH AVE N
39
40
Space
Needle
99
JOHN ST
TERRY AVE N
FAIRVIEW AVE N
MINOR AVE N
EASTLAKE AVE E

41
Pacific
Science
Center
Denny
Park
DENNY WAY

9TH AVE N
8TH AVE N
DEXTER AVE N
WESTLAKE AVE N
E OLIVE WAY

CLAY ST
6TH AVE
E OLIVE ST

CEDAR ST
5TH AVE
8TH AVE
BOREN AVE
TERRY AVE
HOWELL ST
BELLEVUE AVE E

BELLTOWN
E PINE ST

51 **52**
VINE ST
WALL ST
4TH AVE
OLIVE WAY

53
54
1ST AVE
56
57
67
STEWART ST
E PIKE ST

WESTERN AVE
58
61
62
BATTERY ST
South Lake
Union Streetcar
E UNION WAY

59
60
63 **64**
66
LENORA ST
70
5TH AVE
6TH AVE
8TH AVE

ELLIOTT AVE
65
69
71
VIRGINIA ST
SEE MAP 1
E UNION ST

99
5

SEE MAP 6

Broadmoor
Golf Club

MADISON
PARK

Washington Park
and Arboretum

STEVENS

Japanese
Garden

E HELEN ST

E WARD ST

Washington
Park

E ALOHA ST

E VALLEY ST

E ROY ST

E MERCER ST

E HARRISON ST

E MADISON ST

E THOMAS ST

E JOHN ST

E DENNY WAY

E HOWELL ST

E OLIVE ST

E PINE ST

E PIKE ST

E COLUMBIA ST

SIGHTS

2 A2	Lake View Cemetery	**69 F2**	Seattle University
4 B3	Seattle Asian Art Museum		

RESTAURANTS

3 A3	Volunteer Park Cafe	**36 E1**	Sitka & Spruce
9 C2	Cook Weaver	**37 E1**	Taylor Shellfish Farms
10 C2	Altura	**38 E1**	Starbucks Reserve Roastery & Tasting Room
11 C2	Poppy		
13 C2	Witness	**39 E1**	Stateside
16 C3	Caffe Ladro	**40 E1**	Mamnoon
17 C3	Coastal Kitchen	**49 E2**	Oddfellows Café and Bar
19 C3	Victrola		
20 C3	The Wandering Goose	**54 E2**	Quinn's Pub
		55 E2	Grim's Provisions & Spirits
21 C3	Rione XIII		
22 C3	Monsoon	**59 E2**	Spinasse
23 C3	Tallulah's	**60 E2**	Nue
24 D1	Kedai Makan	**61 E3**	Skillet Diner
29 D2	Dick's Drive-In	**66 F2**	Café Presse
30 D3	Smith		
33 E1	Li'l Woody's		

NIGHTLIFE

6 C1	Single Shot	**34 E1**	The Baltic Room
7 C1	Sol Liquor	**41 E1**	R Place
12 C2	Bait Shop	**42 E1**	Linda's Tavern
14 C3	Canterbury Ale House	**46 E2**	Neighbours
		52 E2	Q
15 C3	Liberty	**53 E2**	Neumos
25 D1	Montana	**56 E2**	Unicorn
26 D1	Stumbling Monk	**58 E2**	Cuff Complex
27 D1	C. C. Attle's	**62 E3**	Chuck's Hop Shop
28 D1	Kessler's	**64 F1**	The Hideout
31 E1	Knee High Stocking Co.	**67 F2**	Canon
		68 F2	Rhein Haus
32 E1	Pine Box		

ARTS AND CULTURE

45 E2	Egyptian Theatre	

RECREATION

1 A1	I-5 Colonnade Park	**44 E2**	Cal Anderson Park
5 B3	Volunteer Park		

SHOPS

8 C2	Freeman	**48 E2**	Isla House + Flower
18 C3	Ada's Technical Books and Café	**50 E2**	Totokaelo
		51 E2	The Elliott Bay Book Company
35 E1	Melrose Market		
43 E1	Babeland	**57 E2**	Throwbacks Northwest
47 E2	Sugarpill		

HOTELS

63 F1	Hotel Sorrento	**65 F2**	Silver Cloud Hotel Seattle - Broadway

0   200 yds

0   200 m

DISTANCE ACROSS MAP
Approximate: 2.6 mi or 4.2 km

© MOON.COM

1

2

3

99

Woodla
Park

A

5TH AVE NW

NW 53RD ST

NW 52ND ST

2ND AVE NW

N 51ST ST

PALATINE AVE N

GREENWOOD AVE N

Woodland Park
Zoo
2

Rose
Garden

B

NW 51ST ST

NW 50TH ST

NW 49TH ST

NW 48TH ST

NW 46TH ST

MARKET ST

1ST AVE NW

2ND AVE NW

1ST AVE N

PHINNEY AVE N

DAYTON AVE N

50TH ST

49TH ST

48TH ST

47TH ST

46TH ST

EVANSTON AVE N

ST GREEN

E GREEN

WHITMAN AVE N

WOODLAND

PARK

C

5TH AVE NW

4TH AVE NW

3RD AVE NW

BAKER AVE NW

2ND AVE

NW 44TH ST

NW 43RD ST

43RD ST

NW 42ND ST

1ST AVE N

PALATINE AVE N

FRANCIS AVE N

DAYTON AVE N

EVANSTON AVE N

FREMONT AVE N

N ALLEN PL

44TH ST

43RD ST

N MOTOR ST

LINDEN AVE N

N PHINNEY WAY

WINSLOW PL N

45TH ST

45TH ST

5

6

7

8

9

10

11

To
4 Hale's Ales

D

NW 41ST ST

NW 40TH ST

NW BOWDOIN PL

LEARY WAY NW

CANAL ST NW

13

14

41ST ST

40TH ST

BOWDOIN PL

2ND AVE NW

1ST AVE N

PALATINE AVE N

N BOWDOIN PL

39TH ST

DAYTON AVE N

EVANSTON AVE N

AURORA AVE N

WHITMAN AVE N

B.F. Day
Playground

99

FREMONT

FREMONT WAY N

E

W BERTONA ST

Canal
Park

Lake Washington Ship Canal

NW CANAL ST

PALATINE AVE N

FRANCIS AVE N

DAYTON AVE N

EVANSTON AVE N

36TH ST

36TH ST

15

16

17

18

19

20

21

22

23

24

25

26

27

Lenin
Statue

FREMONT PL N

Fremont
Troll

28

BRIDGE WAY N

ALBION PL N

FREMONT AVE N

F

Seattle
Pacific
University

4TH AVE W

3RD AVE W

W CREMONA ST

W DRAVUS ST

W ETRURIA ST

QUEEN ANNE AVE N

NICKERSON ST

WARREN AVE N

Burke-Gilman Trail

30

31

99

N

SEE MAP 2

4   5   6

WALLINGFORD

Meridian Playground

SEE MAP 6 ▷

SIGHTS

2	**A2**	Woodland Park Zoo	28 **E3** Fremont Troll
23	**E2**	Lenin Statue	36 **F5** Gas Works Park

RESTAURANTS

1	**A1**	Brimmer & Heeltap	14 **D1** Frelard Pizza Company
5	**C2**	Lighthouse Roasters	19 **E2** Fremont Coffee Company
6	**C2**	Pecado Bueno	20 **E2** Norm's Eatery & Ale House
7	**C2**	Paseo	
8	**C3**	Uneeda Burger	27 **E3** Agrodolce
9	**C3**	RockCreek Seafood & Spirits	29 **E4** Manolin
12	**C4**	Tilth	30 **F3** Café Turko
13	**D1**	Tarsan i Jane	32 **F4** The Whale Wins

NIGHTLIFE

4	**C1**	Hale's Ales	21 **E2** The BackDoor
15	**E2**	George & Dragon Pub	22 **E2** High Dive
17	**E2**	Nectar Lounge	24 **E2** The Barrel Thief
18	**E2**	Brouwer's Cafe	31 **F3** Fremont Brewing

ARTS AND CULTURE

10	**C3**	Fremont Abbey Arts Center

SHOPS

3	**B4**	Archie McPhee	26 **E3** Show Pony
11	**C3**	The Book Larder	33 **F4** Evo
16	**E2**	Outsider Comics and Geek Boutique	34 **F4** MiiR
25	**E2**	Les Amis	35 **F4** Brooks Trailhead

0   300 yds

0   300 m

DISTANCE ACROSS MAP
Approximate: 2.0 mi or 3.2 km

Lake

Union

© MOON.COM

Gas Works Park
36

NW 63RD ST

NW 62ND ST

NW 61ST ST

Ballard
Playground

NW 60TH ST

NW 59TH ST

NW 58TH ST

Ballard
Commons
Park

NW 57TH ST

NW 56TH ST

NW MARKET ST

5 Nordic
Museum

4

Burke-
Gilman
Trail

6

8 9

10

11

12

SHILSHOLE AVE NW

BALLARD A

13 Hiram M.
Chittenden Locks

30TH AVE NW

28TH AVE NW

26TH AVE NW

24TH AVE NW

22ND AVE NW

Salmon Bay

SEAVIEW AVE NW

Burke-Gilman Trail

24TH AVE NW

3

NW 65TH ST

34TH AVE NW

32ND AVE NW

2

1

MAP AREA

15TH AVE NW

NW MARKET ST

SHILSHOLE AVE NW

Burke-
Gilman
Trail

© MOON.COM

4 **5** **6**

SIGHTS
- **5 C2** Nordic Museum
- **13 D1** Hiram M. Chittenden Locks

RESTAURANTS
- **1 Ins** Ray's Boathouse
- **2 Ins** Copine
- **3 Ins** Un Bien
- **9 C3** Pestle Rock
- **11 C3** La Carta de Oaxaca
- **16 D4** Bastille Café
- **19 D4** Bitterroot BBQ
- **24 D4** Stoneburner
- **33 E4** The Walrus and the Carpenter
- **34 E4** Staple & Fancy

NIGHTLIFE
- **8 C3** Hazlewood
- **10 D4** Sunset Tavern
- **15 D4** Noble Fir
- **21 D4** Percy's & Co.
- **22 D4** King's Hardware
- **25 D4** The Gerald
- **27 D4** Tractor Tavern
- **30 D4** Lock & Keel
- **31 D4** Conor Byrne Pub
- **32 D6** Stoup Brewing
- **35 E6** Maritime Pacific Brewing Company

ARTS AND CULTURE
- **7 C3** Majestic Bay Theatres
- **12 C3** Venue

RECREATION
- **4 C1** Stone Gardens
- **23 D4** Ascent Cycles
- **36 F6** Burke-Gilman Trail

SHOPS
- **6 C3** Bop Street Records
- **14 D3** Re-soul
- **17 D4** Ballard Farmers Market
- **26 D4** Prism
- **28 D4** Ascent Outdoors
- **29 D4** Monster Art and Clothing

HOTELS
- **18 D4** Ballard Inn
- **20 D4** Hotel Ballard

NW MARKET ST

BARNES AVE NW

NW 54TH ST

TALLMAN AVE NW

RUSSELL AVE NW

NW 53RD ST

NW IONE PL

NW 52ND ST

NW 51ST ST

NW DOCK PL

NW 50TH ST

11TH AVE NW

15TH AVE NW

14TH AVE NW

NW LEARY WAY

NW BALLARD WAY

SHILSHOLE AVE NW

NW 46TH ST

SEE MAP 4 >

NW 45TH ST

0   200 yds

0   200 m

DISTANCE ACROSS MAP
Approximate: 1.3 mi or 2.1 km

36 Burke-Gilman Trail

To **3** Third Place Books
and **4** JuneBaby

SEE MAP 4

Burke Museum of
Natural History
and Culture

University
Village

University of
Washington

University of
Washington

0   300 yd
0   300 r
DISTANCE ACROSS MA
Approximate: 1.4 mi or 2.3 k

Montlake Cut

Marsh
Island

East Montlake Park

SIGHTS
11 B2	Burke Museum of Natural History and Culture	**24 F3**	Japanese Garden
18 C1	University of Washington	**25 F3**	Washington Park Arboretum

RESTAURANTS
4 A2	JuneBaby	**17 C1**	Portage Bay Cafe
8 B1	Thai Tom	**21 D1**	Agua Verde Cafe
16 B3	Din Tai Fung		

NIGHTLIFE
1 A1	The Monkey Pub	**5 B1**	The Blue Moon Tavern

ARTS AND CULTURE
9 B1	Neptune Theatre	**19 C2**	Henry Art Gallery

RECREATION
20 D1	Recycled Cycles	**23 D3**	Husky Stadium
22 D1	Agua Verde Paddle Club		

SHOPS
2 A1	University District Farmers Market	**13 B3**	Amazon Books
3 A2	Third Place Books	**14 B3**	Glassybaby
10 B1	University Book Store	**15 B3**	Tommy Bahama
12 B3	University Village		

HOTELS
6 B1	Watertown Hotel	**7 B1**	Graduate Hotel

SEE MAP 3

To
24 Japanese
Garden ↓

Washington P
Arboretum
25

© MOON.COM

© MOON.COM

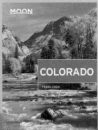

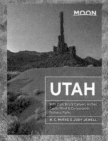

PORTLAND

SEATTLE

TUCSON

VANCOUVER

Explore the city, escape into nature,

75 GREAT HIKES
SEATTLE

101 GREAT HIKES
SAN FRANCISCO
BAY AREA

CALIFORNIA
CAMPING

COLORADO
CAMPING

OREGON
CAMPING

PACIFIC
NORTHWEST
CAMPING

WASHINGTON
CAMPING

WEST COAST
RV CAMPING

or go where the road takes you....

CALIFORNIA
Road Trip

PACIFIC COAST
HIGHWAY

PACIFIC
NORTHWEST
Road Trip

SOUTHWEST
Road Trip

Gear up for a bucket list vacation

MOON
TRIP OF A LIFETIME
ANGKOR WAT

MOON
BARCELONA & MADRID
JESSICA JONES

MOON
ICELAND
JENNA GOTTLIEB

MOON
TRIP OF A LIFETIME
GALÁPAGOS ISLANDS
LISA CHO

MOON
TRIP OF A LIFETIME
MACHU PICCHU

MOON
MOROCCO

MOON
NEW ZEALAND
JAMIE CHRISTIAN DESPLACES

MOON
NORWAY
DAVID NIKEL

MOON
TRIP OF A LIFETIME
PATAGONIA
WAYNE BERNHARDSON

MOON
VIETNAM
DANA FILEK-GIBSON

MOON
USA NATIONAL PARKS
THE COMPLETE GUIDE TO ALL
59 PARKS
BECKY LOMAX

MOON
CAMINO DE SANTIAGO
SACRED SITES,
HISTORIC VILLAGES,
LOCAL FOOD & WINE
BEEBE BAHRAMI

MAP SYMBOLS

■	Sights	◉	National Capital	▲	Mountain	═══	Major Hwy
■	Restaurants	◎	State Capital	✚	Natural Feature	─────	Road/Hwy
■	Nightlife	○	City/Town	🖌	Waterfall	─────	Pedestrian Friendly
■	Arts and Culture	★	Point of Interest	⚑	Park	- - - - -	Trail
■	Sports and Activities	•	Accommodation	⛰	Archaeological Site	ⅢⅢⅢⅢ	Stairs
■	Shops	▾	Restaurant/Bar	🄷	Trailhead	··········	Ferry
■	Hotels	▪	Other Location	🄿	Parking Area	⌐⌐⌐⌐	Railroad

CONVERSION TABLES

$°C = (°F - 32) / 1.8$
$°F = (°C \times 1.8) + 32$
1 inch = 2.54 centimeters (cm)
1 foot = 0.304 meters (m)
1 yard = 0.914 meters
1 mile = 1.6093 kilometers (km)
1 km = 0.6214 miles
1 fathom = 1.8288 m
1 chain = 20.1168 m
1 furlong = 201.168 m
1 acre = 0.4047 hectares
1 sq km = 100 hectares
1 sq mile = 2.59 square km
1 ounce = 28.35 grams
1 pound = 0.4536 kilograms
1 short ton = 0.90718 metric ton
1 short ton = 2,000 pounds
1 long ton = 1.016 metric tons
1 long ton = 2,240 pounds
1 metric ton = 1,000 kilograms
1 quart = 0.94635 liters
1 US gallon = 3.7854 liters
1 Imperial gallon = 4.5459 liters
1 nautical mile = 1.852 km

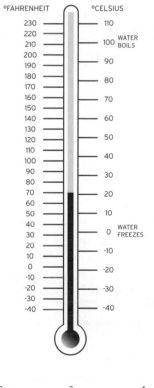

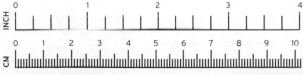

MOON SEATTLE
Avalon Travel
Hachette Book Group
1700 Fourth Street
Berkeley, CA 94710, USA
www.moon.com

Editor: Kristi Mitsuda
Series Manager: Leah Gordon
Copy Editor: Ann Seifert
Graphics and Production Coordinator: Lucie Ericksen
Cover Design: Faceout Studios, Charles Brock
Interior Design: Megan Jones Design
Moon Logo: Tim McGrath
Map Editor: Kat Bennett
Cartographers: Kat Bennett, Erin Greb, Brian Shotwell
Proofreader: Anna Ho
Indexer: Rachel Kuhn

ISBN-13: 9781640492110

Printing History
1st Edition — 2017
2nd Edition — June 2019
5 4 3 2 1

Front cover photo: Dale Chihuly, Glasshouse Sculpture (detail) 2012; 27 x 100 x 23, Chihuly
    Garden and Glass, Seattle © Chihuly Studio
Back cover photo: © Avmedved | Dreamstime.com
Printed in China by RR Donnelley